The five great rules of selling

THE 5 GREAT

McGraw-Hill Book Company, Inc.
New York   Toronto   London

RULES of SELLING

PERCY H. WHITING
Vice-President, Dale Carnegie Publishers, Inc.
Managing Director, Dale Carnegie Sales Courses

Second Edition

Published by the McGraw-Hill Book Company, Inc.
Printed in the United States of America

1819 VBVB 109

This book is dedicated to
    my wife, Gene,
        my boss, Dorothy Carnegie,
            and to the lonesomest man in the world
                THE SALESMAN

I am grateful to these people

I am deeply grateful to the people who "read copy" on this book. They corrected many errors and made innumerable helpful suggestions.

Their names, arranged alphabetically, are:

Miss Marylin Burke, Executive Assistant to Mrs. Dale Carnegie, President, Dale Carnegie Publishers, Inc., Forest Hills, New York.

John Cooper, Assistant Managing Director, Dale Carnegie Sales Course, New York, New York.

Mrs. Isabel Fidler, my secretary, Chappaqua, New York.

Mrs. Lee Maber, Administrative Assistant, Dale Carnegie Sales Course, New York, New York. _____

Mrs. Ethel Knight Pollard, President, Southern Institute, Birmingham, Alabama. (I am deeply and doubly grateful to "Polly" for her editorial help. She read the manuscript of this book twice, with meticulous care. Out of her wide experience in selling she made many helpful suggestions—for which I am grateful and for which every reader of this book *should* be grateful.)

Fred B. White, Administrative Assistant, Southern Institute, Birmingham, Alabama.

and my wife, Gene.

* * *

I have included selling maxims at the beginning of each chapter. A few of them are original; some are partly original; some are borrowed. I have given credit to the authors if I knew them. Often I didn't. Many of the pithy sayings in this book came to me by way of the magazine *Quote*, published by Droke House, Indianapolis, Indiana. Salesmen will find this magazine a fruitful source of maxims, jokes, examples, and inspirational material which they can use in sales talks, sales letters, speeches, and general conversation.

. . . . How this book came to be written—and rewritten

When we were organizing the first Dale Carnegie Sales Course, we couldn't find a practical book to use as a textbook. So I wrote one myself. I called it *The Five Great Rules of Selling*. Salesmen must have liked it, because they have been buying it regularly, and in large quantities, since 1947.

Recently I decided that my readers might benefit from a revision which would incorporate new material I had gathered since the book was first published. Before I went to work on the revision, however, I interviewed 101 of the leading sales trainers in the United States. The combined experience of these men in sales training amounts to over a thousand years! The best of the good selling ideas I gathered from the 101 men, who are the very cream of the country's sales trainers, are now part of this book.

In addition, I have put into *The Five Great Rules of Selling* many useful ideas that I gained in my twenty-year connection with the Dale Carnegie Institute.

Oh yes, in addition, I had a few ideas of my own, gathered in the nineteen years I was a sales manager. They are in the book, too.

If you want a practical book that will tell you how to sell more than you are selling now, this, I hope, is it.

Percy H. Whiting

Contents

I introduce myself
and my subject briefly

CHAPTER 1

They found I couldn't sell,
so they made me sales manager!

*The difference between the successful insurance sales-
men and those who just struggle along—is primarily a
difference in the skill with which they do the job.*
—HOLGAR JOHNSON, OF THE
NATIONAL ASSOCIATION OF UNDERWRITERS

In 1918 I was advertising manager of Central Maine Power
Company of Augusta. The company was trying to sell its preferred stock to its customers in order to finance the building
of a power plant. It had a securities-sales force made up of
four men who had failed as vacuum-cleaner salesmen, and another man who wasn't any good either!

Sales were slow.

One day the company treasurer, Walter S. Wyman, called
me into his office and asked me to run some advertisements
to increase stock sales. I did. I know they were good advertisements because I wrote them myself!

Nothing happened. Sales didn't get any worse. That is one
good features of sales—they can't go below zero, but they can
stay right at zero a long time!

Mr. Wyman then suggested that I go down to Bath, where
the salesmen were "boarding," to see if I could give them an

1

inspirational talk that would stir them up enough to make some calls.

I brought together our entire sales force—all five of them—and gave them what I supposed was a stirring inspirational speech. Especially, I told them how good my advertising was and how much stock they would sell if they would only get behind it—but not too far behind!

When I had finished talking, a tall, gangling Yankee named Clarke stood up and said, "Percy, if your advertising is so good it practically sells the stock, why don't you go out and *accept a few orders?*"

Well, there I was in the selling business!

Though I had never sold anything before in my life, I sold, in the ensuing two weeks—and I say it with all modesty—more stock than all the other members of the sales force put together.

Yes, I sold seven shares—they didn't sell a share!

I was then the sixth worst salesman in the United States.

At the end of two weeks Mr. Wyman called me into his office and said, "Percy, it is perfectly obvious to all of us that you will never by any chance become a salesman, so we are going to make you sales *manager!*"

How I learned what I know

Well, there I was, pitchforked into a job I knew nothing about. What could I do?

I read books on selling; I subscribed to sales magazines; I interviewed sales trainers, sales managers, salesmen, advertising agencies.

Every time I picked up an idea—no matter how wild—I tried it out. Oh, not personally, of course, but through my salesmen.

For example, when I was working for Henry L. Doherty and Company our advertising agency suggested an idea. I tried it out through 1,000 salesmen. One thousand salesmen came back and reported, "The idea is no good." I had learned something!

As a result of this trial-and-error method, I now know over one thousand ways to sell—*that won't work!*

By this process of elimination I arrived finally at the few rules that do work. I have given them to you in this book—and have told you how to make them produce more sales for you.

Thus you can profit by the mistakes of others—and at their expense.

You don't need a lot of rules

My long experience has brought me to these basic conclusions:

1. Just five rules of selling are vital. Not even a score are important and hardly more than a scant hundred are even worth recording.

2. No basic selling rule or principle has been discovered in the last hundred years. We have, however, made some improvements.

3. What salesmen need is not a lot of rules or a dose of fine-spun psychology. They need to learn a few basic principles of selling and to drill themselves in these principles until they habitually use them in their selling.

4. You can't learn selling in a hurry. You must practice faithfully and patiently. You must acquire the ability to use the rules one at a time—by drilling yourself.

The good results of forcing yourself to sell the way successful salesmen sell will amaze and delight you.

You must be patient—you must have faith—to become a topflight salesman.

You can't learn it in two weeks

This yarn appeared in the *Wall Street Journal*:

A country boy came to New York's Wall Street to learn to be a securities salesman. At the end of two weeks he was fired.

When he returned home, one of his friends asked him, "How do you like the selling business?"

To which the ex–Wall Street salesman replied, "It's no good. I'm sorry I learned it."

When I read that yarn I laughed out loud. Yet I have told it to sales groups at least a hundred times and I never raised as much as a faint, wan smile. From that experience, I have arrived at this conclusion: most salesmen actually believe that, *in two weeks*, a man can learn to sell.

After almost half a century of personally training salesmen, (72,000 in all) I can state with some authority, "A man can't learn all he needs to know about selling in two weeks—or two years! But he can start—and the place to start is with the basic rules."

TWO

If you don't *know* it,

how can you *sell* it!

(Product knowledge)

_____ CHAPTER 2

Know your product—or else . . . !

*Never get mad at a competing salesman for knowing
more about your product than you do. It's not his fault.*
——ELIZABETHTOWN (KENTUCKY) *News*
(SLIGHTLY IMPROVED!)

My first day on Wall Street as Employee Campaign Sales
Manager of Henry L. Doherty and Company, my friend Jack
Small invited me to lunch at the restaurant of the Chamber
of Commerce of the State of New York.

As we sat eating, a man came in. Jack nodded toward him
and said, "That man makes more money selling securities, I
believe, than any man on Wall Street. His name is Gerard
Werner."

"He doesn't look like a salesman," was my comment.

"He isn't a salesman," said Jack. "I don't suppose he has
made a sales call in ten years."

"What's the answer?" I asked.

"It just happens," replied Jack, "that Gerard knows more
about securities than any man who is selling them on Wall
Street today. He knows so much that if someone has a million-

dollar fund to invest or a ten-million-dollar estate to settle, he comes to Gerard and asks him to please handle it."

It is astonishing to find how little the average salesman knows about the articles he is selling. Gerard Werner was the exception.

E. E. Kenyon quotes in *American Weekly* this conversation he overheard in a supermarket:

"I notice this loaf of rye bread is 20 cents, and some others are 23 cents," said a customer. "What's the difference?"

"Well," said the clerk, after a pause, "the 23-cent loaf costs more."

Some sales analyst has figured out that, in 75 per cent of retail sales, the customer knows more about the product than the salesman.

While I was instructing a sales class in Seattle in the autumn of 1940, I asked a coal salesman to give me the talk he used in selling coal.

He answered, "I just say, 'It's a hell of a good coal!'"

"What else?" I asked.

He didn't know anything else—that was all.

I asked, "Does it burn down to a nice, clean ash?"

He thought so, but he wasn't sure.

"Does it form a lot of clinkers?"

He didn't have the remotest idea.

"What about BTU content?"

He'd never even heard of a British Thermal Unit.

I asked, "Is it common banded, splint, cannel, or boghead coal?"

He was sure it wasn't cannel coal.

Finally, annoyed by my badgering, he blurted, "What *is* there to know about coal?"

What is there to know about coal! Nothing except that coal is one of the most complicated minerals known to chemists. Nothing except that more tons of coal are mined in the United States than any other mineral.

I had the matter looked up when I returned to New York. The New York Public Library then listed 3,553 books on coal. The salesman was like the mountaineer whose sad story was told in *Fifth Wheel*, the house magazine of the Indiana Motor Truck Association, as follows:

When the examination was over, a teacher in a mountain school told her pupils to write a pledge that they had neither received nor given help. One gangling youth, who was squirming in dismay and mopping a bewildered brow throughout the ordeal, wrote, "I ain't received no help, and God knows I couldn't give any."

Too many salesmen are like that mountain lad.

The magazine *Your Life* quoted Walter Hoving, then president of Lord and Taylor and the youngest department-store president in New York City, as follows:

Although I had taken several courses in college on the appreciation of art and painting, I was so lacking in real knowledge of the subject—which you can readily see is very important in merchandising—that I went for four years to the Metropolitan Museum of Art two nights a week, taking courses in period furniture, old silver, rugs, color, painting, and textile design.

Walter Hoving took the trouble to know many hundred times as much about his product as he would ever use in a sales talk. Perhaps that is one reason why he was, when this was written, head man at Bonwit-Teller's and Tiffany's in New York City.

It isn't enough to know a little something about your product. As Publilius Syrus said, "Better be ignorant about a matter than half know it." And remember, "What you don't know, *somebody* is getting paid for knowing."

*   *   *

Several salesmen of services have complained, in years past, that all through the previous edition of this book we referred to selling a "product"—as though nobody ever sold anything but a "product."

"We don't sell a *product*," they complain. "We sell a *service*."

True. It's also true that some other salesmen sell a *line* (as a drug *line* or a grocery *line* of products). Then we have the *missionary* salesmen, who do not sell anything, directly. Also the salesman of space in publications. Let's not forget, either, the salesman who sells nothing except himself!

Think how impractical it would be to say, "To arouse the interest of your prospect in your product (or service, or line, or space, or idea, or yourself) tell him . . . !"

Therefore we shall, in the interests of brevity, use the word "product" in this book to indicate *anything that a salesman sells*. We hope that salesmen who sell intangibles will understand and will excuse us.

CHAPTER 3

What good is product knowledge to a salesman?

A good rule with respect to product knowledge is: "Know lots—talk little."

One night when I was talking to a sales class about the importance of product knowledge, a coffee salesman in the audience asked, "Why should I learn anything about coffee? Grocers wouldn't let me tell it. If I did, they wouldn't understand it. If they understood it, they wouldn't care a hoot. So I just go in and say, 'Want any coffee today?' If they do, they buy; if they don't, I blow."

All right, what *do* we gain by knowing our product—knowing more about it than prospects, more about it than competitors, more about it than our fellow salesmen—and maybe more about it than our sales manager?

You don't need it to show off. You don't need it to impress competitors, to confuse the prospect, or to startle your boss.

No, here is why you need product knowledge:

REASON 1: You need product knowledge because it is one of the two great builders of enthusiasm.

You will find, in Chapter 4, how product knowledge works miracles in producing the enthusiasm you need to be a great and successful salesman.

Product knowledge sells carpet tacks

For example: Harry Bowser, Sales Development Manager of Dairypak Butler, Inc., told us about it once at a meeting of the New York Sales Executive Club. Here is the story, as reported in the *New York Sales Executives Weekly*:

I went one day with one of our mechanics to buy some linoleum tools and equipment. I saw some carpet tacks and I said, "Do you sell carpet tacks?"

"Do I sell carpet tacks!" he almost shouted as he bubbled over with excitement. "Why, I sell the best carpet tacks on the market, and I can prove it."

Ah! I thought to myself, the sign of a good salesman—a statement of fact backed up by proof. "Do I sell carpet tacks!" he continued as he took a tack from a box. "Look," he said as he admiringly held up the tack, "I sell Presto blue sterilized, rustproof, small, bevel-headed tacks. Unlike the ordinary flat-headed tack that pinches and pulls the carpet and thereby forever exposes its ugly head, this tack when driven into the carpet causes the carpet to flow up over the head and thereby conceals itself in the pile of the carpet. Yes sir, this is by far the best tack on the market!"

I was impressed—I was convinced—I was sold. I bought a box of the darn things even though I don't have any carpets to tack down. I'm in the linoleum division of Alexander Smith, and we don't tack down linoleum; it's cemented to the floor. But I'll tell you this, if I ever do have any carpet to tack down, I've got

200 sterilized, tested, rustproof, bevel-headed tacks, that cause the carpet to flow over its head. I've got all that in a box—200 of them for 26 cents! Who can afford not to buy something like that, whether he has any carpets to tack down or not? I said to this fellow, "You must sell a lot of tacks." He said, "I sell a ton of tacks a month—4,800,000 tacks a year. Brother, that's a heck of a lot of tacks!"

Product knowledge nearly sold me
the wrong house

A couple of years ago my wife, Gene, and I decided to sell our house in Chappaqua, New York, and buy a somewhat larger one. We looked at perhaps twenty-five houses. We nearly bought one we didn't like—all because of the enthusiasm of its owner—an enthusiasm based on knowledge of his product.

This man had all but built this house himself. He had hired his labor, bought his material, drawn his plans, supervised the construction. He showed us through the house. He had a story to tell about every room and every feature. He'd say, for example, "Copper piping all the way through—and let me tell you about that copper pipe. . . ." And away he'd go with facts and figures! Or I would ask, "Is it insulated?"—which would bring down a flood of facts about the insulation and why it was the best in the world.

I'd have bought that house for sure, except that it was the wrong size in the wrong location at the wrong price. If that man had sold me that house it would have been a triumph for enthusiasm founded on product knowledge!

REASON 2: We need product knowledge to give us courage.

A fear that grips all beginners and, alas, many experienced salesmen, is the fear that the prospect will ask questions they can't answer.

The only salesman who fears questions is the one who doesn't know the answers.

REASON 3: We need product knowledge for the personal satisfaction it gives us to be experts.

REASON 4: We need product knowledge so that we can talk confidently with experts. This is especially true when we deal with purchasing agents, engineers, accountants, and other professional men.

An exasperated purchasing agent once told me: "The reason so few of us learn anything from sales talks is that so few people who sell know anything!" I don't subscribe to this belief, but I know, unfortunately, it is true of some salesmen.

The Coca-Cola Company asked some of its larger customers to tell them the outstanding qualities of good salesmen. The answer that led all others was: "A thorough knowledge of his product."

My friend Art Lustig, a Dale Carnegie Sales Course instructor in Chicago, told me how product knowledge enabled him to resell to a group of real estate salesmen a subdivision on which they had "gone dead." Art said:

John Forbes, vice-president and sales manager of Robert Bartlett Realty Co. of Chicago, was concerned about the lagging of sales of their subdivision at Miller, Indiana, a suburb of Gary. They opened their sales campaign with a bang. However, after a few months the Bartlett salesmen lost interest in the Miller property and began bothering Forbes to open up a new subdivision.

One day John said to me, "Art, I sure would appreciate it if you would make a talk to my salesmen about the Miller subdivision. Tell them why they should continue to sell the Miller lots. They are tired of listening to me every Monday morning."

I told John that I would, but that I needed a little time to study the subdivision thoroughly.

I went to Gary, which is about 20 miles from the south side of Chicago, and talked to numerous store owners and individuals about Gary and Miller. I learned: (1) that the people in Gary who wanted to have homes of their own knew little about Bartlett's subdivision; (2) that the water pressure in summer in Gary was low; (3) that a railroad crosses Gary about every four or five blocks; (4) that the people who were building in Gary were moving farther away from the lake, because most of them were under the impression that there was no more shore land available.

After I had studied that subdivision, I made the talk to the Bartlett salesmen. I brought out all those selling points. I stressed over and over again that a fertile field of prospects lay right under their noses in Gary.

Later John told me that the following week their sales jumped over 30 per cent and that in six months they had sold out the entire subdivision.

Product knowledge helps you to
answer objections

REASON 5: You need product knowledge to answer objections effectively.

When the prospect says, "Your machine isn't as well built as the XYZ machine," you had better know your product— and the XYZ product as well—or you are likely to lose the sale.

For many salesmen the toughest of all objections is, "The price is too high." The one answer to that objection is to prove quality and value. To do this you must have thorough product knowledge.

REASON 6: You need product knowledge because the more you know about your product the more advantages to users you will discover in it. You will discover, also, new ways to bring the advantages home to prospects.

William Bloethe gave this example in the *New York World-Telegram and Sun*, of the unfortunate results of a lack of product knowledge by a salesman:

Hotpoint developed a butter bin inside the refrigerator to keep butter soft enough to use. It took $100,000 of tools and dies, plus the original research costs, plus an additional charge on each box, to install them.

So what happens?

Listening in on a salesman as a prospect asked about the butter box, I heard:

"Oh that—why that's just a place to put the butter where it's not in the way of other articles in the refrigerator."

The salesman, because of ignorance of his product, had completely missed the $100,000 point: that the purpose of the butter compartment was to keep the butter at the proper degree of softness for table use.

REASON 7: Product knowledge helps you to meet competition effectively.

What will it profit you to tell your prospect that your product is better than another product unless you can state the facts that prove it?

Know your product and fear nobody

REASON 8: You need product knowledge because it gives you self-assurance, which Webster defines as "a state of mind, free from diffidence, doubt, or misgivings."

In teaching public speaking, we tell men, "To gain confidence in speaking, know a hundred times as much about your subject as you can use." That's a good rule for salesmen, too.

As Socrates said, "Everybody is eloquent enough on what he *knows*."

Somewhere—I've forgotten where—I picked up the story of how product knowledge built self-confidence in one of Hugh Chalmers' salesmen when Hugh was Sales Manager for National Cash Register Co.

Hugh held an annual conference of the National Cash Register agents in Germany. He awarded a prize to the man who had made the best record during the year. He then asked the star salesman to tell the secret of his success. The salesman strode

to the speaker's platform, faced his audience for a moment, and
said, "I defy anyone in all Germany to ask me a question about
the National Cash Register that I cannot answer."

That was his entire speech, but it was sufficient. He knew his
product!

REASON 9: You need product knowledge in order to gain the
confidence of prospects.

If you know your product, prospects and customers will
look on you not as a peddler, but as an expert—a sales coun-
selor for your product.

My boyhood friend John C. Small is an excellent example
of how product knowledge (no matter how gained) gives confidence to customers and helps the salesman to build a
profitable clientele. Jack's story follows:

I was a salesman for eighteen years for the New York Stock
Exchange house of Jackson and Curtis.

I was just an average salesman—you know the kind. If I'd been
any worse, they'd have fired me; if I'd been any better, they'd
have made me a member of the firm.

Product knowledge—even if I had to dig it out—helped me
to broaden my list of clients.

For example, a satisfied client mentioned to me a person she
termed "a widow in distress," who had a list of securities that
totaled around a million and a half. I went to work on them. Of
course I had to look them up. There's no such thing as a man who
"knows all about securities." [This would seem an understatement,
considering that 3,454 stocks and bonds are traded on the two
New York exchanges and an estimated 16,000 stocks and bonds
are traded "over the counter" in New York. I am grateful to J.
Craigen Bruce of the New York Stock Exchange house of Burton
Dana & Co. for these figures. P.H.W.]

I took a week to write the report. The widow acted on my
suggestions. For a year nothing happened. Then four other members of that family called on me for advice—all of which led to
business. Soon the family sent in another widow who had over
$2,000,000 worth of securities.

This kind of service pushed Jack Small up from peddling securities to the exalted position of "consultant." Not many years thereafter Jack retired with a comfortable income from his earnings made possible through product knowledge and a desire to serve!

── CHAPTER 4

You can talk *too much*
about your product,
but you can't know *too much*

The buyer who knows merchandise is a little tough on a salesman who doesn't. —JACK SCHOETTINGER

Do you want to know how much you should know about your product in order to sell it successfully? I can tell you in one word: everything!

In general you should know:

1. Your product and its uses—how it can benefit your prospects.

2. *Why* it is superior, at least in some respects, to competitors' products.

3. Your competitors' goods.

4. The concern you represent—its history, its financial standing, its officers, its reputation, its policies.

While speaking one day to a group of salesmen for a large wholesale grocery jobber in Waco, Texas, I said, "When somebody opens a new grocery store in your territory, do you go to him and try to get him to give your company the business?"

One of them replied, "Yes, I do."

"Suppose he asks you, 'Why should I buy from your company?' What would you say?"

"I don't know."

"You mean you do not know any reason why a grocer should buy from your house?"

"No, I don't."

. Of course, this man wasn't even a good order taker. I learned afterward that he held his job only because he wrote his orders in a good, round hand!

Men like that don't get as much pay as a rural school-teacher, and certainly don't deserve to.

If you aspire to the title "professional salesman"—and to his earnings—know your product!

Question: Where shall I look for information? Answer: Everywhere!

You will have to look for information in many places. Here are some of them:

1. Read magazines—those devoted to your industry or business. Read general magazines—a salesman needs general information as well as specialized information.

2. Read books about your product—and subjects allied to it.

3. Pump your boss dry of information. Interview other officials of the company you represent.

4. Get information from other salesmen.

5. Get information from prospects and customers. W. C. Holman, in his book *Ginger Talks*, gives some good advice about getting knowledge from users of your product. Mr. Holman says:

There's one man who knows a lot about your business and doesn't charge anything for imparting his knowledge. That fellow is the *user* of your article. He is generally a keen observer, and if you go at him right, it's an easy matter to get good suggestions from him.

It pays to be friendly with a user.

6. Visit factories, plants, home offices.

7. If your product is something you can use yourself, use it. When I managed a force which was selling a preferred stock, I insisted that every salesman buy some of the stock out of his first earnings. I wanted him to know how it felt to be a stockholder.

When my friend Billy Wootton of Evansville, Indiana, is promoting a Dale Carnegie Sales Course class through the Jaycees or a service club, he insists that every member of the program committee enroll in the course. "If they don't believe enough in the benefits of the course to take it themselves," says Billy, "they don't believe in it enough to sell it."

N. Fratt, sales manager of the Seattle Gas Co., told me that once a month he made his gas-range salesmen cook a meal—on both a gas and an electric range—then he made them eat the meal they thought was cooked the better.

The trick is to remember it!

Unless you have an amazing memory, like that of my friend Dr. Bruno Furst, who memorizes books just for fun, you should write down what you learn and should file it where you can find it.

I use, for filing information, 8½ x 11 folders with three tabs, assorted. I write on the tabs the subject headings, such as: "Buying signals," and "Overcoming prejudices." Then, as I pick up material, I slip it into the appropriate folder. It will astound you, after a few years, how much useful information you have gathered.

Be careful that your information is true and authentic. I think it was Artemus Ward who said, "I honestly believe it is better tew know nothin' than tew know what ain't so."

Now one last, loud word of warning about product knowl-edge! *Don't talk just to show off your knowledge.*

I once heard a man say, at a convention of direct-mail experts, "I always throw into every sales letter one word I'm sure the reader will not understand. That convinces him I know more than he does!"

That isn't what it would convince me of!

Please, I beg of you, don't ever let your knowledge of the product get in the way of telling your prospect, simply and clearly, what your goods or service will do to benefit him.

A good example of the danger of talking over the prospect's head was given in an article by Ed Graham, Jr., in the magazine now published as *Advertising Agency Magazine.*

A CASE OF TECHNOSIS—THE SALESMAN
WHO TOOK HIS PHONE APART

Once upon a time there lived a successful telephone salesman who traveled all over the country selling shiny black telephones faster than his company could make them. "Tell me the secret of your success," a friend who sold vacuum cleaners asked him one day.

So the telephone salesman thought and thought, but there was no secret to tell. "I just explain that telephones allow people to talk to their friends without getting out of bed"—he said—"and for only a dime."

The vacuum-cleaner salesman laughed heartily. "That's the silliest excuse for a sales story I ever heard," he roared. "You don't even tell them how your machine *works.*"

"I don't really *know* how it works," the telephone salesman confessed. At this his friend laughed and laughed.

That night the telephone salesman decided to take one of his phones apart. Within a short time he became so involved in what he found that he went to the library and took out 56 books—each of them explaining how telephones work. He discovered that the simplest call had to pass through a central switchboard with 24,835 wires in it. He learned how a dial system works, and he read that there are 92 million miles of aboveground cables stretched across the state of Massachusetts alone. After he had memorized all this, he threw a gross of shiny black phones into a suitcase and went into the field to make more sales.

"The telephone is a most remarkable instrument. It took 43

laboratories filled with 43 engineering staffs 43 years to perfect our No. 2 voice amplifier alone," he told the first lady.

"I'm busy," she said.

"Not as busy as the Alpha Home Company," the salesman answered. "Alpha devotes 336 man hours a week just to inspect the brass parts for interconnecting switches."

"That's the sillest excuse for a sales story I ever heard. When I want to know how to run a telephone company, I'll get in touch with you," said the woman, as she picked up an old cane and drove the salesman out of the house.

MORAL: The *least* SILLY excuse for a sales talk is what the product does for the customer. . . .

If the moral of that story isn't clear to you, you'll never be a salesman anyway—so why go into it!

CHAPTER 5

What a salesman should know
about his prospects

Unless you know your customer's needs, why take his time!

Exactly what should a salesman know about his *prospect* before he starts to make his sales talk?

That depends, of course, on the prospect and on what the salesman is selling. Here, however, are some "prospect-knowledge" questions that apply most of the time to most salesmen, most products, and most prospects.

1. What is your prospect's problem that might be solved by your product? (Your aim should be to *serve* the prospect rather than merely to *sell* the product.)

2. What are the prospect's (*a*) needs and (*b*) wants? (DEFINITIONS: *need*, "Something useful, required or desired,

that is lacking"; *want,* "a *desire* for something, a craving.")
That is, find what the prospect wants to accomplish, which
your product will help him to accomplish.

3. What are your prospect's hobbies, his outside activities,
his politics, and his habits? What about his family?

4. What is your prospect's name and how does he pro-
nounce it? What are his titles—in his organization and out?
(And does he like his titles used? Some Ph.D.'s like to be
called "doctor." Some don't.)

5. Is your prospect in a position to buy? Someone once
wisely said, "Many a sale is lost because a misinformed salesman either underestimated or overestimated his prospect's
buying intentions and purchasing power."

6. What is the best day and the best hour to see the prospect?

Find it out—write it down

If you are selling items that run into big money, you may
want to find out, in addition to the prospect's needs, the competition you are likely to meet; probable savings or profits
which will result from using your product; and the most desirable equipment for this particular prospect, and the like.

Be very sure to write on your prospect card all information
you secure. No matter how good a memory you have, it is
probably not good enough to carry this information indefinitely.

Use these facts about your prospect to help build up your
sales talk. This will be discussed in succeeding chapters.

To sum it up: find the *want*

"The indispensable foundation for every sale," says W. L.
Barnhart in *Printers' Ink,* "is absolute knowledge on the part
of the salesman that the prospect needs the goods and can
profit greatly by purchasing them."

If you don't know how your prospect can profit from owning your goods and can't find out—*get out.* A salesman who
does not know this before he starts his sales talk has little more
moral standing than a pickpocket.

So, to sum it up, you should find out what your prospect
wants and needs and should talk to him about it. If you do,
you have a good chance to succeed. If you don't, you have an
even better chance to fail.

––––––––––––––––––––––––––––––– CHAPTER 6

What the pre-approach is
and how you can use it
to make many more sales

*The man who knows everything about his product is
an expert; the man who tells everything is a bore!*

The primary cause of poor approaching is poor pre-approach-
ing. I found that out over twenty-five years ago, by making a
sales error so incredibly stupid that I blush to think about it.
It was such a blundering performance that I haven't the heart,
even now, to name names, but here's what happened: I called
on the treasurer of a gigantic and completely solvent company to sell him a financing job for one of his subsidiaries. The
conversation had not gone far before I learned, to my humilia-
tion, that, though the parent company was solvent, the subsidiary was bankrupt. What the subsidiary needed was not
an investment banker, but an undertaker. The subsidiary had
no more chance to float a loan than an inmate of the county
poorhouse.

I made this hideous selling mistake because I disregarded
this basic rule of selling:

Before you make a sales talk, get enough information about your prospect's needs and wants so that you can talk intelligently to him about how your goods or services will benefit him.

Disobey this basic rule and you will probably fail as a salesman.

The late G. Lynn Sumner wrote:

The most important development of modern selling is recognition of the value of selling not the article itself, but the use of it.... The seller must know everything possible about the use of his article in order to sell all its uses to the best advantage.

This information-getting step in the selling process is usually called the "pre-approach." This title is misleading because often the information is not secured *before* the approach is made, but after. A better name would be: the "information-getting step."

To shorten it, let's call it the "info step."

Whatever you call it, this fact remains: in most forms of selling, unless you get the information about your prospect and his needs before you start your presentation, you cannot make an effective sales talk.

Failure to observe this rule results each year in literally millions of puny pitches and "sunk" sales.

Why so many salesmen ignore the "info step"

Why do salesmen ignore this "info step?"

We have, at various times, asked this question of several hundred men and women who were taking the Dale Carnegie Sales Course. Here are the five top reasons, as given by these salesmen, why they and other salesmen so often fail to take this "info step":

1. Overeagerness. Salesmen are in such a hurry to make a sale they feel they can't take time to prepare.

2. Inadequate training. Nobody told them how to do it— or sold them on its importance.

Lots of salesmen never even heard of the "pre-approach." A few months ago I taught the first session of our sales course to an extremely high-grade group of real estate salesmen in Plainfield, New Jersey. I said to the class, "Will all here who know what the word *pre-approach* means please put up their hands?"

Only one hand went up—mine!

Charles W. Mears, in his book *Salesmanship for the New Era,* gives this example of men selling carbon paper:

The untrained man comes in and says, "Any carbon paper today?"

The well-trained man comes in and says, "I would like to ask you a question or two about your carbon paper. Would you mind telling me all the different uses you make of carbon paper? What size sheet? What color? How many copies do you make? How much carbon paper do you use in a month? How often do you buy it? About how long will your present supply last? With this information, I will see if I can't help you."

3. They don't know where to get information about the prospect and his needs and wants—or how.

4. Laziness. (NOTE: *I* didn't say that—no, but several hundred salesmen did.)

5. Failure to include the "info step" in *planning* the day's work—if they planned it at all.

Maybe you think this step is not important

Here are some of the reasons why I believe that the "info step" is important to you:

1. It saves you from making mistakes.

Under the heading "Know Your Customer" the magazine *Sales Management* recently gave this example:

A bride of a few months complained to her relatives about her husband's continued drinking. "If you knew he drank, why in the world did you marry him?" asked Aunt Kate.

"I didn't know he drank," replied the tearful voice, "until one night he came home sober."

We had an example, right in my own home not fifteen minutes before I wrote this, of what may happen if you skip the "info step."

Someone called on the phone and asked for Mrs. Whiting. It was a saleswoman for a neighborhood photographer. The dialogue ran like this:

Saleswoman: "I want to talk to you about having some free photographs taken of your children."

Gene: "I have no children."

That ended the pitch—and any chance that photographer had of ever doing business with us.

2. Knowledge secured in the "info step" may enable you to "qualify" your prospect—that is, to find out if he could use your product. For example:

COLUMBIA, La. March 5. (AP)—William Heard received a letter from the circulation department of a Little Rock, Ark., newspaper advising him that his subscription would expire March 8.

Heard replied, in part:

"I wish to inform you that, if you read your paper as closely as I do . . . you would know that I will be hung on March 7."

3. In the "info step," you can find out what information you need in order to talk effectively in the interest step, the conviction step, and the desire step. Without this information, you must sell blind!

4. Getting the information you need in advance of your call keeps purchasing agents, space buyers, and other prospects from hating you.

Why make prospects dislike you?

The indignation of purchasing agents against salesmen who do not bother to find out what a prospect makes or sells, was well expressed in an article in *Printers' Ink*, headed "Why Don't Salesmen Stop Wasting My Time?" and written by A. E. R. Peterka of The Lamson & Sessions Co., Cleveland. He said:

Nine out of ten space peddlers—at the very least—call without even bothering to learn what The Lamson & Sessions Co. makes.

We make fasteners—all kinds of fasteners. We do not make conveyor systems (that's another Lamson) and we have no relation to clockmaking (that's another Sessions).

Those salesmen who do seem to have at least an inkling of the kinds of fasteners we manufacture usually have no knowledge whatever of the way we market.

Unless you are deliberately trying to antagonize a prospect, you'd better make it a policy to find out how your product fits into his plans—or stay away from him!

Printers' Ink asked 108 representative advertisers to name objectionable practices of the advertising salesmen who called on them. The most common objection named—the one placed number one on this list of selling ineptitudes—was "trying to get our business but knowing nothing about our problems."

E. W. Hull, in charge of sales training for Railway Express Agency, told me, "One of the things we teach our salesmen is 'Don't call on a prospect unless you have something to offer the prospect that *he can use.*' The main purpose of the pre-approach is to find out how the prospect can use your product or service!"

5. The "info step," properly taken, helps a salesman to keep up his courage.

If, when a salesman faces his prospect, he is just loaded with knowledge about the prospect and his wants and needs, he has little cause for fear. He is vastly better off than he would have been if he had gone in with no ammunition but a canned sales talk—guaranteed to fit all prospects, and probably suited to none.

If you know—and your competitor doesn't!

6. Having ample knowledge gives you an advantage over your competitors—assuming they have not done as good an info-getting job as you have.

Morton Bailey, a top man in the *Saturday Evening Post* organization, said recently: "We all feel that the more we can find out about our customers and our customers' business the better advantage we have over competitors."

An excellent example of the effectiveness of a good pre-approach in meeting competition was given me by W. J. Newhouse of the Chase Bag Company. He said:

The Woburn Chemical Company at Newark had a packaging problem. As soon as inquiries were sent out, representatives from competitive companies in the packaging field called at the Newark office. Included was Lloyd Wise of the Chase Bag Company.

By asking questions Mr. Wise determined the nature of the product to be packaged, the protection that it required, and other information.

Then, and not until then, Mr. Wise told the purchasing agent, "I know exactly what you need. I will immediately get samples for you for test packaging."

The representative of the Woburn Chemical Company said, "Thank heavens! At last I have run into one of you fellows who knows his business. I'm in the *chemical* business, *not* in the *packaging* business. I have had three other representatives in my office today. In each case they asked me, 'What kind of package do you want?' That is what I wanted to learn from them! If I had known what I wanted I would have ordered it. You go ahead and provide those samples. If they are satisfactory, you certainly will get this business."

The samples did prove satisfactory, and an order for 20,000 bags resulted.

To sum it up, the primary items the salesman needs to know before he starts his sales talk are: (*a*) the needs of the prospect and (*b*) the wants of the prospect as they relate to what the salesman is selling. (NOTE: Salesmen should not get the mistaken idea that *wants* and *needs* are the same. I might *need* castor oil—but I wouldn't *want* it. Equally, I *want* a color television set, but I don't *need* it.)

—————————————————————————— CHAPTER 7

Some rules for getting the information you need to make an effective sales talk

Every sale will be easier if you can
discover the prospect's chief interest.

The method of getting information from a prospect differs according to the *prospect* and even more according to the *product*.

The door-to-door brush salesman is lucky if he learns a housewife's name before he calls on her. It usually takes him not over 30 seconds to get it—usually from the next-door neighbor.

Yet the man planning to sell a complete new harbor installation at some undeveloped port in South America might spend a year or two on his pre-approach.

A vast amount of time is spent on the pre-approach by men who sell highly technical equipment. My friend Warren Stubblebine, sales manager of the Connecticut Hard Rubber Company, told me of a long-pull pre-approach:

This pre-approach took eight months and landed a half-million-dollar contract

In our organization, an engineer and a salesman work together. Recently one of our engineer-salesman teams learned of a redesign and change of military function of an airplane. The engineer went to work with the customer's engineers on a study of the needs, if any, for electric heating assemblies.

The entire process of designing and developing this heating unit took eight months. The salesman finally obtained the order—for half a million dollars!

The best way to get information is usually to ask for it

Here are a few general suggestions for getting information about the prospect and his needs:

A. *Interview his friends and associates.* These men will know his personality, his hobbies, his family situation, perhaps his dominant buying motive.

B. *Use your eyes.* As you go into the man's place of business, or as you sit in the waiting room, look at the walls, the tables, the bookcases—maybe something there will give you an idea.

C. *Ask questions.* The receptionist may be willing to give you some information. Some waiting salesman may give you a pointer or two.

D. *Get permission to interview a subordinate.* Phone the prospect, state your business, and do just enough selling to get the man interested. Then say, in substance, "I do not know for sure whether or not our proposition would fit into your needs. May I talk to an associate of yours who could answer enough of my questions to help me determine whether our ... [whatever you sell] is something that might be of service to you? With whom would you suggest that I talk?"

E. *Ask questions of the prospect.* Almost any man will answer at least a few questions about his company and himself. He is human—hence he likes to talk about himself. While he talks, you listen—attentively.

How they do it in Hawaii

A few months ago, when I was in Honolulu teaching a Sales Course Instructors School, J. Edwin Whitlow of Honolulu, who offers the Dale Carnegie Courses on the Hawaiian Islands, said, "Be sure to ask your questions in a sincere, friendly, helpful way—a way that indicates that you want this information so that you can render the prospect a service. Here in Hawaii we teach salesmen to tell the prospect substantially this: 'Mr. Prospect, I believe I have something here that will be of considerable value to you. In order to be *sure*, I need to know a little more about your particular situation. Is it all right for me to ask a few questions?'

"Then we train salesmen to ask the questions that will bring out the needs and wants of the prospect. By so doing, we cease to be salesmen, we become counselors.

"I suggest this wording to salesmen because each prospect seems to feel that his situation is just a little different from the other fellow's. And when you tell him you need to know a little more about *his particular situation*, believe me, he's ready to talk!"

Let the prospect talk

Get the prospect to admit that he has a problem and that he should do something about it. Then you know how to plan your attack.

Ask the prospect to tell you how *he* thinks his problem can best be solved. When he tells you that, he has left himself wide open for a strong sales attack.

Remember the rule, "To be popular with prospects, *ask questions.*"

Lug a lot of "info" into your second call

If a salesman needs, for his first call, lots of information about his prospect and his prospect's problems, he needs vastly more for his second call.

A prospect is charitable, indeed, if he listens to a salesman who comes in half prepared for his second selling attempt.

Here's an interesting point made by J. E. Sorrell, advertising manager, The Lamson & Sessions Co., in an article in *Printers' Ink.*

If you can't thoroughly convince yourself that your product can be profitably fitted into your prospect's schedule, and if you can't corral more than enough facts to prove it, then save yourself some time: *don't make the second call.* Get on to the next prospect and qualify him in the same way before you uncork your full presentation complete with easel and gestures!

Really prepare for that second call

Remember, for one sale made by luck, ten are made by planning.

It is not enough merely to get all the information you need in order to make an effective second call; you must *plan* your sales talk according to this information. Here are some suggestions:

1. Analyze the information.
2. Arrange your sales points in the proper order.
3. Determine exactly how your proposition will benefit the prospect.
4. Consider how you can word each point so that you will talk not about the product, but about the *benefits* of this product *to the buyer.*
5. Then go back through and check to be sure that every point will be presented from the viewpoint of the buyer.

6. Try to think of some way to put drama, showmanship, and excitement into your talk.

7. Then memorize not the *words* but the *ideas* you plan to present.

8. Finally, rehearse it—perhaps in front of a mirror.

When you have done these things, you are ready to make the second call—effectively.

§THREE

You have to *see* your prospect

to *sell* him

(The secret of "getting in")

―――――――――――――――――― CHAPTER 8

How to get in to see your prospect

The law gives salesmen full right of protection, but makes no provision for the casket. —SALESMAN'S SAYING

If you expect to find, in this chapter or anywhere else, an unfailing rule for getting in to see the man you want to see at the time you want to see him, you should harden yourself for disappointment.

No such rule is known to man. No universal door-opener exists.

Two groups of salesmen have the problem of getting in to see the prospect: door-to-door salesmen and office-to-office salesmen. Let's see if we can help the salesmen of each of these groups to solve one of their meanest problems.

Let's take the former group first—

NOTE: Don't skip this just because you are an office-to-office salesman. You may get some ideas here that you can use.

Gifts unlock doors for salesmen

Let's look first at the greatest discovery of the greatest door-to-door salesman of all time—Alfred C. Fuller.

33

This man, in the winter of 1906, made some brushes and started selling them.

His gross sales the first week totaled $6. Today, more than 7,300 Fuller Brush men push more than one hundred million doorbells annually—for total sales of $53,000,000. From A. C. Fuller's start in 1906, Fuller Brush men have sold about three-quarters of a *billion* dollars' worth of brushes.

Fuller's great discovery was that almost any salesman can get past almost any door—with a *gift*.

American Business tells the story thus:

Getting inside the housewife's door has always been the number one problem [of door-to-door salesmen]. Fuller's major contribution to the art of legal entry came in 1915, when he got Fuller Brush men to give away a vegetable brush.

Fuller Brush salesmen are taught to carry the sample in the sample case, to call it a *gift* instead of a *sample*, and to present it inside the house rather than on the doorstep.

A Fuller Brush man was taught how to handle a housewife who wanted to take the sample without seeing his line. (With a helpless gesture he would indicate the impossibility of opening his sample case out there.)

If the housewife said she was too busy, he should say he would just step in for a minute. If she didn't want the brush he should say, "I get credit for giving them out."

Nobody, as far as I can learn, has ever improved on the Fuller method of getting past that solid barrier between salesmen and housewives—the front door.

Many other companies which sell door-to-door use gifts. The salesmen of Real Silk Hosiery Mills, Inc., of Indianapolis still use, as a door-opener, a mending kit for silk stockings. It is now called an "emergency kit." Other "good will items" used by Real Silk salesmen are a plastic case, a comb, and a razor blade.

If you sell door-to-door, these rules are for you

Here are some suggestions for door-to-door salesmen about getting past housewives and into homes so that they can display their product and attempt a sale:

1. Don't work door-to-door up one side of a block and down the other. This advertises the fact to watchers—and lots of housewives are watchers—that you are a salesman. Then, when you ring the doorbell of one of these watchers, she's out—and so are you!

2. Never work in a block which is being worked by another salesman.

3. Try to get—and always use—the name of the woman you are calling on. Try to get the names of her children.

4. Walk up to the house briskly, as though you were on important business. Give the prospect plenty of time to answer the ring.

5. When the prospect opens the door, take a step backward—which is a disarming gesture.

6. Smile, talk slowly, clearly, and in not too loud a tone.

7. A greeting used by successful salesmen is "Good morning. Are you Mrs. Brown?" After she admits it, the salesman says, "I am Mr. Jones—may I step in?" Then he makes a confident step toward the door—or reaches for the screen door, as if to open it.

8. Never make your sales talk at the door. Either get in, or get out and try again later.

CHAPTER 9

How office-to-office salesmen can get through the "buffer zone"

If an important man were to take time to see everybody who wanted to see him, he wouldn't be important long.
—SALESMAN'S SAYING

The Constitution of the United States does not give salesmen an inalienable right to take the time of a reluctant prospect. Important men use receptionists and secretaries to sort out and turn back unimportant and unwanted callers. They have to!

A salesman should not be annoyed when a secretary says, "Please tell me your business." It's part of her job to separate the wanted from the unwanted.

You must be prepared to sell the receptionist or the prospect's secretary—or perhaps both—that you can render the prospect a real service and thus that you are justified in asking for enough of his time to explain what your product or service will do to benefit him. Frequently you have to sell the prospect himself on the idea that you are entitled to an interview.

Some salesmen, when they have trouble selling the interview, say, "I'm not going to ask you to buy anything. I just want a chance to tell you how our product will . . ."—and then he launches into buyer's benefits.

Don't underestimate the private secretary

Sometimes it pays to give your presentation to a private secretary—certainly enough of it to convince her that you have a message her boss ought to hear.

Sometimes you have to detour around the private secretary. You may have to call the prospect at his home to ask for an appointment if he is very important, or you may tackle him as he leaves his office for lunch or for home. Don't expect the prospect to be delighted with such an intrusion. One salesman who uses "detours" opens his talk with the prospect by asking, "Mr. Blank, do you have enough influence with your secretary to persuade her to let me in to see you?"

If the prospect is important and the barrier between you and him seems as impenetrable as a vault door, you may be able to get an introduction through the officials, directors, or banker of your company. You may enlist the aid of the people from whom you buy, or a friend, a member of your lodge, club, or fraternity.

Here are some rules for getting in

Some rules for getting past receptionists and secretaries and into the presence of the prospect follow:

Rule 1: Feel as though you had a right to be ushered in. You get this feeling by knowing so much about your product and what it will do, so much about your prospect and what he needs done, that you would feel sorry for your prospect if you did not get in to see him.

For example, when I was in charge of sales promotion for the Dale Carnegie Institute, if an unknown printing salesman called, I always referred him to Dick Fay, our purchasing agent. But when Fred Peck of George Bosch and Company called, I always saw him. Fred knew so much about printing and had made such a study of our particular problems that his sales talks were worth listening to. He had helped us distribute our printed matter at meetings, had kept a line on the results of our mailing campaigns, and knew what we were trying to do.

Fred Peck always got in to see me because he had earned the right to get in.

Good clothes help to make you look important

Rule 2: You must *dress* the part.

For example, a man who called on me one day when I had my own company on Wall Street wore a cutaway coat, striped trousers, a plug hat, and a carnation, and carried a cane. He looked as though he had just stepped out of a society wedding. When he announced, "I have come to see Mr. Whiting," he managed to make it sound as though he were conferring a favor on me. He told me he was rarely refused admittance.

What was this sartorial specimen selling? Magazines!

I don't recommend cutaways and plug hats for ordinary salesmen, but I do recommend that they dress like successful businessmen. Good clothes pay cash dividends for salesmen. Buy the best you can afford—maybe a little better.

Good clothes build good morale

I recall that, in 1918, when $100 would buy a lot of fine clothes, my sales manager, Austin Brown, dug up a wreck of a salesman. This man, who had once been a highly successful securities salesman, had sold a security that went sour, had been sick, had been and still was broke, had been drinking too much. Naturally, his morale was wrecked.

Austin said to me, "Will you gamble $100 on a wreck?" After I heard the story I said, "Yes."

So Austin took the salesman to a clothing store and bought him a complete outfit. The result was miraculous. This man's morale was soon brought back to normal, his courage was built up, and he started selling successfully and kept on selling successfully as long as he was with us.

Rule 3: You must *talk* the part. Don't talk like a beggar or a pack peddler. "Will you please tell Mr. Blank that..." tells the story better than "I'd like to see Mr. Blank." The former makes for action; the latter invites questions.

Rule 4: You must *act* the part. Remember, if you *act* as though you expected to get in, you will probably *feel* as though you expected to get in.

How do you *act* the part?

(*a*) Walk in briskly.

(*b*) If you have to wait, don't slouch down in your chair as though you had come to spend a week end.

(*c*) Make it a general rule not to wait longer than fifteen minutes for anyone. (Naturally, you have to make exceptions.)

Don't talk "on the doorstep"!

Rule 5: Get inside to make your talk.

Suppose your prospect comes out of his office and into the reception room and insists that you state your business there—what should you do? The rule is: Don't hit him! The provocation is great but the results are bad.

Try some of these remarks:

(*a*) "Let's step back into your office, where we can talk without interruption"—and start walking. Unless he is an utter boor, he will follow. Maybe he is a boor! In that case, try one of the following:

(*b*) "I'm sorry you are too busy to see me now. May I see you Thursday at 9:40?"

(*c*) "I'm here to talk about your . . . , Mr. Blank. May I go into your office where we can talk freely?"

In other words, meet it head on.

What is the rule if the prospect says, "Go ahead and tell me your story right here"?

The rule is: Don't tell it.

I can *imagine* exceptions but I never saw one. You lose your self-respect when you talk in "no-man's land," and you rarely make the sale.

P.S. If you have trouble getting in to see your prospect, read David D. Seltz's book, *250 Successful Door-openers for Salesmen.*

CHAPTER 10

A good personality is a good door-opener

It seems so easy to be good-natured, I wonder why anyone takes the trouble to be anything else. —JERROLD

Let's see what we can do to improve our chances of getting in to see hard-to-see prospects.

If a "buffer" takes one look at you and then says to herself, "I like that man," you are already more than half in. If she likes you better as the interview with you progresses, you are three-quarters in—maybe all the way.

Why will "buffers" like you? Because you have a good personality and because you use good human relations—because you know how to win friends and influence people.

Our best advice to salesmen who sell office-to-office, and especially to those who have trouble getting past the "buffers," is: read again Dale Carnegie's *How to Win Friends and Influence People* and observe the advice it gives you.

Here are a few suggestions for getting in that may help you:

Rule 1: Be courteous, smiling, considerate, and appreciative.

Thomas Fuller, who lived over three hundred years ago, said, "All doors open to courtesy." That's a slight exaggeration—but courtesy certainly helps to open doors. So be unfailingly tactful, polite, and thoughtful.

Don't bluster. I once heard my secretary, Maryann McGaffin, say to the receptionist, "That man talks mighty big— he's a windbag. He'll never bluff his way in to see my boss"— and he never did.

Of course you shouldn't expect that your courtesy will always be echoed by "buffers" or prospects. An example of what prospects sometimes say to salesmen was given in *Tracks*, the house magazine of the Chesapeake and Ohio Railway.

The big businessman had died and gone to—well, not to heaven. He had hardly settled down for a nice long smoke when a hearty hand slapped him on the back, and into his ear boomed the voice of a persistent salesman who had pestered him on earth.
"Well, Mr. Smith," chortled the salesman, "I'm here for the appointment."
"What appointment?"
"Why, don't you remember?" the salesman went on. "Every time I entered your office on earth you told me you'd see me here!"

Again I say, if you often have trouble getting in to see your prospects, read *How to Win Friends and Influence People*.
Especially observe these four Dale Carnegie rules:
(*a*) Smile.
(*b*) Show appreciation. Thank people who help you.
(*c*) Remember names—not only the names of important people, but also of the seemingly unimportant ones. Take a memory course or a course in public speaking in which memory is taught.
(*d*) Make people feel important. You certainly impress the average secretary when you say, "Do you realize, Miss Jones, that you are the only person who can perform the miracle of getting me in to see your boss?"

Be friends with everybody

Rule 2: Try to make friends with everybody in every office where you call. Salesmen who have been kept out by secretaries have often been smuggled in by an office boy.
My friend the late Walter Jenkins was always able to walk in on one of the most important space buyers in New York City. I asked him once how it happened.
He said, "I helped to raise that boy. When I started in as

an advertising solicitor, he had just started in as an office boy.
I liked him, was nice to him, and made a fuss over him. He
has never forgotten it and is never likely to."

Rule 3: Don't lie.

Your business is not strictly "personal," rarely "confidential,"
and probably not too "important" to anyone but you.

Don't be dishonest. The man you fool once will rarely let
you fool him a second time.

Rule 4: Don't be turned down too easily. When you face
the "buffer" is a good time to develop "no" deafness. If you
make a practice of hearing the first "no" you will soon be in
another business or in the poorhouse.

CHAPTER 11

You need courage and ingenuity to get in to see the hard-to-see people

*What most of us need is more horsepower and less
exhaust.* —*Texas and Pacific Topics*

Cy Burg wrote, in an article, "Training Salesmen for Post-
war" (and I've forgotten which war he meant):

It is startling the number of salesmen I can get rid of over the
phone.

"Can I see you?"

"No, I am too busy."

"Well, when can I see you?"

"I don't know."

It is surprising how many salesmen quit at that point.

We have a policy to see any salesman who calls at the plant, so
most salesmen get in.

When a jelly-backboned salesman gets into my office, right away,
regardless of what the guy has to sell, I don't want it. My attitude

is *no*. Sometimes I say it so loud I, figuratively speaking, blow the salesman out of the office. Many jelly-backboned guys get out and write to the boss, "Oh, what a tough bird this Burg is." But the guy who has enough backbone will say, "Wait a minute, I am not through yet. I haven't told you this story," and he won't take no. Don't let your men become discouraged. Don't let them take *no*.

Perhaps the most common turnaway technique of private secretaries is to say, "Mr. Prospect is too busy to see you."

We recently heard of a successful New York salesman who, though his clients were big businessmen, rarely had difficulty in getting an appointment. This astounding record he explained by the fact that he always asked for an appointment *at an odd time*. That is, instead of suggesting eleven o'clock, for instance, he would specify 10:50. Of course the busy executive would have another engagement at eleven, but probably no engagement at such an odd hour. The executive also somehow got the idea that this salesman's time was valuable and that he would be interested in making the interview as concise as possible. —*Manager's Magazine*

There is always a way to get in to see anybody

Rule 5: Use some ingenuity.

An ingenious salesman can almost always find a way to get in—if he will only take the trouble to look for it.

A story in *Gas Age Record* tells of the clever strategy of Morton M. Chorost, sales manager for the State Appliance Company, Newark.

Mr. Chorost called on a barber; the barber was busy and said, "Go 'way, mister, I no gotta time. Goodbye, please!"

Morton M. Chorost didn't hesitate. He flipped his hat onto a hook, doffed his coat, and seated himself in the barber's chair.

"Give me a shave, John," he said.

But that was one time when the barber didn't do the talking. He listened to Chorost. It took a total of four shaves in as many days for Morton to get his story across, but when he got out of the chair for the last time, the barber had signed an order for a gas-fired unit heater installation.

Walter Horvath, in his book *How to Overcome Objections in Selling*, told of another salesman who, when the secretary said the prospect was busy, replied in substance, "Oh, I just stopped in to make an appointment. Will you please ask Mr. Jones when he will be free?"

You may have to spend time on it!

Another good example of ingenuity in getting an interview was given by Joseph Luchs of Philadelphia, in an article in *Printers' Ink*—a method which he used when he was a cub space salesman for the Philadelphia *Inquirer*.

The cub was given, as a prospect, a drug company which advertised in other Philadelphia papers but never in the *Inquirer*. Every new salesman for twenty years had been given that account—and every one had failed.

Here was the method Mr. Luchs used to get an interview with the druggist: Almost every day for three weeks he went into the store, walked to the rear, bought some inexpensive article. Then, as he passed the boss's desk, he smiled at him and said, "Good morning."

One day, after three weeks of this treatment, the druggist asked, "So you have your office in this neighborhood?"

Mr. Luchs replied, "I'll answer that question gladly, if you'll answer one in return."

The druggist agreed and the salesman was "in." He walked out with the order.

CHAPTER 12

Office doors can be unlocked—
if you have the right key

*If you got in, ask yourself why, and try to repeat; if
you failed, ask yourself why, and try not to repeat.*

The problem of getting in to see important people is not exactly new. Since the days when our savage ancestors began having rulers, people have had trouble getting interviews with men of importance. So the problem dates back maybe ten thousand years before you were born—maybe a hundred thousand!

The salesmen who, for the past hundred years at least, have been studying the problem of how to get past "buffers" naturally have dug up some effective plans. I shall try to give you, in this chapter, a few of the best of these keys for opening office doors.

Key No. 1: Use letters to get in, or to prepare the way. How? Here are some suggestions:

(*a*) One way to get in, via the U.S. mails, is to send the prospect a letter signed by the head of your company. If your company and its president are well known, this letter will almost always get you in. In Dale Carnegie's lifetime, we found that a letter signed by him practically always assured us admittance.

Henry Bayer, who, in my days in the investment business, was one of the best investment men in upper New England, once told me, "Phone a prospect, then write him a letter, then phone, then write. Any salesman who keeps this up long enough not only gets in, but he makes sales."

Some salesmen object to having letters sent out ahead of

their calls. They say it gives the prospect time to think up a good reason to turn them down. They feel that the prospect is likely to say, "Yes, I read your letter and the circular and I'm not interested because...."

The successful pre-approach letter should arouse either curiosity or interest, without divulging too much, or it should show the prospect that your goods or service will really benefit him. Letters that do this make it easier for a salesman to get in—and to sell successfully.

(*b*) Another way to get in is to send the prospect an *I'll-call-unless* letter. B. W. Brown, who was once a sales manager for Henry L. Doherty & Company, used to send important men a letter that said, in substance: "I would like to talk with you briefly about a matter I am sure is of importance to you. Unless I hear to the contrary, I shall call at 3:45 on Wednesday." He found that a certain number of men would neglect to head him off. He felt he was justified in calling on the men who had not answered his letter and saying to their secretaries, "I have an appointment at 3:45 with Mr. Blank." This is slightly "high-pressure"—but "B.W." told me it was a real opener.

Letters in longhand are magic!

(*c*) Try writing letters in longhand. Almost anybody, no matter how important, will read a letter written in longhand, especially if it is on good stationery.

An oil-royalty salesman told me, "If I write five longhand letters a night I can get enough prospects to keep going."

Be sure to call within two or three days after the letters are received by prospects.

Key No. 2: Promise a survey of the prospect's problems which might be solved by your product or service.

This is standard practice by many of the country's big companies. National Cash Register, for example, uses it.

Key No. 3: Ask for advice. If it is done sincerely, it is a compliment.

An excellent example of the successful use of this technique was given by John S. Clement, president of Sandura Co., Inc., of Philadelphia in *Printers' Ink's* interesting series, "The Sale I Never Forgot."

Back in 1914 Mr. Clement took the job of selling for a company which had put out an untried floor-covering product. This product was full of "bugs," and brought grief to dealers who sold it.

So naturally when Mr. Clement called back on these dealers and sent in his card, with his company's name on it in red, he was usually invited to get out before he was pitched out. So he threw away his cards and, when he called on an important dealer, sent in word, "I have come to you for advice." He did not give the name of his company or his product.

Once in, Mr. Clement explained to the dealer that his company had put out an untried product. He explained that the product had now been improved, that the "bugs" were out, and that the company had started national advertising. (He still hadn't mentioned the name of the company or the product.) He then asked the dealer for suggestions about how to sell this product. The dealer outlined a plan. Let Mr. Clement tell what happened in one case:

I asked the buyer, "If this product is floor covering and I presented this proposition to you, would you take it on?"

He hesitated a moment, then, "By the way, what is this product?"

I told him.

He didn't know whether to laugh or get angry, but decided for the former, thank fortune.

We went to work, and before the day was over I had an order for a carload of goods for which I received hearty commendation from the home office. The order was for $3,100.

Key No. 4: Offer benefits. If you can truthfully send in word to your prospect that you can show him how to increase production, cut costs, save on his income tax, or cut ten strokes off his golf score, do it! The more specific your claim is and the more truthful it sounds, the more likely you are to get in.

Key No. 5: Treat secretaries with the respect which is due them for their intelligence and their position. To get cooperation from receptionists and private secretaries, observe these *don'ts:*

Don't No. 1: Don't call her *babe* or *dear.* Don't be affectionate.

Don't No. 2: Don't waste her time with chatter. Secretaries don't interview you for the purpose of hearing funny stories—especially risqué ones.

Don't No. 3: Don't bother to tell the secretary how wonderful *you* are.

Don't No. 4: Don't bluff. Remember, she had met salesmen—and bluffers—before she ever saw you.

Don't No. 5: Don't expect a "buffer" to remember your name. You're not especially important to her. But be sure you remember *her* name. *She is especially important to you!*

Don't No. 6: Don't hold back information to which any "buffer" is entitled.

Secretaries usually have a right to know the purpose of your call. As Margaret Brown said in *Printers' Ink:*

We [secretaries] would be the best friends salesmen ever had if they'd give us the chance. Do you think for a minute a woman who has a responsible position is proof against a sales suggestion like: "Miss Brown, if I could show you how your company could save a thousand dollars a year in office expense, would you give me ten minutes of your time?" Or, "Miss Brown, I've got a market study here that Mr. President would find valuable. Should I go into the details with you—or to whom should I talk?"

Getting past "buffers" and into the presence of your prospect is a life-and-death problem. If you don't solve it, you're dead—as far as that job goes! Conscientiously and enthusiastically observe the "Do's and the Don'ts"—and you *will* lick the problem!

§ FOUR

The "Five Great Rules"

and why they work

CHAPTER 13

**A normal sale goes through
the five simple steps
of the selling process**

*A sale isn't a thing—it's a process. It isn't standing still
—it's moving. It isn't one long job—it's a series of
smaller jobs.*

The five steps of the selling process are:
(1) attention, (2) interest, (3) conviction, (4) desire,
(5) close.

The normal sale goes through these five steps. Perhaps the
salesman doesn't carry the prospect through all of them. Advertising often carries the prospect through some of these
steps—occasionally through all of them.

Somehow or other, however, the purchaser of any item more
important than a package of gum or a pack of cigarettes goes
through these steps in making a purchase. (Maybe you
learned another set of names for them. No matter. Let's not
argue over it—the names are not important.)

These five steps of the selling process make good sense.
They are based on good psychology. They work! So let's have
a closer look at them. Let's analyze them a bit, as follows:

1. Unless you get your prospect's attention, unless he lis-

49

tens to you, why make your pitch? (No listen, no hear; no hear, no sell.)

2. You want your prospect to keep on paying attention, so you get his interest. If a prospect is interested because he believes that your product or service will benefit him in some way, he gladly listens.

3. Next you must convince your prospect that it will be a wise move for him to buy your product—an intelligent thing to do, because of the benefits he will gain from owning and using your product.

4. He may be interested in your product, may be convinced that it is a good article, and still not reach for his wallet. (You are *interested*, for example, in looking at the Grand Canyon. You are *convinced* that no better canyon exists—but still you have no *desire* for it.) Therefore, after you have *interested* your prospect in your product and after you have *convinced* him that it is a good product, and that it will benefit him, you must, as a rule, make him *want* to own it before you can make the sale. That is, you must arouse *desire*.

5. Even if your prospect is *convinced* that your product is as good as you claim, even if he *wants* it, he still may not sign the order blank. For example, I have taken the first four steps of the selling process with respect to a color television—and I can afford it. Yet I don't own one, because no salesman has helped me to take that final step. So the next step is to close.

This formula is flexible

Please note these three points:

1. Often you can combine two steps into one—notably the attention and interest steps.

2. You do not necessarily have to take the steps in the order given. The alert salesman, for example, may try to close a half-dozen times in the conviction step.

3. You do not always have to take all five steps. For example, the prospect may be familiar with your product before

you call, may feel that it is the best on the market. In this case, you may skip the conviction step. Once in a great while, before you talk to him, a prospect may have taken, perhaps as a result of advertisements, all the steps except closing. This happens with considerable regularity in the automobile business, where, it is estimated, 65 per cent of all cars are not *sold*, but *bought*.

However, when we talk about what you must do to sell more, we shall assume that a sale goes through the five steps— attention, interest, conviction, desire, close.

You probably know this a-i-c-d-c formula now. If, however, you cannot zip it off, forward and backward, you should learn it before you read another line. You will want to use it the rest of your selling life.

The five great rules of selling are the rules for carrying your prospect through these five steps of the sale.

§FIVE

How to switch the prospect's attention
from his work to you
Step 1:* Gaining attention

——————————————————————— CHAPTER 14

How to gain favorable attention

Every living creature loves itself. —CICERO

* Great Rule 1. Get your prospect's attention by talking to him briefly about something in which he is interested.

I should blush to present a rule so idiotically simple as this —if I had not heard so many thousands of sales talks that violated it.

Most salesmen open their talk with a stranger by making some such stirring statement as, "I am John Brown. I am with the Smith Printing Company."

Who cares!

Surely not the prospect. It is entirely immaterial to him who you are and probably hardly more important whom you are with.

That "I am So-and-So" opening violates good sense and our rule. The salesman who uses it does not "talk briefly about something in which the prospect is interested." Instead he talks about something in which only he, the salesman, is interested.

Oh, I agree with you—this matter of how a salesman introduces himself isn't important, but why not start your talk

53

with something in which the prospect *is* interested? Then, after you have said something interesting to the prospect, give your company's name—then your own.

Do you know why most salesmen use that "Big-I-am" opening? Because they have not thought as long as ten seconds about those critical opening words.

Of course, if your company is well known, you are justified in using its name.

You will get attention if you say, "I am with U.S. Steel, or, "I am with General Motors."

Sometimes it pays to use part of your interest step at the start of your introduction of yourself, as "I am here because I can show you how you can increase your sales at least 10 per cent. I am with the Dale Carnegie Sales Course. My name is John Jones."

Another idea was presented by John Wesley Coates in a talk made before the Sales Managers Association of St. Paul. Mr. Coates said, in part:

> When I go in to call on a man, I never tell him whom I am with, or what I am selling. I make him ask me. I go in and I shake hands with him, and I tell him where my office is.
>
> "Oh, yes, I know So-and-So in that building."
>
> Pretty soon, we are talking about people; the most magical subject in the world. Soon he will say, "What business are you in, Mr. Coates?" He doesn't say to himself, "Here is a high-powered salesman trying to get my money."

After all, it isn't what you say when you introduce yourself that is important—it's what you say immediately afterward.

Nobody invited you—you just came

What you say after the introduction should be governed largely by the fact that you are not there by invitation. The prospect didn't beg you to come—you invited yourself.

The prospect does not want to see you—you want to see him.

Before you call on a prospect, normally you should do several things. One of the first is: Find out, by observation or by inquiry, some subject in which the prospect is interested.

One thing, with respect to gaining attention, you are sure of: every prospect is interested in himself and his work—and often in little else. For example: The wife of a millionaire gave a dinner party. Her husband, who had made his fortune by inventing a rat poison, was silent during the meal. As the ladies left the room, the millionaire's wife whispered to him, "What's the matter with you tonight? Why don't you talk to anyone?"

"Talk?" he replied testily. "What is the use of talking? Not a single person here knows anything about rat poison!"

For convenience, I am dividing the following attention-getters into:

1. Those useful to the general run of salesmen.
2. Those applicable especially to jobbers' salesmen.

Some attention-getters under both these classifications can be used to advantage by retail salesmen.

How most salesmen can get attention

Don't get into the rut of using just one kind of attention getter—until you have tried many and have learned which is the most effective for you.

Here are some reliable attention-getters:

1. *The question opener.* This is one of the easiest of openers. If your prospect answers your question he must pay attention.

For example, a laundry company equipped its route men with big badges on which appeared the question, "Can you drink it?" It got attention by arousing curiosity.

Insurance men use a table that shows the "money value" of a man. They get attention by asking, "Do you know that the amount of insurance that insurance companies will let you buy depends on your 'money value'?"

Tire companies teach distributors' salesmen to ask, "Have you had any tire trouble lately?" The normal answer is, "No, why?" That response by the car owner is practically an invitation to the salesman to give his sales talk and to explain that 90 per cent of all tire trouble comes in the last 10 per cent of the tire's mileage.

A question is especially effective when it bears on some subject in which the prospect is keenly interested. For example:

> Hamlin Garland once found himself seated at a formal dinner in London beside dour Henry M. Stanley, the man who found Livingstone in darkest Africa. Stanley was morosely silent until Garland had an inspiration.
>
> "By the way," he remarked, "I've heard so many pronunciations of the name of that famous African fly; I wonder how *you* pronounce T-S-E-T-S-E?" Stanley brightened—and they were off to the races.   —ROTARIAN

Jack Farmer, a divisional manager for the Confederation Life Insurance Company in Ontario, starts his new men out with, "Would you mind telling me why you bought life insurance?"

WARNING: Avoid banal, trite, or irrelevant questions. (The insurance salesman who once opened a talk with me by asking, "What did your grandmother die of?" got a quick answer!)

2. *The startling statement or "explosion" type of opener.* A punchline can be an effective opener. So can a startling statement, if it really is startling. It should apply, directly, of course, to what you are selling.

The magazine *Specialty Salesman* tells of an insurance salesman who opened his talks with, "Mr. Jones, when I tell you what my business is, you are going to throw me right out of that window."

3. *The mystery opener.* To use the mystery opener, you

must start your talk by saying something that arouses your prospect's curiosity. If dignified and relevant, this mystery opener is one of the most effective attention-getters.

I once heard a salesman open his talk to the owner of an automobile agency with, "I overheard one of your salesmen making a pitch yesterday and I was shocked by what he said."

At that point the dealer was wondering what in heck his salesman had said. He was paying attention!

Another example of the curiosity opener: A catsup salesman walks into a store and asks for "a bottle of your best catsup." He opens it, whips out a spoon, and asks the grocer to taste it. Next he brings a bottle of his own catsup out of his pocket and asks the grocer to try that.

Quite obviously he gains the grocer's attention by this piece of curiosity-arousing showmanship.

From *The Postage Stamp* magazine comes this example of getting attention by arousing curiosity:

Tom Lowry, before his death some years ago, was known beyond the limits of his home city, Milwaukee, as a utility tycoon—and as a man in whom the gambling urge was well developed.

He was also known to insurance agents as the man who couldn't be sold.

One day an up-and-coming young agent decided he was going to sell Tom Lowry. He learned that Lowry was the sort of man who would bet on the way a hoptoad would hop. The salesman strode into the great man's outer office and said, "I want to see Mr. Lowry about a bet!" He was admitted immediately.

"Mr. Lowry, I'll bet you $100,000 to $1,800 that you'll not die within the next year."

Insurance hadn't been presented to Tom Lowry like that before. It aroused his curiosity. He paid attention—and before the talk ended, he paid for a policy!

4. *The famous-man, or big-name, opener.* If you say, "John Smith thinks our machine is the best in the world," it is not a striking utterance; but if you can honestly say, "Henry

Ford II told one of our salesmen that . . ." you get attention by
the use of a big name.

5. *The screwdriver opener.* If you sell something that may
need servicing, an effective opener is to look over your prospect's equipment and make any minor adjustments or screwdriver repairs. From *The Howe Salesmen* come these suggestions for men selling scales:

> Carry a screwdriver with you. And a can of metal polish. And a
> piece of polishing cloth. Approach the prospect with a suggestion
> that you'd like to look over his scales and see if they are working
> all right. . . . Use the metal polish and polishing cloth on the
> scale beam. Adjust the balance ball, if it needs it. . . . Twirl the
> wheel of a truck. If it runs sluggishly, ask for an oilcan and drop
> some oil on the axle.

By the time you have done a few acts of service, you have attention, and perhaps have learned a number of facts that will help you
later in your sales talk.

6. *The exhibit, or "here we have," attention-getter.* If your
product is one that provides you with a good exhibit, you can
often use it as an attention-getter.

A salesman talking to a Dale Carnegie Effective Speaking
class one night opened with the statement, "This little gadget
may revolutionize the world." He then exhibited an electric
eye, which at that time was quite new. He had the attention
of everyone present.

When I was directing the sale of preferred stock for Central Maine Power Company, we used to supply our salesmen
with short pieces of copper wire used in our high-tension lines.
The salesman would place a piece in the hands of a prospect
and ask him if he realized what a miracle it was that all the
power furnished by the company in that city was brought
along strands of wire just like that.

One life insurance salesman introduces himself by saying,
"Mr. Blank, I sell money for future delivery—here is my
business card," and hands the prospect a crisp dollar bill.

7. *The gift attention-getter.* Fuller Brush salesmen made the "gift opener" world-famous. Other direct-selling organizations have used the idea effectively. So have salesmen in other lines.

If you use gifts, try to get something odd, different, and exclusive. Vincent Blunt of Montgomery, Alabama, inherited a collection of old one-cent pieces. (The one he gave me is dated 1822 and measures an inch in diameter.) He had these mounted in glass as paperweights and uses them to get the attention of important prospects.

8. *The "referral" attention-getter.* This one is often used by insurance salesmen. Get a customer to give you the name of a prospect—and permission to use his (the customer's) name.

Then your attention-getter is something like this: "Your friend Bill Jones thought you might be interested in. . . ."

A related approach is to mention the name of some friend or acquaintance who is a satisfied user. The salesmen of the Iron Fireman Company of Cleveland used to get attention by saying, "I'm from Iron Fireman. We have been able to furnish automatic heat and to save money for your neighbor, Mr. John Blank."

Such an opening almost certainly gains attention.

9. *The insult.* Once in about a hundred years or so, you meet a man with a rough exterior and a keen sense of humor whose attention can be gained only with an insult.

Back in the nineteen-hundreds one man who would not give attention to a salesman was George F. Baer, president of the Reading Railroad. The primary reason he couldn't be sold was that he would not let a salesman get as far as the attention step of his pitch.

Once the famous and immensely successful salesman "Diamond Jim" Brady called to sell Mr. Baer some railroad cars.

Mr. Baer refused to see him.

"I'll wait," said Jim. He did—all that day, all the next day, all week!

Finally, Mr. Baer broke down, let Jim into his office, and then
yelled, "Don't you know I never see salesmen? What have you
been waiting for?"

With a sweet smile, Jim said, "To tell you you can go straight to
hell!"

An hour later Jim departed with an order for $5,000,000 worth
of cars.

(NOTE: We don't recommend this attention-getter for ordinary
use—but for "Diamond Jim" Brady it got attention and Jim got
the order!)

10. *The compliment.* Some form of sincere compliment is
one of the safest and best general-purpose, heavy-duty attention-getters, but it must be sincere. For instance: "Congratulations on winning that golf tournament, Mr. Blank," or "This
is a wonderful office—and what an amazing view you have of
the city!" If there is a framed photograph on the desk, some
complimentary remark on that is safe and usually effective.
Or, "I expected to find a much older man in your position,
Mr. Jones." (Sure-fire if the man is past fifty—and if the remark is sincere.)

Remember, mothers are always proud of their children;
doctors and dentists of their equipment; businessmen of their
offices; neat men of neat desks; disorderly men of disorderly
desks; purchasing agents of their efficient buying; old men
of their youth; young men of their age; and women of their
beauty—whether they have it or not!

11. *The news item, or "it just happened," attention-getter.*
Become a traveling newsgathering bureau. Remember and
pass along any news you hear. Read trade papers and magazines. Read books, read papers from other cities, and get news
items and market information out of them. Remember the
news which dealers give you.

A grand opening phrase is, "I just heard that. . . ."

If it's news, it's interesting.

Example: When I was doing some work for a small chain-store group, a man came in one day and said, "The Colorado Supreme Court has just rendered a verdict that lumps voluntary chains with regular chains and makes them both liable for chain-store taxes." Because this was exciting news to me that day, the salesman had my full and interested attention.

Dale Carnegie said, in one of his newspaper columns, "Try to be the bearer of good news. The news need not be important. If you have heard someone speak well of him, tell him so; or that you saw his name in the paper; or that you have thought several times of something he said at a former meeting."

WARNING: Be careful about passing around news about competitors to competitors. Don't tell secrets or violate confidences. Give news, not gossip!

Be a walking "compendium of useful information"

12. *Helpful suggestions.* Of course, the salesman who brings suggestions that increase sales for the dealer is more than welcome.

So your job is to get yourself into a position where you can give suggestions. They will probably fall into one of these classifications:

a. *Advertising ideas.* You are likely to get attention if you say to a dealer of poultry supplies, "John Smith, up in Smithville, wrote this advertisement himself and ran it in the local paper at a cost of $25. It brought him seventeen incubator sales. I have some extra copies of the advertisement, if you'd like one."

If you are a jobber's salesman, your company probably supplies you with plenty of advertising copy. One of your jobs is to find out how a given piece of copy has worked for one merchant, so you can tell another noncompeting merchant.

To say to a merchant, "My company thinks this is a good advertisement," is not impressive, but when you say, "John Smith ran this advertisement at a cost of $25 and made sales of $450," you get immediate attention.

b. *Selling ideas.* Pass along anything that helps the merchant to sell your product—or any product except your competitors'. Dealers will welcome any man who can show them how to make more money.

How jobbers can get attention

We've talked about how specialty salesmen can get attention. How about jobbers' salesmen?

Melvin H. Poretz, director of sales promotion for the Ideal Toy Corporation, gave this list of ideas a salesman could offer a dealer to get his attention: merchandising ideas, promotional ideas, display ideas, traffic-building ideas, excitement-firing ideas, hot-item ideas, department layout ideas, customer self-selection ideas, sales-training ideas.

If your job requires you to call on the same dealers, buyers, and purchasing agents again and again, try to give some information or help on each call that will keep these men from getting sick of the sight of you.

"So you're here again" is the best greeting that a lot of jobbers' salesmen deserve from customers. Don't be satisfied with that sort of greeting. You can avoid it by being interesting and helpful. Certainly, if you are alert, you can often find opportunities to use the two attention-getters above.

Ideas? You have to hunt for them

Where should you look for ideas about advertising help, sales helps, and news items?

Printers' Ink gave this list, which was supplied by a group of successful salesmen:

1. Information supplied by your company.
2. Industry and trade publications.
3. General business publications.
4. Discussions with competitors' salesmen.
5. Discussions with salesmen of other lines who service accounts.

Also mentioned were current-events publications, financial newspapers and magazines, company and industry sales meetings and sales conferences, on-the-spot observations, and talks with customers, including discussions with buyers concerning competitors' products and competitive salesmen.

A few useful ideas passed along to prospects are worth a million that you forgot! So record them when you find them—so you can find them when you need them.

CHAPTER 15

Observe these fifteen rules and you'll rarely fail to get attention

I to myself am dearer than a friend. —SHAKESPEARE

If you will observe the rules for gaining attention which follow—which you can do easily—you will surely get the prospect's mind off what he has been thinking about and focused, momentarily at least, on you.

Rule 1: Give heed to your personal appearance. Look like a person who is worth listening to.

W. Wallace Powell, director of merchandising, Hoover Company, in an article in *Specialty Salesman*, said:

When you're planning your presentation, don't ever forget this: you have only one opportunity to make a first impression.

All other impressions are secondary. I'm firmly convinced that in your first impression—your first ten seconds, when your eyes meet the eyes of your prospect—something dynamic happens. That first impression must be planned and it must be good.

Carefully prepare your attention-getting remarks before you come face to face with your prospect. Don't depend on inspiration.

Elmer Wheeler, in his book *Tested Sentences That Sell*, says, "The first ten words are more important than your next ten thousand." A wild exaggeration, of course—but an effective one.

Rule 2: Never start with an apology. In fact, the old rule: "Never apologize, never explain, never retract, get it done and let 'em holler," is worth thinking about—even if you don't follow it unfailingly.

Rule 3: Get your prospect saying "yes." I doubt if this "yessing" method is quite as important as some salesmen seem to think, yet it is a useful technique. It is usually as easy to get "yes" answers as "no" answers. For example: "Is it all right if I hang my hat here?" "You have an amazing view from this window, haven't you?" "You can be proud of having offices in a building like this, can't you?"

Rule 4: Don't—I implore you—*don't* use the "I just happened by" introduction. If you haven't a better reason than that for calling, don't call.

Rule 5: Make your attention-getter brief. If you spin it out you may first get attention and next lose it.

Hugo Münsterberg of Harvard used to illustrate the point that attention is hard to hold by telling of the alchemist who sold a recipe for turning eggs into gold. The buyer was to put the yolks of a dozens eggs into a pan and stir these yolks for a half hour without ever thinking of the word "hippopotamus." Thousands tried, but of course none succeeded.

If people can't keep their attention on one thing for thirty minutes to win a pan of gold, they aren't likely to give attention very long to your sales talk, unless you can show them how they can make a "pan of gold." So, as soon as you have your prospect's attention, move quickly to the interest step of your talk.

He never got down to his sales talk

I once heard F. W. Nichols, then vice-president and general manager of International Business Machines, tell this story:

A friend of mine was talking to a visitor in his office the other day when a salesman was announced. My friend said that, just as a demonstration, he would give the salesman five minutes of his time.

As soon as the salesman entered, the executive began talking about the general economic situation. The salesman responded in a like vein. At the end of the fifth minute the executive said, "Well, nice of you to call on me. I enjoyed meeting you. Thank you very much." And so the salesman was shown out.

How can you switch from a general conversation into the serious subject of selling your goods? Herbert N. Casson once answered this question thus: "Ask the buyer questions that relate to your goods. This keeps the buyer talking but it makes him talk *on the right subject*." This question method will keep *you* in control of the interview.

Rule 6: Never force your prospect to shake hands. If he seems to expect it, shake; if not, don't.

Rule 7: Try to sit or stand reasonably close to your prospect. But don't get too close. Never get so close that it interferes with your gestures. Your breath, also, may have some bearing on the distance you should sit from your prospect. If it is sweet, don't worry. If it is bad, keep your distance!

Oh, yes, if you are afflicted with objectionable underarm or other body odors, do something about it.

Rule 8: Don't loll or sprawl in your chair. You should have a message of importance for your prospect and should act accordingly. Sit straight.

Rule 9: In general, do not smoke while you are making a sales talk. Especially, never smoke unless your prospect is smoking. There are exceptions, of course. But if in doubt, don't. Don't chew gum in the presence of your prospect—or anywhere else in public! Also, don't drink (if you must drink at all) until after your last sales call, because some hard drinkers and most teetotalers hate to talk to a man with a liquor breath.

Rule 10: Avoid talking to your prospect when others— especially uninterested people—are present. If you find a third person present, you can say to your prospect, "Pardon me, I did not know that you were engaged. When will you be able to see me?" This frequently causes the third person to withdraw—or gives you another date for the interview.

If you are forced to talk in the presence of a gallery, talk not to one person, but to all of them.

Rule 11: Smile. You *can* learn to smile naturally and effectively. I almost learned to do it myself—in seventeen years. Most people accomplish it faster! You do it by "thinking a smile." Before you go in to see your prospect, say to yourself, "I like people. I am going to like this man. It's a good world. I have my health and a lot of other blessings. Surely I feel like smiling."

Don't dismiss this as foolishness. It works.

A smile made him a champion salesman

Does smiling pay salesmen? At a Dale Carnegie effective speaking class session in Boston, a girl told this story:

> Several years ago a small boy walked into my office one day and said dolefully, "Want to buy a *Saturday Evening Post?*" I said, "No, I'm busy." So he went out. On my way to lunch, I met the lad at the elevator, and I asked him if he had sold any *Posts*. He said he hadn't. So I said, "I'm no salesman but I'll give you one selling rule. When you say, 'Want to buy a *Post?*' you smile."
>
> One week later this boy breezed into my office, gave me a big smile, and said, "Want to buy a *Post?*" Almost unconsciously, I

reached for my purse and handed him a nickel. (Yes, it happened years ago—before inflation!)

Soon that boy led all *Post* boys in the Boston area. He was a leader until he grew too big to peddle magazines. Many times he has told me, "I owe it all to my smile."

On the other hand, don't be a perpetual smirker. After the smile of courtesy, get down to business and look businesslike.

Rule 12: Don't try to be too clever in your opening. A good friendly remark is safer than shooting off a skyrocket or standing on your head.

Rule 13: Get the prospect's name right. You will get attention if you mispronounce it—but the wrong kind! Don't hesitate to ask your prospect how to spell his name—your interest in his name will please him. If it is an unusual name, comment on that.

The other day, I overheard a salesman compliment a man on his unusual name. The man swelled with pride. "I'm the only Zirul in the telephone book," he said.

Rule 14: Avoid openers that millions of other salesmen use. The first man who used the remark, "I've come here today, Mr. Jones, to show you how you can make more money," was smart—but he died of old age before you were born. By the time a prospect has heard that remark ten or twenty thousand times, it bores him.

So, heed this advice: find out what attention-getters other salesmen are using—and use the other kind!

Rule 15: Arouse curiosity. For example, there was the door-to-door salesman who said to a housewife, "You should have heard what I just heard next door! May I step in and tell you about it?" (But don't repeat gossip or scandal!)

Don't do these "don'ts"

Don't No. 1: Don't lie or cheat to get attention.

When a vacuum cleaner salesman says, "I'm here to get your opinion of this cleaner," he perhaps gets attention; but, unless the prospect's mind is oversimplified, the salesman is not likely to make the sale.

Don't No. 2: Don't start with a joke—unless it is at your own expense.

Don't No. 3: Don't be loud or boisterous.

Don't No. 4: Don't talk about your troubles, your problems, or your health. Your prospects are interested in their own. Don't peddle bad news, rumors, or gloom. Bring glad tidings or don't bring any.

Don't No. 5: Don't overdo a man's hobby. It's hard to lead from a ball game into a boiler or a computing machine.

Is the attention step important?
Of course it is

Perhaps you will feel that we have given too much space to the attention rule, which you may consider the least important in the selling process. However, please remember:

1. Most beginners and many experienced salesmen fear the approach. Once they have secured attention, their fears usually depart.

2. If your prospect does not pay attention to you, you are finished at the start! It is vital to get his attention.

Lastly, remember: to grab attention is easy, to hold it is difficult. Attention can be kept fixed only if it is kept moving.

Which brings us to the Second Great Rule of Selling—the rule for keeping attention fixed by converting it into interest.

Before we consider it, I want you to ask yourself, "Exactly what do I want my prospect to be thinking when I end the attention-getting step?"

The answer is simple and brief. You want him to be thinking, "Here is a salesman."

SIX

Why should your prospect

listen to your talk?

Tell him!

Step 2:* How to arouse interest

————————————————————————— CHAPTER 16

If your product will benefit your prospect, it's easy to get his interest

> *Selling, to be a great art, must involve a genuine interest in the other person's needs. Otherwise it is only a subtle, civilized way of pointing a gun and forcing one into a temporary surrender.* —H. A. OVERSTREET

Great Rule 2: Arouse your prospect's interest by telling him what your goods or services will do to benefit or serve him.

You may ask at this point, "Why do I have to have both an attention step and an interest step?"

You don't.

In actual selling you occasionally use only one. Now and then you combine the two steps. Some authorities consider the two steps together and call this step the *approach*.

However, I recommend that, as a rule, you take both steps. Why?

Let's take, as an analogous case, the start of a ball game.

The umpires are getting into position. You, as one of the

players, are chatting with another player. At the moment you aren't thinking of the game.

Then the umpire says, "Play ball." That's the attention step. Immediately you pay attention—but still you are not completely interested.

Then the umpire says, "Batter up"—at least they used to say that when I was a baseball writer. That's the interest step. You are the first man in the batting order. You are now completely interested in the game.

Of course, the umpire could have omitted the attention step and started off with "Batter up." Somehow that would have seemed too sudden! Everybody is better pleased when the umpire takes both steps.

How do the attention and interest steps differ—basically?

Let's take an imaginary case. Suppose an automobile salesman comes in to your office to sell you a car—and that *is* imaginary—at least in my experience of buying a car every other year for thirty-eight years. They never come to see you— you have to go see them!

Well, anyhow, when the salesman steps in, you are studying the sales report. You can't seem to figure out why your sales slipped off a bit last month.

The automobile salesman says, "I hear you still lead the sales force. Congratulations." That's his attention step.

For the moment you have stopped thinking about last month's sales. You say to yourself, "That automobile salesman is in again."

Still you're anything but interested in the automobile salesman. You've practically decided to drive the old ark another year.

Then the salesman says, "I've talked the boss into offering you $50 more on that old ruin of yours." That's the interest step.

Now you've forgotten about last month's sales; you've almost forgotten that a salesman is facing you. Why? Because you are interested in this new, more liberal offer for your old car. The salesman has gained your interest by telling you of a deal that will benefit you—$50 worth!

Admittedly, the automobile salesman could have opened his talk by saying, "We'll boost the offer for your car $50." Somehow that's too abrupt. Your mind isn't quite ready for it.

So don't begrudge the time you devote to getting the prospect's attention. Often it takes not over ten seconds. It should rarely take over one minute.

The attention step pays—so don't skip it.

Then, after you have gained the prospect's attention, go on to develop his interest.

Why should your prospect listen?

If you will ask yourself, "Why should this man listen to me?" you will make more sales. Many salesmen seem to think that they have some God-given right to take the prospect's time.

"But," protests the salesman, "why shouldn't I take his time? I'm here to do this man a service—to sell him something he really needs."

True, I hope. But does the prospect know it?

Your prospect's natural and justifiable attitude is, "Whatever you're selling, I don't want any!"

When Nicholas H. Maarchalk retired after forty-five years of selling for the Holland-American Line, a *New York Times* reporter told this story about him:

Years ago Mr. Maarchalk once volunteered to see a tough old shipper who had earned a reputation for refusing to see salesmen. When he arrived at the shipper's office, he was told that he couldn't see his man that day. "I sat down and waited while his secretary tried to get me to leave," he narrated. "Finally, when the shipper let me in, he said, 'It's no good your being here because I'm not going to listen to you anyhow.'"

The young solicitor astonished the shipper by replying, "You're not fit to hold your job! You're not fit to hold it if you're too busy to hear somebody tell how your company can save money."

Mr. Maarchalk then presented his facts and figures. He walked out, ten minutes later, with the business for his company.

This illustrates the fact that the way you can get a prospect (even a notoriously tough prospect) interested in your proposition is to talk to him about what your product or service will do to benefit him or his company.

National Cash Register meets this "I-don't-want-to-buy-anything-anyhow" attitude by having their salesmen say, "Let us analyze your business to see if we can help you."

Talk in terms of your prospect's interests

A prospect becomes interested only when you have tied up his business or pleasure with your product. Your job is to do the tying.

An example of gaining interest by asking questions to tie up the prospect's business with the salesman's product was given me by W. H. M. Stover, president of Leadership Training Institute of D. C., in Washington. Mr. Stover wrote:

One day while World War II was in progress I walked into the O.P.A. office, found the fiscal officer, and asked him just two questions:

1. "How many weeks delinquent are your payrolls?"
2. "Do you know how the Justice Department pays 28,000 people on time and keeps its payroll records totaled, posted and balanced?"

Right there and then I had his interest. He wanted to hear more of this example of payroll efficiency. So I told him the story of the accomplishment of the Justice Department in keeping its payroll up to date, took him to see it in operation, surveyed his O.P.A. payroll problems, presented a written proposal, demonstrated its fitness for his problem.

Shortly thereafter I had his order for $55,000.00. And O.P.A had a current payroll system with a resultant annual saving of some $200,000.

Here's a sound piece of advice: Tell the prospect what he will gain from owning your product, and don't waste any time in doing it.

As Gene L. Powers, manager of sales training for Swift and Company, told me once, "If your prospect hasn't found out in your first twenty-five words what you can do for him, you are probably out—and you deserve to be."

In what are your prospects interested?

How can you know your prospect's interest? You can answer that question by asking yourself another: "In what one subject are we all interested?" Ourselves, of course. Hence, to interest your prospect, talk to him about *himself*. Since you are there to make a sale, you should tell him *how your goods will serve him*.

Gail Lehmberg, who presents the Dale Carnegie Sales Course in Milwaukee, gave me this incident of the effectiveness of talking in terms of the prospect's interests:

Recently one of my friends was in the market for an electric range. After he and his wife had visited three dealers in town and had received three sales talks on as many different ranges, the husband asked his wife, "Which range do you like best?" Her answer was, "Why, I just couldn't buy from anyone except Mr. Wilson." When I asked the wife why she felt she must buy from this salesman, she answered, "Mr. Wilson seemed to have our interests at heart. He asked many questions about *our* family needs and *our* baking needs. He talked about what his range would do for us."

Do you always deliberately arouse interest?

This rule of getting the prospect's interest by talking about what your product will do to benefit him seems so obvious—so

in accord with practical psychology and good selling sense—
that you may wonder why I stress it. If you have ever trained
salesmen in thousand lots, as I have, you know that it takes
threats, rewards, drills, cajoling, and abuse to get many salesmen to make it a regular practice to arouse interest before
they begin to tell the facts about their products.

As John Wilson says in his excellent book *Open the Mind
and Close the Sale,* "Failure to arouse the prospect's interest
before the salesman begins to discuss benefits is the greatest
criticism of most selling presentations."

This rule for arousing interest is as old as civilization—
probably older.

Ben Franklin used this rule

One of the first men to use this rule in an advertisement
was Benjamin Franklin. He tells about it in his autobiography,
which is required reading for all ambitious salesmen.

Franklin was commissioned by General Braddock, back in
April, 1755, to secure for him 150 wagons with four horses to
each wagon. These the general wanted for what proved to be
his ill-fated expedition against Fort Duquesne.

Franklin went to Lancaster, and on April 26, 1755, published an advertisement. The purpose of the advertisement was
to get the farmers interested in supplying the wagons. What
did it contain? One single paragraph about what *Braddock
wanted* and six numbered paragraphs about *what the farmers
would get.* Good salesman that he was, Franklin told the farmers *how they would benefit* from the transaction.

Franklin comments in his autobiography on the "great and
sudden effect it produced" and says further, "In three weeks
the one hundred and fifty wagons, with two hundred and fifty-
nine carrying horses, were on their march for the camp."

Suppose that instead of arousing the interest of the farmers
by telling them what *they* would get out of it, Franklin had
told them what Braddock wanted—would he have secured
equally good results? We don't have to guess. Braddock had

tried it previously in Maryland, on a "we-want-wagons-or-else" basis. The net result, wrote Franklin, was "... twenty-five wagons and not all of those in serviceable condition."

Surely then, your question, "How do I get the prospect interested in my product?" can be easily answered: tell your prospect how he will benefit from owning it. Remember that, in this step of the selling process, he wants to know not what your product *is*, but what it will *do* for *him*.

Back in the old days, a man named E. J. Weir sold stoves so successfully that they made him general sales manager for his concern.

In explaining his success, Mr. Weir said, "To sell to retailers, jingle the dollars. Tell them how to get profits and prestige. The phrase 'Profits today you never dreamed of' is a line that never failed."

Yes, but what about purchasing agents?

"That's all right," you say, "if you are selling direct to consumers. But I sell largely to purchasing agents. They don't benefit, no matter what they buy."

Many salesmen consider the purchasing agent as a sort of machine, into which are fed prices, specifications, terms, and the like, and out of which come decisions to buy from the salesman who offers the best combination of quality, price, service, and terms—usually with most of the emphasis on price.

That appraisal is not quite fair to purchasing agents, because it omits one factor: the purchasing agent has to please others besides himself. He has to satisfy the president of the company, the treasurer, the board of directors. Yes, and he must also satisfy the people in his organization *who use or sell what he buys*.

If a purchasing agent buys something that works and lasts he gets little credit. but if he buys something that doesn't work, he hears about it.

Remember: purchasing agents are *human*—all reports to
the contrary notwithstanding!

Your job is to stir up interest

Leo McGivena wrote, "Last year over a million quarter-inch
drills were sold—not because people wanted quarter-inch drills
but because they wanted quarter-inch holes." So, to get their
interest, talk "holes."

"What will it do for me?" prospects ask. A story from *The
Informant* illustrates how one salesman answered this question:

A printing salesman, who called on a Swedish sawmill owner
in Washington State, told the millman what wonderful printing
his company did. Finally, the shingle man said petulantly, "I don't
want to buy printing—I like to sell shingle, you bet!"

"Why should anyone buy *your* shingles?" parried the salesman.
The millman told him.

The salesman left but was back in two days with copy and layout
for a $225 job. And the gentleman from Sweden bought it with
these words, "Aye tank you smart fella—Aye gamble."

Another way you can gain the immediate interest of a retailer is to tell him some new way to merchandise, such as an
original display stunt, or a tested advertisement.

Lewis Greene Bissing was quoted in *American Business* as
follows:

...I claim selling is easy when the salesman's goal is to do
something for his customers. Not long ago a wholesaler asked us
to call on a druggist with him.

I let our factory man do the talking. First thing he did was to
take out some pieces of stainless steel to show the druggist the
kind of materials used in our fountains. Then he told him the
price of the fountain. Plainly, the customer was not interested. Our
man was talking too much about us, too little about the customer's
problems.

The fountain was at the rear of the store. A cigar counter was right up in front. The neighborhood was such that sales of cigars would be confined to cheap brands, bringing little profit.

"If I were in your place I would move the fountain to the front of the store where people will see it," I said to him. Right away the druggist declared he didn't want to spend a lot of money for new fixtures. I explained that I was not recommending new fixtures, just a rearrangement of the old ones.

This bit of helpful advice opened the way to the sale of a fountain.

If you use your brains, you will usually find an interest-getter that will break through any "I'm-not-interested" attitude. Arthur J. Hand, writing in *Sales Scrap Book*, said, in substance:

The company I represent sells a credit and collection service. If I approached a prospect with "I want to tell you about our credit and collection service," you know what he would answer? "We are well taken care of. I'm not interested."

What I do say is, "I want to tell you about a service that reduces risks for you and minimizes losses."

Almost always the prospect says, "What do you mean?"

Thus he has asked for my presentation.

Be ready to skip any step

When can you skip the interest step in the selling formula?

When you are absolutely sure that your prospect is already interested.

For example, a man once came in to see me at the Dale Carnegie Institute and said, "Because I have to make a series of speeches this summer, I have to take a public-speaking course right now!" That remark showed his interest. Consequently, I could jump right into the conviction part of my talk—could give him facts as evidence that he would be wise to take the Dale Carnegie Course.

Let's take some of our own medicine. Suppose you ask me,

"Why should I be interested in what you have just said?" My answer is, "It will help you to sell more." I know you can't honestly say, "I'm not interested in selling more."

In this chapter, I know that I have repeated the same thing over and over. I have done it deliberately. By iteration and reiteration I hope I can drive home the point that the interest step is important to *your* success.

I ask you and every person who reads this book to take this pledge: "On my honor, I pledge myself that I shall never again present the body of my sales talk until I am sure I have the prospect's interest."

You may say, "I know men who sell successfully who don't use this rule."

So do I. Bob Bale and I did a job years ago for the Halliburton Oil Well Cementing Company. We found one man in that company who was selling quite a bit with this opening remark, "Joe, I want to sell you some Halliburton equipment. The boys in the field get a commission!"

The miracle in such case is not that the salesman sells, but that the prospect buys!

Arouse interest deliberately

Now to sum it up: Don't assume that your prospect is interested. Instead, take it for granted that he isn't.

Before you call on any prospect, ask yourself, "How will my product benefit this particular man?" Then get in your mind, before you even walk into the presence of your prospect, what you are going to say to him about this benefit.

Keep doing it consciously until it becomes a habit. When your subconscious mind has taken over the job of reminding you to arouse interest in every prospect, you are at last in a fair way to become a professional salesman.

Just by way of review, I ask you this question: "What do you want your prospect to be thinking at the end of the *interest step* of the selling process?"

The correct answer is, "I want my prospect to be thinking, 'Maybe this product will really do something I want done.'"

—————————————————————————— CHAPTER 17

These rules will help you to get interest— and hold it

The ideal of service is the basis of all worthy enterprise.
—PRINCIPLES OF ROTARY, 1905

Rule 1: Ask questions to arouse interest. (Keep on asking questions all the way through the first three steps of the selling process. Don't stop asking questions until you come to the desire step.)

United States Rubber salesmen answer questions with questions in the approach step of the sale. For example, if a prospect says, "What is the price of a tire such and such a size?" the salesman does not give the price. Instead he asks, "For what kind of service do you use your car?" If necessary, he explains that he must know the kind of service for which the car is used in order to know which tire to recommend.

Salesmen say, "Many a man has been jailed for making a statement, but no man was ever arrested for asking a question."

Rule 2: Be sure your interest step is really interesting. It will be interesting if it tells the prospect what your goods or service will do to benefit him.

Vash Young, once one of the most successful insurance salesmen in the world, told me that he called on a prospect every seven days for fifty-two weeks before the prospect would even give him an appointment. When Vash finally faced the prospect, this man said:

"I'm not interested in insurance."

Vash replied, "It isn't very interesting, is it?"

"But I thought you were in the insurance business," said the prospect.

"I am," continued Vash, "but the interesting thing to me is not insurance, *but the possibility of your having an income for life.*"

Vash then sold him an annuity that called for an annual premium of $10,000.

Rule 3: To get the prospect interested in anything you can show or demonstrate, let the prospect see it, feel it, ride in it, drive it, taste it, smell it. When I managed a securities-sales force in Maine, we used to hand prospects a sample dividend check and say, "How would you like one of these rolling in every three months?"

Rule 4: Avoid exaggerated claims about your product. Baltaser Gracian, writing in 1653, said, "Exaggeration is a branch of lying." Exaggeration is always dangerous, but *at the beginning* of a sales talk it is often *fatal.*

The late Guy P. Gannett once told me, "When I was buying bonds for the Augusta Trust Company, I often had to turn down bond salesmen. If the salesman started out with an exaggeration it was easy. I'd call him on it. Then, every time he made a statement, I'd ask him if that was an exaggeration, too. Once you catch a man in an exaggeration, he has no defense—and he quickly fades out."

Rule 5: Avoid using an interest-getter to which the prospect can say, "I'm not interested." If the salesman says, "I want to show you a new XYZ lamp," the prospect can say, "I am not interested." If you say, "I want to show you how you can cut down your electric-light bills," how can the prospect truthfully say, "I'm not interested!" To repeat: when you tell the prospect how he will gain something by using your product, he *must* be interested.

Rule 6: Be sincere always—but be super-sincere in this part of your talk. The day when salesmen opened with "I'm here to give you a valuable book" or "You have won a lot in Shaky-Deal Subdivision" is about gone, though the young man selling magazines to pay his way through college is still with us.

Nobody likes to take losses

Rule 7: In your approach, get your prospect to think about his loss or disadvantage as a result of not owning the goods or service you are selling. Make him dissatisfied with his present situation. Suppose you are selling dictating machines and you say, "Isn't your secretary sitting around several hours each day, either taking your dictation or waiting to get it?"

Thus you get your prospect thinking about a disadvantage that results because he does not use a dictating machine.

Chauncey M. Depew, head of the New York Central Railroad back in the days when being head of a railroad meant something besides grief and woe, said, "I would not sit up all of one night to make a hundred dollars—but I would sit up all of seven nights to keep from losing a hundred dollars."

Don't chisel—serve!

Rule 8: Don't think about yourself when you open your talk—think about your prospect. Put out of your mind thoughts of your commission. Put into your mind thoughts of benefits to your prospect. The prospect's interest in your goods will die at exactly the time when your interest in yourself and your commission begins. It will be written all over your face.

Rule 9: Talk to your prospect about his problem, his profits, his advancement, his home, his business, his health, his family, his cause, his religion. Then you can defy him to be uninterested.

The journalism professor was passing out a few hints on writing. "A good introduction," he explained, "is highly important. Always remember the young man who, desiring to marry Angus Mac-

Pherson's homely daughter, opened his interview with, 'Sir, I'd like to show you how I can save you some money.'"

Rule 10: Gain interest by telling a story—by giving an example of how your product benefited somebody.

Sales talks, speeches, and short stories have this in common—they must get the interest of the listeners at the very start.

Liam O'Flaherty started one of his stories like this:

By the hokies, there was a man in this place one time by the name of Ned Sullivan, and he had a queer thing happen him late one night and he coming up the Valley Road from Durlas.

Why was that thirty-eight-word sentence a good interest-getter? Because Liam started right quick with an incident—something that happened to Ned Sullivan!

Why don't you get the interest of your prospects the same way?

You might say, for instance, "There's a man down in Jonestown by the name of John Smith. I got him to run the advertising series we proposed—and a queer and pleasing thing happened to him. Let me tell you about it."

Of course your prospect would listen—because you had secured his interest with a story—with an example.

Rule 11: Keep reminding yourself of the Dale Carnegie rule: "Become genuinely interested in other people."

"Old stuff," you say.

Old indeed—older than you think! Publilius Syrus, writing before Christ was born, said:

We are interested in others when they are interested in us.

He might have said, "We buy from others who are interested in us."

"Old stuff"—old before Christ was born—but have you learned it? Did you use it today? Will you use it tomorrow?

Never write "Not interested" on a prospect card. Write instead, "I failed to interest him."

SEVEN

How to talk "benefits"
and prove claims
about your product
Step 3:* Producing conviction

CHAPTER 18

How to convince your prospect
that your product
will benefit him

Never forget the power of plain facts. —WINANS

*Great Rule 3: Give your prospect enough facts, and no more, about your product and how it will benefit him, to convince him that he is justified in buying.

If you have been successful in the interest step of your sales talk, you have made the prospect say to himself, in substance, "If this thing will do for me what this salesman says it will do, I'd like to have it." Maybe he has added to himself, "But I don't believe it will."

Perhaps you have said to him, "This refrigerator will save you enough electric energy in five years to pay for itself—so it really costs you nothing." The prospect says to himself, "I'd buy one if I thought I'd get it for nothing."

You have claimed, in the interest step, that your product

will benefit or serve the prospect. Now you must make him believe it.

Maybe you're not so good as you think—few are!

I have rarely known an experienced salesman who suffered from a feeling of inferiority about the way he presented the conviction part of his sales talk.

"I may slip on the interest and desire steps," he says, "but I can surely give 'em the facts." And he does! His talk usually has all the dullness of the encyclopedia with little of its dignity.

Does this statement seem unduly pessimistic and cynical? Not if you have, as I have, through a period of over thirty-eight years, made ten thousand calls with a thousand salesmen, yawned at the dullness of their talks, and flinched at the wildness of their misstatements.

The conviction part of your sales talk is the defensive part. If you do not effectively present the facts, you will probably not close the sale. It is like a baseball game. If a team can't field, it can rarely win a championship.

So learn to present your facts effectively.

You appeal here to the prospect's mind
—not his emotions

What do you do in the conviction part of your talk? You convince your prospect that your product will do what you claim it will. You give him facts, evidence, testimonials. You pile up enough evidence to prove your claims.

Your prospect wants answers to five questions about your product.

1. What is it?
2. What does it do?
3. What does that mean to me?
4. Who says so?

5. Can you prove it?

If you boil the conviction step down to brief rules, you have these three:

1. Tell your prospect what your product is and what it will do *to benefit him.*

2. Tell him—and, if practicable, *show* him—that it works satisfactorily.

3. Support your claims about your product with evidence.

Some additional rules for convincing your prospect follow:

A. Give the prospect all needed facts—but no more.

B. In most instances when you give a fact, give the related benefit. (See Chapter 16, which tells you how to use "buyer's benefits.")

C. Don't expect, in the average sale, to arouse the prospect's desire to own your product with a mere statement of facts and benefits. You usually have to carry him through the desire step of the selling process, to make him want to own your product.

D. Close the conviction part of your talk with the question, "How do you like it?" (This suggestion comes from Frank Bettger, who says of that question, "It's magic!")

You may say, "I sell nuts and bolts to purchasing agents. I don't have to prove that they work. What am I supposed to talk about?"

My answer is: Unless you have some advantage over your competitor in goods or service, terms or price, why bother to learn about selling? If you know your facts, you can usually tell a good story about nuts and bolts but a better one about your engineering service or terms or whatever your best talking point may be.

But I'm a jobber's salesman

"You can't mean *me*," say jobbers' salesmen. "Why, we just go around to the same old people and take the same old orders."

All too true! You just take orders—and yet you wonder why your pay hasn't been increased for ten years!

I have often asked jobbers' salesmen this question, "Suppose you were calling on a dealer who was about to start in business and he asked you, 'Why should I trade with your company?' What would you answer?" I am usually appalled by such replies as, "Well, it's a fine company. It's been in business a long time. We offer good service. I'd like to have your account." Vague, windy, general claims. No facts. No reasons. No benefits.

Yet Bertrand R. Canfield, in his book *Salesmanship*, quotes a survey which shows that purchasers consider the *company* to be over five times as important as the *product*.

So, if you are a jobber's salesman, be prepared to tell the story of your company and its service. Try to have one good sales point about your company to present each time you call.

"Yes," says the jobber's salesman, "but generally I just call back on the same old dealers."

True, of course. But don't you usually have a deal, a promotion plan, or a new sales idea to offer? Don't you have to give your customers facts about your company or about its products, its deals, or its advertising? Don't you have some news or advertising ideas to give to dealers?

If you are not willing to put some selling into your work, if you are going to "just take orders" all your life—well, friend, your best chance to get rich is to marry money!

CHAPTER 19

It's easy to convince prospects— just follow the rules

No prospect objects to how much a sales-
man says, if he says it in a few words!

To present the conviction part of your sales talk effectively,
use the following rules:

Rule 1: Be brief. Don't give any more facts than your prospect needs. Some cynic once defined a watch as "a spheroidal
metal device, filled with machinery, which the salesman
glances at as he starts his sales talk and then forgets until it
runs down."

Too many salesmen talk until they run down. They tend to
substitute talking for thinking. Remember the old farmer's
advice, "When you're through pumpin', let go the handle."

If you talk too long in the conviction step, the prospect may
develop an eager desire to get rid of you—and may even tell
you so.

As my friend W. J. Newhouse puts the idea, "A hint is a
hint! If the prospect reaches for a club, the salesman should
reach for his hat."

Salesmen often say to me, "I don't need to work on the conviction part of my talk. I can rattle off the facts."

And that's just what they do—rattle them off with no
thought of clarity, continuity, connections, or coherence!

This story of the briefest successful sales talk on record
gives you an idea of what can be accomplished in the way of
economizing on words:

Anthony Dimock was eighteen years old when he started selling.
He sold bonds on Wall Street. A few days after he started work,

he was sent to offer a bond to the president of the National City Bank—one of the largest banks in the world.

While Dimock was waiting his turn to speak to the president, he overheard him say to an employee, "Get to the point, get to the point."

This was a warning to Dimock to make his sales talk brief. He did. When his turn came, he walked up to the desk, took out a bond, placed it on the president's desk, and made the world's shortest sales talk—this one word, *"Par."*

The president looked up, smiled, reached for his check book, made out his check for the amount, and took the bond.

Ten years later, Dimock was worth a million dollars.

How long should you talk?

How long should the conviction part of your talk last? Long enough to convince your prospect—and no longer. The story of creation is told in Genesis in 400 words; the Ten Commandments contain only 297 words; Lincoln's Gettysburg Address is but 266 words in length, and the Declaration of Independence required but 1,321 words to set up a new concept of freedom. Make your presentation brief, too.

Watch your prospect—if he begins to act bored, quit! "If you don't strike oil in two minutes," quotes Albert Beveridge, "stop boring."

You can usually sense when to stop

"How shall I know when to end the conviction part of my sales talk?" you ask.

It ought to be enough of an answer to say, "When you have presented all important facts about your proposition." Alas, "all of it" is frequently too much! If your prospect becomes bored by your talk—and usually even a beginner can sense that point—you should either put on more steam, or move briskly along to the desire step.

Don Marquis once wrote, using the editorial "we," "We

were at a dinner the other evening, and we were called on to say a few words. It suddenly occurred to us, after we had made certain dull and inept remarks, that we really didn't have a damn thing to say, and so we sat down." That's the way salesmen usually find out when to stop.

Two purchasing agents were talking about a new product. One said, "I want to know more about it." The other said, "Ask the salesman." "Oh," said the first one, "I don't want to know *that much* about it!"

Rule 2: Locate the key issue and confine your talk largely to that. As Stanley Resor, the great advertising man, phrased it, "What you've got to do is to discover what makes this product the white pea in the pod."

If the prospect for a car is primarily interested in gasoline economy, talk chiefly about that. Why worry about the paint job, if his chief interest is "miles per gallon"?

How do you locate the key issue? By asking questions, of course. After you have made each important point in your sales talk, you ask such questions as, "How do you like that feature?" or "Is that important to you?" or "Will that be a lot of help to you, or is it not too important?"

After you ask such questions, encourage the prospect to talk. Listen carefully and usually you will locate the key issue.

Leonard Lyons ran this item in his column, "The Lyons Den:" "Joseph M. Proskauer, the former Supreme Court Justice . . . subscribes to the London *Times*. . . . Not that he doesn't feel that the New York newspapers supply sufficient news coverage. It's just that he believes that the London *Times* has the finest crossword puzzles in the world."

Therefore, if you were trying to sell Judge Proskauer a newspaper, you wouldn't talk to him about news coverage; you would talk to him about his key issue, crossword puzzles.

The following example of a sale that was nearly lost because the salesman did not dig out the key issue at the start

of the negotiations was told to me by Harold E. Lee, of
Harold Lee Realty Co., St. Louis, Missouri.

"I'm sorry, Mr. Lee," Mrs. Miller said on the phone one morning recently, "but my son found a much larger home last night and
is so enthusiastic about it that he is signing a contract for it this
afternoon."

With such a firm turndown, Mr. Whiting, the normal reaction
would be to bow out. Fortunately, I remembered two rules I had
learned in the Dale Carnegie Sales Course. The first was, "Never
give up until the prospect has said 'no' at least seven times," and
the other, "Find the key issue." So I decided to find out what the
prospect's chief interests really were.

"Mrs. Miller," I said, "please tell me about the house you are
going to buy."

She told me about its fine construction, its huge lot, its spacious
rooms. Somehow, I sensed that she was overemphasizing size. So,
I asked her simply, "Mrs. Miller, do you *like* the house?"

She answered, "I'm afraid of all the housework," and then
added, "I didn't mean to say that—my son is so enthused I wanted
him to be completely satisfied."

I complimented her on being so considerate of her son and then
suggested, "In all fairness to yourself, Mrs. Miller, will you mention to your son, as you did to me, about the housework that
'frightens you'?"

That afternoon young Mr. Miller called with the glad news,
"I've decided to buy your house—let's sign the contract."

Housework was the key issue. Once Mr. Lee located it, he
made the sale.

The facts and benefits about the key issue are probably
more important in making a sale than all the other facts and
benefits heaped together!

How much do you know?

Rule 3: Know at least one hundred times as much about
your product as you use in your sales talk. This gives your talk
a tone of authority that can be achieved in no other way.

Don't be afraid to repeat

Rule 4: This is one way to get people to believe what you say: repeat it again and again. Be sure, however, to repeat it in different words and from a different angle.

As that mythical Irishman, Mr. Dooley, once said, "I'll belave anything at all, if you'll only tell it to me often enough."

Rule 5: Sometimes you may skip the conviction step entirely.

This is especially true in most retail selling, in some wholesaling, and in intangible selling—life insurance, for example. The life insurance salesman usually spends little time telling the merits of his wares—he appeals to the emotions. He talks benefits rather than facts.

When I was managing my first sales force, I tried to get my five-man team out of a slump that threatened to be perpetual. I offered a handsome leather Gladstone bag to the first man who sold any Central Maine Power Company preferred stock.

I made the offer at the end of a brief morning meeting. Four of the men started off at high speed. The fifth, Perley Clark, the fattest and laziest man on the force, strolled into a haberdashery shop next door, walked up to the proprietor, and said, "Wouldn't you like to buy some of our preferred stock?"

The prospect replied, "I've been thinking about it for some time. I may as well buy it now."

Inside of ten minutes after I had offered the Gladstone bag, Perley walked back with an order and a check, and picked up the prize! He had skipped not only the conviction step—he had skipped the interest and desire steps as well. Perley made a guess that the haberdasher knew that the stock was safe and good. It happened that his guess was right!

_____ CHAPTER 20

Lots of salesmen talk lots—
when they should be listening

*When you say, "To make a long
story short," it is generally too late!*

Here are some more rules for making the conviction part of
your sales talk really convincing:

Rule 6: Ask a lot of questions and *listen to the answers.*

Get your prospect's story before you tell all of yours. The
early part of a sales talk should usually contain more questions
than statements.

This story, from the Wright & Co. house magazine, gives
an idea of how people dislike a man who talks too much—even
when the talker is President of the United States:

President Theodore Roosevelt, before leaving the White House,
was making detailed plans for his African big-game hunt. Hearing
that a famous British big-game hunter was in the country, President Roosevelt invited him to the White House. Thus the President hoped to gain some pointers for his trip.

After a two-hour conference, during which the two were not
disturbed, the Englishman came out.

"What did you tell the President?" a reporter asked.

"I told him my name," sighed the wearied visitor.

Apparently, Theodore Roosevelt had the instincts of a misguided salesman!

Walter Mack, president of National Phoenix Industries,
Inc., ended a talk before the Sales Executives Club of New
York with a story of a Pullman porter on a train coming up
from Washington. The porter had a big cut on the side of his
face. Walter asked him how he got the cut. The porter replied,

"I was talking when I should have been listening." Salesmen, heed that moral!

"Much talk, much foolishness," says the Talmud.

Let the prospect sell himself

John Batdorff of Cleveland told me this story about the good result of being closemouthed in a sales situation:

> I've been in the real estate business off and on for eighteen years. A little over a month ago I read in your book the rule, "Don't try to do all the talking yourself—let the prospect do his share." So I tried it. I was showing an expensive house to a wealthy man. I unlocked the front door with "Well, here it is," and ushered him in. I stayed outside. He came out in a half hour or so and said, "I sort of like it. May I show it to my wife?" Did I offer to show it? I did not. I handed him the key. In an hour he was at the office, all smiles. "Well," he said, "I sold it to my wife." He sold it, but I got the commission!

John's method, of course, is not recommended for daily use. His experience is evidence, however, that silence sometimes sells.

One of the great selling delusions is "The more talk, the more sales." Don't fall a victim to this fallacy.

Rule 7: A good way to test interest in the conviction step of your sales talk is to stop now and then, look the prospect right in the eye, and say, "Have I made it clear?"

From the *Arkansas Baptist* I culled this example of what may happen when you ask the prospect if he understands what you say.

A salesman who had managed to get himself and his prospect confused in the explanation of a not too complicated piece of machinery paused to ask, "Do you follow me?"

"I have so far," the prospect answered, "but I'll say frankly, Mr. Jones, if I thought I could find my way back, I'd quit right here."

Nail down your points

Rule 8: To be sure you are really convincing your prospect, nail down the important points as you make them.

Suppose you have been giving a prospect your reasons for believing that your tire is a safe tire; you can say, "When you consider these facts, you agree with me that this is a safe tire, don't you, Mr. Jones?"

That is, after you make each important point, clinch it with a question about that point, to which the prospect must answer "yes." Gradually, you are building up your case. If the prospect has agreed, as you have carried him through the sales talk, that your product is the only one that exactly fits his wants, he will find it difficult to say "no" when you ask for the order.

The National Cash Register Company used to recommend that its men list, on a large writing pad, the points they wanted to cover. Their instructions for nailing down these points follow:

As each important thing is covered, question the merchant in order to find out if he understands you. For example, "I believe you will agree with me, Mr. Blank, that this is a better way of handling this transaction than your present method, won't you?" If he is not convinced, explain to his satisfaction before going farther.

"Yes," you say, "but suppose when I say, 'You agree with me about that, don't you?' the prospect says, 'No, I don't!' Where does that leave me?"

It leaves you in a better position than you were, because you have smoked out a resistance. Your next move is to go back and answer his hitherto unexpressed objection. If you had not smoked it out, that one objection might have cost you the sale.

Be specific—avoid generalities

Rule 9: Be specific all through your sales talk, but especially in the conviction step. That is, be definite and explicit. Remember, "One hard fact may outweigh all logic and rhetoric." State facts, not unsupported claims.

A *Printers' Ink* survey showed that talking in generalities was regarded as the next-to-worst fault of salesmen. (The worst was "Trying to sell without knowing the business" or "Lack of product knowledge.")

Another poll by *Printers' Ink* shows that buyers of advertising space also object to these kinds of generalities: (*a*) plain boasting, (*b*) broad, meaningless claims, (*c*) too much blue-sky talk, (*d*) wild ideas, (*e*) exaggerated statements, (*f*) talk —without proof, (*g*) vagueness.

How many of these faults are *you* guilty of?

"The biggest poison in salesmanship," says Paul W. Ivey, "is the poison of indefinite statements." And Aristotle, writing over 2,200 years before Paul was born, said, "Generalities are the refuge of weak minds. Generalities are usually dull. Eschew them."

Earle Doucette, writing in *Coronet* on "The Super-salesman of Freeport, Maine," gave an excellent example of the sales power of specific facts. He wrote:

During World War II, L. L. Bean [an authority on outdoor apparel] was in Washington as a consultant to the armed forces.

For cold-weather wear the Army wanted leather-topped rubbers with 16-inch tops. Bean thought 12-inch tops and a lighter rubber would be better.

Getting nowhere with verbal argument, he whipped out a pencil and began a furious calculation. "Gentlemen," he said presently, "do you realize that, if you insist on the higher-topped boot, in a day's march of 36,980 steps each soldier in the Army will be lifting 4,600 unnecessary pounds?"

Awe-stricken by this down-East way of figuring, the Army capitulated.

If this book taught you nothing except to be specific, it would be worth ten times what you paid for it.

To sum it up: As a rule, be exact, be specific, give facts, not guesses. Broad generalities will not disguise your ignorance. Buckle down and learn the facts about your product. Then eliminate from your vocabulary loose generalities such as "high-grade," "best quality," and "and so forth"!

Don't let me give you the idea, however, that you must never use a generality. Sometimes you can't avoid it—sometimes you don't want to avoid it.

Generalities are handy to soften unfavorable facts. For example, you could be specific and say, "Our washer sells for $34.75 more than the next most expensive one on the market," or you could state it in more general terms: "We are proud to tell you that our washer is high-priced."

—————————————————————————————————— CHAPTER 21

Every big-league salesman must use these rules or go back to the minors

Selling is easy. All you have to do is find out what people want and then tell that your product gives it to them.
—CHET BOWLES (with the word "selling"
              substituted for the word "advertising")

Here are a few more rules that every salesman should know by heart and use always:

Rule 10: Be concrete. To learn what concreteness is and how important it is to salesmen, see Chapter 32.

Rule 11: Be clear. While I was general retail sales manager of the securities department of Henry L. Doherty and Company, a client called our New York office one day from Connecticut and said, "Your salesman, R. F. D. Lemon, came by my place yesterday and sold me something and ... er ... would you mind looking up your records and telling me what it was I bought?"

I suppose most salesmen aim in the direction of being clear, but most of them miss the bull's-eye—and some of them miss the whole blamed target! Their talks are so hard to follow they practically constitute an intelligence test.

Anthony Hope, the novelist, understated it when he said, "Unless one is a genius, it is best to aim at being intelligible."

Your prospect buys, not because of what you say, but because of what he *understands* of what you say. Keep asking yourself (not the prospect), "Is he following me? Is he understanding me?"

If he isn't following you, it's probably your fault.

Your talk will be clear if you make it clear

"Everything that can be thought at all can be thought clearly," said Ludwig Wittgenstein. "Everything that can be said can be said clearly."

When I was in charge of selling preferred stock for the Central Maine Power Company, I got out a circular which included a map printed in several colors. The salesmen took delight in "selling from the map." One day, I went out with Arthur Campbell. Mr. Campbell ordinarily was an exceptionally effective salesman. On this occasion, however, when he was about half through his canvass for the preferred stock, his prospect said, "No, I don't think I want to buy a *map* today."

Arthur had completely failed to make his prospect understand what he was offering.

You can speak clearly, and here's how

How can you be sure to use clear, understandable language in your sales talk?

(*a*) Have your subject clearly in your own mind. About half the fuzzy selling in this country today is due to fuzzy thinking.

One night, when I was teaching a public-speaking class, I made this comment on a speech, "It isn't exactly clear to me."

The speaker replied, "Well, I'm not surprised. It isn't exactly clear to me, either!"

(*b*) In order to make your talk clear, use short, familiar words. Don't be what Cy Frailey calls a "googler"—and defines as "a man who never uses a short word if he can think of a long one with the same meaning." Remember what St. Paul said: "Except you utter words that are easy to be understood, how shall it be known what is spoken?"

Remember also that, of the 266 words in Lincoln's Gettysburg Address, over 185 have only *one* syllable.

(*c*) Don't talk too fast. Think ahead of your prospect but talk behind him. Pause often.

(*d*) Don't expect customers to understand the jargon of your trade or profession or business. Here's an example.

One afternoon, Mark Twain, who lost more than one hard-earned fortune by investing it in harebrained schemes, observed a tall, spare man, with kindly blue eyes and eager face, coming up the path with a strange contraption under his arm. Yes, it was an invention. The man explained it to the humorist in technical language. Mark listened politely but said he had been burned too often.

"You can have as large a share as you want for $500," said the man. Twain shook his head; the invention didn't make sense.

He didn't understand the explanation he had heard. The tall, stooped figure started away.

"What did you say your name was?" the author called after

him. "Bell," replied the inventor a little sadly, "Alexander Graham Bell."   —VANSANT CORYELL IN
                                              The Christian Science Monitor

The chances are the inventor of the telephone had failed to make clear what his contraption was or what it would do, because he talked in technical language, unfamiliar to Twain.

Bell lost a backer—Twain lost a billion!

Rule 12: Manage the interview—don't let your prospect manage it. If he tries to carry the conversation off the track, show only mild interest in the unrelated and immaterial subject. As soon as good manners permit, you could say, for example, "Let's see, what were we talking about?" and then get back into your sales talk.

Rule 13: Speak good English.

How?

Buy any one of a dozen books on correct English (preferably pocket-size) and go to work. Then buy another and another. Never stop as long as you live. (My personal preference is *The Handbook of Composition*, by Woolley. It's old, but good. It's published by D. C. Heath and Company. Price, $2.20.)

Is English important to salesmen? Yes, vitally so. The salesman who habitually uses bad English is offensive to a considerable number of people. Often, bad English annoys even people who do not speak correctly themselves.

Professor Austin Phelps said, "The common people know good English when they hear it; they understand it. Men crave it who never use it."

So give people what they crave.

Sell the gadgets too

Rule 14: Don't pin all your faith on one or two major selling points of your product or service.

One of the first security sales I ever made was to a woman who lived a few miles north of Augusta, Maine. She bought so easily that, after she handed me the check, I asked her what she liked particularly about the stock.

Her answer was, "The money comes to me every three months by check." That minor selling point was the major point in her case.

Rule 15: Don't use profanity in a sales talk. A cuss word is always a poor substitute for the right word.

I once said to a profane salesman, "I notice that the best salesmen do the least cussing."

He replied, "Well, what the hell have they got to cuss about?"

Don't get bored with your own sales arguments

Rule 16: Don't discard selling points, examples, or testimonials just because *you* are tired of them. The smart salesman holds on to the old just as long as it is good, and does not grab the new until he is sure it is better.

Do you want to know how to keep from getting bored with saying the same sales talk over and over?

Back in 1902, I interviewed Joseph Jefferson, then perhaps the most distinguished actor in America. He was playing *Rip Van Winkle* in the Vendome Theatre in Nashville. He had played "Rip" thousands of times. So I asked him, "Don't you get tired of playing the same part over and over?"

He smiled when he replied, "Mr. Whiting, lots of people ask me that. And it is true, I used to get bored with the repetition. One day I faced the issue. I said to myself, 'Joe Jefferson, are you playing the role of Rip Van Winkle for your own amusement—or for the amusement of those people down front?' As soon as I forgot myself and got to thinking of my audience I was never bored again by that or any other part."

So if you are bored by repeating your sales talk over and over the one right way, just tell yourself, "Stop thinking about yourself—start thinking about the prospect."

Rule 17: Don't seem too eager to sell. Go a step farther, if you can do it honestly: make the product seem hard to get.

Perhaps the greatest salesman of his time, Joseph Duveen, who sold art in million-dollar lots, including one $25,000,000 lot to Andrew Mellon, was expert at the technique.

Duveen practiced this psychology continually. When a visitor to his exhibits or storerooms asked about any particular item, Duveen was usually reluctant to sell it. He had halfway promised this picture to Mr. Widener, or he had such an affection for that one that he wanted to keep it for himself.

He was following the old horse-trading rule: never seem anxious to sell.

"Duveen didn't want to sell his stuff, but they always badgered the poor fellow till he gave in," said Mrs. William Randolph Hearst, one of his good clients. She saw through his strategy, but liked it nevertheless. —FRED DE ARMOND IN *Specialty Salesman*

CHAPTER 22

Mention facts but stress benefits

A lot of salesmen are so intent on telling what the product is that they forget to tell what it does.

In one of the Dale Carnegie Sales Course classes we asked a salesman to present the conviction part of his pitch. We told him that he was to assume that he had secured attention and aroused interest. We asked him to jump into the body of his talk. He started thus:

"This General Electric Automatic Blanket has double-bed control; it is 72 inches by 86 inches; it weighs 5 pounds; it is 50 per cent wool, 25 per cent cotton, 25 per cent rayon; it can be washed; it is bound with 5¾-inch rayon satin with boxed corners; it has a device that compensates for normal changes in room temperature."

What did that salesman omit?

The benefits.

Presenting a conviction step without benefits is like "closing" without asking for the order.

After we drilled the class on buyer's benefits, the same salesman started his talk this way:

"This blanket has a control on each side of the bed, so you and your husband can each have the temperature you want. The blanket measures 72 inches by 86 inches—so it is large enough to fit any double bed. It weighs only 5 pounds, so it will not press down on you as a pile of heavy blankets would. It can be washed, hence it can easily and inexpensively be kept clean."

That sales talk, coupling facts with benefits, would have a real chance to sell—because it told the prospect how she would benefit from owning and using the blanket.

People buy benefits—so talk benefits

"Customer benefits determine whether or not you close the sale," said John Wilson in *Open the Mind and Close the Sale.*

William J. Tobin, editor, Research Institute of America, in an article in *Printers' Ink*, told about a salesman so good that he sold 41 per cent of all the business available in his field. Mr. Tobin explained this man's success in this way:

All the time he was selling he was on the customer's side of the fence. What was the customer looking for? What did he need to operate more effectively? How could the customer use his product to accomplish his business objectives in a minimum of time, for less money, to his greater advantage with profit?

Wm. E. Robbins, manager of Field Training, Firestone Tire and Rubber Company, gives this advice to Firestone salesmen: "Keep coming back to the question, 'Do you know what this will do for you?' " (That is, "Do you know the benefits?")

A good example of the magic of benefits was given by W. Bernard Jones, Jr., of Sumter, South Carolina, in his book *How to Rush*, as follows:

In the little town of Pinewood, South Carolina, the owner of the local drugstore told me this story: "The best sale I ever heard of was made by James C. Bryan. A local bachelor in a neighboring community had bought a cemetery plot. He had bought his coffin. He came in to see Mr. Bryan about getting a suit in which to be buried.

Mr. Bryan sold that man a suit with two pairs of trousers!"

Mr. Bryan accomplished the miracle of selling a man a coat and two pairs of trousers to be buried in! He did it by pointing out to his prospect that he didn't wear a coat much anyway, so he could wear the coat occasionally and one pair of pants frequently and thus have a coat in fairly good shape and a new pair of pants to be buried in!

Actually, he pointed out a benefit.

"What does it do for me?" asks every prospect

The idea of talking *benefits* was stressed by Hal Bergdahl, manager of Dealer Sales for Crane Company, Chicago, in a talk before the Sales Executives Club of New York.

In closing, he launched into a jingle (whether his own or somebody else's he didn't say), part of which follows:

> I see that you've spent quite a big wad of dough
> To tell me the things you think I should know
> How your plant is so big, so fine, and so strong;
> And your founder had whiskers so handsomely long.
>
> Your machinery's modern and oh, so complete;
> Your "rep" is so flawless; your workers so neat.
> Your motto is "Quality"—capital "Q"—
> No wonder I'm tired of "Your" and of "You"!

So tell me quick and tell me true
(Or else, my love, to hell with you)
Less—how this product came to be;
More—what the darn thing does for me!

So here is one of the near-great rules of selling:
After you state a fact about your product, immediately tell
the prospect the benefit to him that results from that fact.
For example:
"It weighs 5 pounds, so it is easy to carry."
"This garbage disposal unit has a wide mouth, so it gobbles
up big hunks of garbage."
"This machine operates by remote control—you can turn it
on and off from any part of the room."

Avoid benefits that don't benefit—like this one:

Salesman of high-priced car talking to prospect: "Driving is
virtually effortless, leaving your entire mind free to figure out how
you will meet the payments."

Buyer's benefits help in answering objections, too

Here is an example of how buyer's benefits can be used to
overcome the objection, "Your price is too high." It was given
me by Blake Davis, a salesman for the Molin Manufacturing
Company, of Montgomery, Alabama, makers of commercial
refrigerators.

When I was taking the Dale Carnegie Sales Course, the class
members worked for a week on buyer's benefits. That week I
called back on a prospect whom I had called on twice and failed
to sell.

While I was going through the conviction part of my sales talk,
the prospect told me that our price was $1,000 higher than that of
one of our competitors. The prospect said that if we would cut our
price $1,000, he would buy from us.

We not only didn't cut our price; we didn't even talk about it. Instead, we talked the buyer's benefits that would accrue to him if he installed our refrigeration.

The prospect kept coming back to the price item. The more he talked about price, the more we talked about buyer's benefits.

After thirty minutes of this price-versus-benefits, the prospect turned to his partner and said, "Oh, well, let's go ahead and trade with them tonight."

Important? I should say it is!

I wish I could make you realize the importance of this "buyer's benefits" rule. Maybe *you* observe it—always. Some salesmen do; many don't. Based on the observations of our instructors in the Dale Carnegie Sales Courses, not over 10 per cent of the salesmen in our classes, before they took the course, made an unfailing practice of tying a benefit to every sales fact they presented.

Occasionally the benefit from a fact about a product is so obvious that it need not be mentioned. However, if you are in doubt, mention it!

People don't buy *things*—they buy *what things will do for them.*

──────────────────────────────── CHAPTER 23

Use evidence to prove your claims

The key to selling something is to prove that it's every-thing it's supposed to be. —ALFRED C. FULLER

Some salesmen expect prospects to believe their unsupported claims. They say, for example, "This washing machine will get out the deep-down imbedded dirt," or "This dishwasher

will sluice off hardened eggs." Then they wonder why the
prospect does not wrench the order blank away from them and
insist on buying this miracle-worker!

Prospects want evidence. For example:

At a religious soapbox meeting at Hyde Park Corner, an atheist
was heckling the speaker. "If I made a universe, I certainly would
do a better job than God."

The speaker answered, "I don't want to challenge you on this,
but would you mind, for the time being, making a rabbit, just to
establish confidence?"

—DR. KARL STERN, IN *Catholic Hour* BROADCAST

Smart prospects do not buy expensive items on *claims*. They
want *evidence*. (*Webster* says that evidence is "something that
tends to prove.")

The smart salesman is prepared to supply enough evidence
to constitute proof.

Some of the forms of evidence available to salesmen to
prove that their product is as good as they claim are:

(*a*) Testimonial letters.

(*b*) Testimonial phone calls—that is, calls to users who
have agreed to give testimonials over the telephone.

(*c*) Guarantees.

(*d*) Photographs, charts, diagrams, and other visual evidence.

(*e*) Articles from books, general magazines, trade journals,
government publications and newspapers.

(*f*) Examples (or "instances") of the successful use of the
product. (An instance may be defined as "an event that is
adduced to prove and support a general statement.")

(*g*) Demonstrations.

(*h*) Facts.

(*i*) Statistics.

(*j*) Analogies.

(*k*) Expert testimony.

(*l*) Bulletins.

Many salesmen gather testimonials, photographs, and clippings in a ring-binder book for effective display.

Gather and use testimonials

In the Dale Carnegie Sales Course, we frequently ask a class, "How many of you carry with you any form of evidence to support your claims about your product?"

Rarely do as many as ten out of forty put up their hands. The other thirty have no evidence—not even testimonial letters.

Yet what better evidence of the value of a product is readily at hand than a statement by someone who has used the product?

So be prepared to produce written evidence of what your product or service or organization has done to benefit users.

WARNING: be careful about telling one competitor what another competitor has accomplished by using or selling your product.

The greatest enthusiast about your product is the man who uses it. He will sometimes make claims about it so fantastic that you would not dare make them in your sales talk.

As an example of a fantastic testimonial, I heard a fine-looking young woman stand before an audience of several hundred people in the Morrison Hotel in Chicago and state that she had been insane—that she had been confined in an Illinois state asylum—that she had been discharged as "incurable but harmless." She declared she had been completely cured by taking the Dale Carnegie Course in Effective Speaking! As evidence that she was cured, she stated that she had held a job for a couple of years for an advertising agency in Chicago—and that she was still employed by them.

Imagine what would happen to a salesman who claimed that any public-speaking course could cure insanity. Yet this woman's claim was true!

You don't need fantastic facts for your testimonials. Good, conservative, specific facts are best.

So use testimonials as evidence that people have tried your product and have been satisfied with results. Original letters are best; facsimiles are almost as good; mere copies will do, if nothing better is obtainable.

Never use a testimonial unless you can give the name and address of its author. The more specific the testimonial is, the more convincing it is as evidence.

Where do you get testimonials?

1. From your company. Your sales manager should have some available.

2. Dig up testimonials yourself. Go to satisfied users and ask for testimonials.

Here's bad news about testimonials—users almost never say in a testimonial letter what you want them to say. So if you want an effective testimonial:

(*a*) Ask the prospect what he is willing to say.

(*b*) Write the testimonial yourself.

(*c*) Then ask the prospect to have the testimonial copied on his own stationery and to sign it.

Then you should have a worthwhile testimonial!

Telephone testimonials are effective

Dale Carnegie told me that he was once considering spending a vacation in a camp in Maine. Naturally, he wanted to know that the camp was a nice place before he committed himself to spend a vacation there. The owner of the camp said, "Here is a list of people in or near New York who have been to my camp. Some are right here in Forest Hills (Dale's home town). Call any of these people and ask them what they think of my camp."

That was convincing evidence!

Remember, a whisper by a satisfied user is louder than a shout by a self-interested salesman.

So if your product is one that should be supported by strong evidence, ask some of your enthusiastic users to give you permission to use their names as "telephone references."

Let's see what salesman Don Cordi of Portland, Oregon, gained by using a "telephone testimonial."

One day, Charlie, one of our salesmen from the Pet Milk Company, and I called on P. H. McMoore, owner of Moore's Food Center, Portland, Oregon. McMoore had refused to let us handle a promotion for him. In fact, he had committed himself to our competitor. We called to see if we could salvage this particular promotion, which meant to us a huge volume of merchandise.

We explained to McMoore all the benefits to him of our promotion. In spite of all the benefits, he would not budge.

Finally I said, "Mac, we've been handling promotions for Phil Walter. They have increased his volume of business tremendously. Don't take my word for it—pick up the phone and ask Phil what he thinks about our promotions."

Mac reached for the phone.

Because Phil was flattered that an important dealer would ask for his opinion, and because he was delighted with the extra business our promotions had brought him, he gave us a strong testimonial.

McMoore thereupon agreed that we should handle the promotion.

If you have a strong guarantee, use it

Most business organizations guarantee their products. If yours does, carry the guarantee with you.

Be sure you use the exact wording your company recommends. A guarantee signed by the president of your company is most effective. So is the label of Good Housekeeping Institute, National Institute of Fire Underwriters, or other recognized authorities.

If your claims about your product can be supported by such visual evidence as photographs, charts, or diagrams—by all means use them.

Printed evidence helps

Martial, who lived nearly 2,000 years ago, wrote, "I will not believe it until I have read it." That's true of many prospects. So try to have printed evidence for them to read.

Don't make the mistake that so many salesmen do of claiming broadly, "Statistics show that...," or "Our product is used in the Waldorf-Astoria."

If "statistics show it," have the statistics with you. If the Waldorf-Astoria uses it, have a letter from the hotel stating that it does use it.

Remember, your own enthusiasm for the product is perhaps the best evidence that the product is as good as you claim it is.

*   *   *

The next form of evidence—*examples*—is so important that I shall give it a chapter to itself.

——————————————————————— CHAPTER 24

Use examples—they will work miracles for you

*No prospect ever fell asleep
listening to a lively example.*

To liven up the conviction step of your sales talk and to make it clear, to make it interesting, to make it convincing, use examples—instances, stories, incidents.

"People are interested first in people, then in things, last in ideas," said G. Edward Pendray in a magazine article. So talk "people"—how "people" used your product and benefited, what "people" gained, how your product worked miracles for "people."

Examples are magic—examples work miracles. A salesman once told me, "Examples are the world's greatest closer of sales."

Please stop right now and ask yourself, "Do I use examples to liven up my talk and to support my claims about my product? If so, do I use them often enough?"

George F. Taubeneck, in his book *One Foot in the Door*, quotes John Patterson, the father of modern selling, as follows:

Tell a story when you present a point. Look at the sales of books. People buy umpteen times as many novels as they do serious dissertations. Look at the magazines—ten stories to one serious article. Let that be your guide when talking to a prospect.

Use examples to make
your sales talk interesting

Seneca (who died in 39 A.D.) wrote, "Rules make the learner's path long, examples make it short and successful." He might well have said, "Facts make the sales talk long, examples make it short and successful."

Suppose you were selling insurance and you said, "Every husband ought to figure out how much money his wife would need to support herself and educate the children in case of his sudden death."

Not very exciting, is it?

If, instead, you had supported this point, as Donald A. Nash of Chicago did, with the example which follows, your talk would have been more interesting. Here is Mr. Nash's example:

I tried several times to sell a policy to the owner of a filling station where I buy my gas. He thought he had enough. He had $4,000!

One day, however, he said, "Nash, can you stop over at the house tonight? Maybe I'll take a little more insurance."

I asked him what had happened to make him want to discuss life insurance.

He said, "My sister has been married about a year and a half and she has a newborn baby. Her husband had only $1,000 of life insurance. He was going to buy $5,000 more as soon as he had his coal bill paid. But he developed pneumonia. We have just returned from the funeral and there is my sister with a newborn baby and five tons of coal—and only $1,000 in insurance!"

Surely one example is more interesting than three dozen facts!

A good deal of the conviction part of most sales talks is necessarily instruction—the imparting of facts about your product. And most instruction is dull.

So, to balance off the dullness of most facts, fill the conviction part of your talk with examples.

Convince your prospect with examples

Examples make the conviction part of your sales talk more convincing.

"Any fact," to misquote Emmons slightly, "is better established by two or three good examples than by a thousand arguments."

For example, if I were selling the Dale Carnegie Sales Course to a salesman I could say, "Many salesmen who take the course increase their business in a sensational way."

That is true, but not convincing. It is a mere claim. But if I had followed it with, "For example, please note this letter from C. C. Davis, division manager, Air-Way Branches, Inc., Gadsden, Alabama. Mr. Davis writes: 'After the first session, I had an unbelievable and astonishing 302 per cent increase in business. At the end of a full month of your Sales Course, my business had levelled off to an amazing 276 per cent increase.' "

Surely that example is more convincing than an unsupported fact or a bland claim.

Examples are bread and butter to insurance salesmen. Here is one used by an agent in Montgomery, Alabama.

I went to pay a claim to a widow. In conversation with her, she said, "I want to show you the highest-priced refrigerator in the world." She took me into the kitchen and showed me a $300 machine.

"That refrigerator," she said, "cost me $10,000. My husband wanted to buy a policy from your company for $10,000. I stubbornly held out for a refrigerator first. My husband was killed in an accident the day after we bought the refrigerator."

Every good product needs examples more than arguments.

Examples are where you find them

Once you realize the amazing value to you of examples to back up your facts and claims, you will become an avid collector of examples. You will find it more interesting and vastly more rewarding than collecting stamps, coins, arrowheads, buttons, or unpaid bills!

Where do you look for examples? Anywhere, and also everywhere!

Get customers to tell you how they have used your product successfully in some interesting and unusual way. Get examples from the manufacturer of the product you sell. If he hasn't supplied any, ask him for some. Get examples from other salesmen, get them from competitors, get them from your superiors. Watch newspapers, trade magazines, general magazines for examples.

Ultimately you should have at least one convincing example to back up every important point in your sales talk. Of course you may not use them all, every time. It is possible to satiate a prospect with examples—possible but unlikely! Know his needs, watch his reactions and use the examples that apply to his situation and hold his interest.

By the way, you can use examples in other parts of your

sales talk besides the conviction step. Instances can be used to gain attention, to arouse interest, to answer objections, and to close.

--- CHAPTER **25**

How to make your examples effective

> *A sales talk without examples is like a ball game*
> *without home runs—it's tolerable but rarely exciting!*

If you want your examples to be effective, you should observe these rules:

1. *Tell the truth:* or, to put the same rule in another way, don't invent your examples.

As Rudyard Kipling expressed it:

> Ah! What avails the classic bent
> And what the cultured word
> Against the undoctored incident
> That actually occurred!

The best reason for not using invented examples is that they *sound* invented. Unless you are an actor, you can't tell them so that they sound real and convincing.

The best examples of all are usually the ones that happened to you. You can tell them better. But be sure you are not the hero of the example. Don't tell an example to glorify yourself. Tell it to glorify your product.

2. *Be specific:* or, to put it negatively: avoid generalities and claims.

If you say, "For example, a number of grocers in nearby towns have found this a fast-moving item," you haven't convinced anyone. If, instead, you say, "Here is a list of grocers in this county who have stocked this item. Here's a clipping from *The Journal* about what John Smith of Smithville, president of the State Grocer's Association, stated...," you have said something convincing.

Any talk with enough explicit examples is likely to be both interesting and convincing. But note the word *explicit*.

3. *Make your examples move.* Examples should have a "plot," should tell a story, should have action. In a story-example, you should tell something that happened to somebody.

This rule might not be too clear without an example. Here is one I used in talking to prospects for the Dale Carnegie Leadership Course:

Katherine Ankenbrandt was a paid worker for a charity organization in New York. She and another girl had similar jobs at the same pay. Finally a job opened up that paid twice what these girls were getting.

Both girls were so competent and had such fine personalities that their superior asked them just one question: "Can you speak in public?"

Katherine couldn't. The other girl could, and she got the job.

What happened to Katherine? Shortly after that, she married a rich man from Chicago and lived happily ever after.

It wasn't a very exciting example, but at least it moved.

4. *Your example must be relevant.* That is, an example must tend to prove what you are trying to prove. To determine whether or not any given example is relevant, ask yourself these questions: (1) What am I trying to prove? and (2) Does this example tend to prove it?

To sum it up:

A. Find examples

B. Polish up examples.

C. Use examples.

Examples will perform selling miracles for you.

_____ CHAPTER 26

Understatements are powerful—
even if you don't believe it!

*A salesman's reputation for truthfulness, once broken,
may possibly be repaired, but prospects will always
keep their eyes on the spot where the crack was!*

The next rule (No. 5) is another rule so important that we are
going to devote a whole chapter to it.

Rule 5: Avoid exaggerating, misrepresenting, prevaricating, equivocating, flattering, fibbing—and just plain lying!

Remember, Lincoln said, "No man has a good enough
memory to make a successful liar." Remember, also, this great
truth, "Understatement is stronger than overstatement."

If you get the reputation of being a liar, prospects will not
believe you, even when you are telling the truth. (We'll skip
the other reasons—ethical and moral—why you should not
tell lies when you sell. But remember, no such thing exists as
a slightly spoiled egg or a slightly untruthful salesman and
even a stupid prospect begins to have suspicions if your stories
don't hang together.)

This discussion of exaggeration can be boiled down to two
brief rules:

Rule 1. Never lie.

Rule 2. Understate some of your claims about your product.

"Why should I ever understate anything about my product?" you ask. Here are some of the reasons.

1. It keeps you from exaggerating.

2. It keeps your talk from sounding like "high-pressure."

3. It favorably impresses your prospect.

4. It is convincing. If you say, "This dictating machine will

save your secretary over an hour a day," it isn't convincing. It is convincing, however, if you say, "I believe this machine will save your secretary an hour a day and the reason I believe it is that the head of the typing department of the Smith Mail Order Company told me yesterday that these machines are saving their secretaries nearly two hours a day."

So, instead of exaggerating, *understate.*

John D. Murphy, contributing editor of the magazine *Salesman's Opportunity*, wrote an article headed, "Use Words to Win Confidence." In it he gave these examples of sales talks that understate:

A fountain-pen salesman says, "If you do most of your writing under water, or standing on your head, this pen won't do. It won't etch in glass or dig up concrete. But if you want a fountain pen to write under ordinary conditions, this is it."

A washing-machine salesman says, "Lady, I can't promise you this machine will make your clothes like new—but it will get them clean without injuring or aging them."

Should you try to understate all facts about your product?

Of course not. All understatement would be no understatement.

Facts can be presented:

1. By overstating them. ("This boat will run on a heavy dew.")

2. By stating them accurately. ("This boat draws seven inches.")

3. By understating them. ("I don't know the exact draft of this boat, but I tried it in 8 inches of water and found that it floated clear.")

Numbers 2 and 3 are desirable; Number 1 should be avoided.

Here's a good practice for you: run through the facts and buyer's benefits that you usually present in the conviction step of your sales talk and whittle down the overstatements into understatements. This will strengthen your talk considerably.

A good example of the effectiveness of understatement came from a recent Lord Calvert whisky advertisement. The advertisement said simply, "It costs a little more, tastes a little better." A statement like that sounds honest and believable and convincing to me—even if I don't use the darn stuff myself.

Prospects want to believe—why make it hard?

The best explanation of the reason for the strength of understatement that I ever read appeared in an article in *Printers' Ink*, written by Frank Denman. I present part of it here, with this one change: I have substituted *selling* for *advertising*.

I do admire the genius of the British for understatement. They seem to be trying so hard to avoid any appearance of immodesty that you feel compelled to step in and say it for them.

That is perhaps the secret of the strength of understatement. When a sales talk seems to be claiming too much, our suspicions start trimming it down to size. Often we trim off too much and end up believing less than the simple truth. On the other hand, when a salesman is obviously leaning over backward to avoid false claims, our eager imagination tends to supply the adjectives we feel an overconscientious salesman has omitted.

Remember this: no prospect ever asks you to prove an understatement.

How do you cure the bad habit of exaggerating?

Perhaps you say, "Many of us have been exaggerating a bit in all our sales talks all our lives. How do we break ourselves of this bad habit?"

Here are a couple of suggestions:

(a) As pointed out earlier in this section, you should do a little thinking as to how you can understate facts about your product in a way to make those understatements convincing.

You don't have to go quite to the extreme of the amateur gardener who, when asked how his potato crop had turned out, replied, "Splendidly, old man. We've just dug 'em. Some are as big as marbles, some as big as peas—and, of course, quite a lot of little ones!"

(*b*) Know the facts.

Much of a salesman's exaggeration is due not to natural mendacity, but to his tendency to *invent* facts when he does not *know* them.

The man who said that truth is stranger than fiction never listened to a salesman who didn't know his facts.

Ignorance and exaggeration are blood brothers.

You have forgotten that the circulation of your paper is 67,421—so you say, "It's over 75,000."

You can't remember whether the tests show that the car you sell makes 22 or 24 miles to the gallon, so you play safe and say, "It gives about 30 miles to the gallon."

So, to avoid exaggeration, know your facts.

(*c*) Don't let your enthusiasm run away with you.

Be warned by this statement of A. J. Balfour's: "It is unfortunate, considering that enthusiasm moves the world, that so few enthusiasts can be trusted to speak the truth."

And remember what Arthur Dunn said: "If the truth won't sell it, don't sell it."

EIGHT

Demonstrations

and showmanship

CHAPTER 27

Talk less—demonstrate more

If you think you can't demonstrate *your* product please read this paragraph

"But, Mr. Whiting," you say, "I sell an intangible —I have nothing to demonstrate."

The truth is: practically any product or service can be demonstrated.

My friend Wally Powell of the Hoover Co. once told me, "I defy any man to make any product that someone cannot demonstrate. You can *show* more in five minutes than you can *tell* in one hour."

So don't skip this chapter just because you sell insurance or bonds or correspondence courses. Instead, read it thoughtfully—you may discover a way to demonstrate a hard-to-demonstrate product.

"*A good product doesn't need arguments; it needs demonstrations.*"

"A simple demonstration is more convincing than 10,000 words. It will sell more in a minute than gab will sell in a week," G. A. Conwell, then San Francisco Manager of Proctor & Gamble, wrote in the house organ *Moonbeams*. Mr. Conwell gave evidence of the truth of his claim with the following example:

121

The hardest dealer to sell I ever met lived in a two-store town. He carried everything. On my first call he was most friendly, listened intently, and closed the interview with a polite "nope." I did learn, however, that he was an ardent hunter.

On five more calls I threw every punch I knew, but always got the same "nope."

On the eighth call I found the dealer in an argument with an old crony about the powers of their .22 rifles. I offered them a way to settle the question. I explained how Waltke's Extra Family Soap was of such high quality and consistency that it would give a perfect demonstration of the striking and penetrating power of a .22 rifle bullet.

The resulting barnyard demonstration proved the friend's rifle the better.

Most important of all, *I learned the power of demonstration.* Again I reminded the dealer of Extra Family's high quality as proved by the neat cone-shaped holes made by the bullets. Mr. Prospect said, "I might take twenty-five cases." I had found the key!

Demonstrations aren't all informal, back-yard performances. The Ethyl Corporation has a traveling demonstration—in fact, it had (in the spring of 1956) eleven shows on the road— including one in Canada and one in Venezuela. This demonstration has been presented 4,500 times to 200,000 service-station people. Its purpose is to *demonstrate* quality.

Seeing is believing—and buying

Why are demonstrations so effective in interesting prospects? Because prospects like a show. They like to see things moving—happening.

Demonstrations do something more, however, than merely make your talk interesting. They make your talk convincing. What the prospect sees with his own eyes he must believe in his own brain.

Find the drama—build your demonstration

An interesting demonstration kit was described in a recent issue of *Sales Management*.

Van-Packer Corp., Bettendorf, Iowa, produces a masonry chimney which can be installed in three hours. Actual chimney materials accompany the salesman into the prospect's office—in a sample case.

Says Sales Manager O. E. Collins: "That important fellow across the table has the opportunity to *participate*. Flue section construction is brought vividly to his attention as he sees, feels, and hefts the masonry. If the prospect wants to, he can actually apply joint cement.

An excellent article on the value of demonstrations appeared in the magazine *Specialty Salesman*. It was written by Wallace K. Lewis. Mr. Lewis said:

Showmanship has been selling products for hundreds of years.

The Wright Brothers had a machine in which, so they said, a man could fly. But they didn't expect anyone to take their word for it. So they *demonstrated* their flying machine.

Thomas Edison held over 1,300 patents on inventions ranging from a camera that took moving pictures to a machine that talked. Can you imagine anyone buying such contraptions without a demonstration?

Westinghouse salesmen might say, "Our Snapper-Disc thermal cutouts really protect our motors from overheating. These discs are so sensitive that they act when the temperature of the motor changes only a little." The prospect might believe that statement or he might not. Here is how the salesman makes him believe. He warms a small snapper disc in his hands. He presses it down on the prospect's desk. When the disc cools it snaps high in the air.

After that demonstration, any prospect must believe that the Westinghouse Snapper Disc is extremely sensitive. The salesman proves his claim as to the sensitiveness of the disc by demonstration.

Almost any product can be demonstrated

A recent quiz on the methods of 213 sales managers indicated that a dramatized presentation—an appeal to both eyes and ears—was eight times as effective in getting over a sales point as an appeal only to the ears.

If your product is an intangible, perhaps you can demonstrate with films, charts, diagrams, photographs, or some sort of analogy.

A demonstration will give your sales talk something it probably needs: a place where you stop talking and replace words with action.

I picked up the following example of how a demonstration got a salesman out of a hot sales spot from Bill Wischman of Michigan Consolidated Gas Co., in Detroit.

The stove was hot—so was the sergeant

Bill once took a radiant heater to demonstrate to the wife of a police sergeant in Detroit. Before he started the demonstration, Bill pulled down the curtains in the living room to show how the heater lighted up the room.

Just as he was making the demonstration—with the curtains down—the police sergeant came in unexpectedly to find his wife in a darkened room with a strange man.

"What are you doing here?" the sergeant inquired, not too politely.

Bill explained.

"If we want to buy a heater we'll go to the office. Now get out of here."

Bill said, "I'll leave just as soon as the stove cools off so I can pick it up."

The police sergeant walked into the next room.

In a few minutes, Bill picked up the stove and started out.

When he passed in front of the police sergeant he said, "Gosh, it's hot," and set down the stove.

The stove was right in front of an open fireplace. So Bill said to the sergeant, "Do you mind if I push this in the fireplace—to give you an idea of the size, so when you come down to the shop you'll know the size you want?"

Without waiting for permission, Bill put it in. As he did so he said to the sergeant, "You paid at least $200 for this chimney in your house—and that money is tied up—you are paying taxes on an extra $200 which is being wasted because you don't have a heater in this fireplace."

A half hour later Bill "got out," but the heater never did!

How various salesmen demonstrate

Perhaps you can get an idea of how to demonstrate your product by knowing how other successful salesmen demonstrate theirs. Here are a few examples:

Simmons Company salesmen demonstrate the independent coils of a Beautyrest mattress by placing a glass of water on it and pressing down some coils near it to show that one coil can go down without pulling the others down.

How Owens-Corning Fiberglas Corp. salesmen demonstrate the insulating qualities of their product in selling to small groups was explained in *Printers' Ink* as follows:

At the beginning of a typical show, the master of ceremonies asks a member of the audience to come up on stage and light the oven of a kitchen range. [Today Fiberglas insulates a high proportion of the ranges in America's kitchens.] After the oven regulator is set for a certain temperature, the M.C. displays a roll of Fiberglas material, the same used to insulate the range. Next he wraps a quart of ice cream in it, pops the ice cream into the oven. Beside it he puts a cherry pie ready for baking.

Then a pot of hot coffee is wrapped in a blanket of Fiberglas and placed in a refrigerator standing next to the stove.

The show proceeds—the ice cream and pie in the oven, the hot coffee in the refrigerator apparently forgotten. When it comes time to take out the nicely browned pie, out comes the ice cream, too. It is unwrapped and found to be as firmly frozen as when it went into the oven. Next the pot of coffee is taken out of the refrigerator, the Fiberglas blanket removed and the contents poured. The steaming cups are accepted with *ohs* and *ahs*.

A manufacturer who makes nonwilt shirt collars has his salesmen dip a shirt in a goldfish bowl—completely equipped with water and goldfish.

More examples of how salesmen demonstrate

Revere Copper and Brass, Inc., wants to prove that the copper-clad stainless steel they use in cooking ware transfers heat more readily than ordinary steel. They supply their salesmen with "heatsticks." Half of the "stick" is made of ordinary stainless steel, the other half with "Copperclad." The prospect is asked to take hold of the "stick" at each end. The salesman places a lighted match under the middle. The prospect drops the Copperclad end before the other end is more than comfortably warm.

What the prospect has felt he must believe!

Goodrich Life-Saver tires are demonstrated by letting the prospect drive an ice pick into a cross section of the tire.

Firestone uses a tire section to show prospects that 70 cents of each tire dollar is invested in the body of the tire, only 30 cents in the tread of the tire.

Optical Gaging Products, Inc., can't carry their *comparators* into a man's office—they weigh about 1,200 pounds—so they provide their men with a kit which contains small machine parts and photographs.

Yes, but what about intangibles?

The salesman of intangibles may readily object that all the examples of demonstration given here are of tangible products. True enough. Admittedly, it requires quite a lot more ingenuity to devise a demonstration for an intangible than for a tangible.

One of the best substitutes for a demonstration is to make sketches or draw plans or diagrams. At least this substitutes action on the part of the salesman for a steady flow of words.

John H. Patterson, the father of modern selling, was an inveterate pad-and-pencil addict. He enlivened his speeches and sales talks with rough sketches. He followed the advice of the man who said, "Draw less on your imagination, more on your scratch pad." He trained his men to "talk with pencils." They carried pads and soft black pencils, and were taught how to draw diagrams, graphs, and rough sketches that made clearer their sales arguments.

In selling the Dale Carnegie Course in Effective Speaking, we ask recent graduates to stand up in front of the audience to tell why they took the course and what they got out of it. Incidentally, they are demonstrating their ability to speak in public—something they learned in the course.

Now, for a novelty, I'm going to give you an example about myself taken from another man's book—two men's, in fact. It is from *Showmanship in Business,* co-authored by Zenn Kaufman and Ken Goode. Here it is:

Percy Whiting, in selling an investment trust service, shows a prospect two lists of securities—each list worth the same $1,000 five years ago. The lists appear evenly balanced. He asks the prospect which list he would have bought. Turn the page! Current market figures reveal that one list went up. The other went down. [This stunt was used as evidence that the normal man is a poor "guesser" as to whether stocks will go up or down.] The bare statement of this fact, without the "Which is which?" introduction, couldn't possibly impress the prospect so definitely. Or hold his attention. This stunt has also a nice element of *conflict.*

Perhaps you can dramatize the *advantage* of your product as Dick Borden, America's top sales consultant, used to point out in one of his talks. Said Dick, "The insurance salesman, for instance, can display a set of college catalogues as he invites his prospect to *see* the educational opportunities a certain policy will guarantee the prospect's son."

G. Ray Schenks, branch manager, Atlas Auto Finance Co., Jacksonville, Florida, uses pieces of pasteboard the size of a greenback to demonstrate a sales point in connection with his service.

The explanation of the sales talk that Ray uses would be too complicated to present here. In general, Ray uses piles of pasteboard to indicate what dealers get from various sources: (*a*) if they use his finance system, and (*b*) if they use a competitor's system. He adds the pasteboard slips to one pile, and then the other, and finally has a pile about twice as high for his deal as for the competitor's deal.

Another good example of how a tangible article can be used to sell an intangible was given by James Maratta in his book *How to Make People Buy Hard-to-Sell Things.* He wrote:

A score of salesmen have tried to sell me accident insurance. I have never had an accident and so I have always scoffed at accident insurance. One day a man entered my office, handed me a piece of inner tube with a large hole in it, and said: "Two weeks ago that innocent piece of rubber killed two persons and maimed three others." Then he showed me a picture of the accident in which three cars figured. Now I own accident insurance.

*   *   *

To sum it up: (*a*) if you don't use demonstrations now, try to find a way to do so; (*b*) if you do, try to find new and better ways to demonstrate. Demonstrations make selling easier.

_____ CHAPTER 28

How to make your demonstration a real sales tool

Anybody can demonstrate, but only an expert can demonstrate well.

How can you become expert in making demonstrations? Here are some suggestions:

1. Write out the words you use in your demonstration. Mull over the talk, polish it, shorten it. Work *out* the words—work *in* the action. Plan to have places in your demonstration where you don't say anything. (Maybe that will be a big relief to your prospect!)

Don't "just demonstrate"—demonstrate effectively

2. Rehearse your demonstration. Go over it again and again. Have your wife hear it, your sales manager, your fellow salesmen. Ask for criticism—and don't be disappointed if you get it!

Keep drilling on your demonstration until you do it and say it so smoothly that it looks easy and sounds easy.

3. Remember "buyers' benefits." Make your demonstration apply to the specific prospect you are talking to. Focus it on him. Tell him—or show him—how your various sales points will benefit him.

4. As you demonstrate, fit your product into your prospect's business; don't ask him to fit his business into your proposition.

5. Let your prospect handle it—let him demonstrate it for himself. Good advice to a salesman is, "Don't let your prospect handle it unless you want him to buy it."

Maxwell Droke, in one of his books on salesmanship, tells of a pack peddler in the old days who specialized in decorative mantel clocks. If this man failed to close a good prospect he would say, "I have far to go and my pack is heavy. Let me leave this clock until I come this way again. Then I will pick it up."

This peddler rarely picked up a clock. By the time he called on the prospect again, the clock had become virtually a member of the family. The clock made the sale—it demonstrated itself.

Eastman Kodak Company tells its salesmen, "Pass the camera to the customer so that he can examine it."

6. Take your product away from the prospect before he is tired of operating it. This increases his desire to own it.

7. Nail down each sales benefit as you demonstrate. Get your prospect to agree that the point is important—to him.

For instance, "Your wife will like this automatic transmission, won't she?" or "This machine will help your secretary finish her day's work on time, won't it?"

8. Try to keep your props out of sight until you are ready to use them.

9. Handle your product respectfully—even lovingly.

Note that the expert shoe salesman polishes off a shoe before he lets you try it on; the jeweler pulls out a piece of heavy velvet on which to display his rings.

If your product is light enough to handle, hold it up and admire it—turn it around for the prospect to admire.

10. Put lots of action into your demonstration. Don't just show your machine—show it in action. Don't just show a diagram—draw it.

11. If you can't demonstrate your product, demonstrate something that works on the same principle.

The Iron Fireman people used to say, "The coal is carried from the bin to the furnace by a worm gear. This works just like your meat grinder." Then, with a common meat grinder, the salesman would show the prospect how coal is carried from bin to furnace.

And now to summarize: Demonstrate your product. Study your demonstration and rehearse it until you do it well.

Effective demonstrations will help you to close sales.

CHAPTER 29

Make your sales talk sparkle with showmanship

Do you want to brighten up your sales talk—and especially your demonstrations? Then use showmanship.

"What is showmanship?"

Webster says, "Showmanship is skill in presenting anything in an interesting and dramatic manner." (It also says that *dramatic* means "full of action, highly emotional, vivid, exciting.")

Showmanship in selling is most commonly used in connection with the demonstration of a product. In fact, many salesmen have come to believe that the words *showmanship* and *demonstration* mean about the same. Of course this isn't true. You can have a demonstration without showmanship or showmanship without a demonstration.

An example of the difference between the two came from the world of sports.

This incident happened in the fifth inning in the third game of the World Series in Chicago in 1932.

Babe Ruth was at bat. The Cub players started to razz him. Babe, perhaps baseball's greatest showman, pointed his bat at a point in the centerfield bleachers. The Cubs knew this meant that he would try to hit the ball there.

The pitcher threw the ball, the Babe swung, the bat cracked, and the ball sailed into the centerfield bleachers—and landed in the area to which Babe Ruth had pointed.

If Babe had merely hit a home run—that would have been a demonstration. But to announce, in effect, that he was going to hit a home run, then to indicate where he planned to hit it —and then to hit it there—that was showmanship!

The showmanship that is available to salesmen comes in many forms.

Wearing clothes which are extreme in cut or color is showmanship—though I advise against it.

Talking with extreme vocal and physical animation is showmanship—and sometimes good showmanship.

"Diamond Jim" Brady's diamonds were showmanship.

Throwing a fountain pen under the wheels of a moving truck to prove its sturdiness is showmanship.

Barney Oldfield, most famous of racing drivers back in the days when I was a sports editor, never appeared in public without a cigar in his mouth—very large and very black. That was showmanship.

Jim Farley makes it a point to remember names—showmanship. (He didn't remember mine the only time he had a chance, but I don't hold it against him.)

The showmanship that interests most salesmen is the showmanship we can use in demonstrating our product.

If you are interested in showmanship and are willing to work at it, I suggest that you read one or all of these three books:

Showmanship in Business by Zenn Kaufman and Kenneth M. Goode, Harper and Brothers.

Profitable Showmanship by Zenn Kaufman, Prentice-Hall.

Showmanship in Public Speaking by Edward J. Hegarty, McGraw-Hill Book Company. (Though Ed's book deals with public speaking, it contains ideas that will be useful to salesmen in selling.)

Some suggestions for putting showmanship into your selling follow:

1. Do something dramatically different. For instance:

The Walter Kidde & Co.'s fire-extinguisher salesmen needed something to rouse shipowners to a realization of their need for fire-fighting apparatus. So one salesman rented a cargo ship; doused hold, bilges, and engine room with gasoline; invited a group of prospects down to the dock.

He ignited the gasoline and thus created a roaring blaze, big enough to frighten everybody—including himself. Then he released into the boat a smothering cloud of carbon dioxide gas. The fire was out, the sales engineer was a "hero"—and Walter Kidde & Co. has ever since been a firm believer in spectacular demonstrations.

Kidde men carry portable units around with them; take prospects out into the backyards of factories; start fires of all kinds and quench them quickly.   —*Sales Management* MAGAZINE

Don't let your effort to be dramatic get you into trouble. The following example of misguided showmanship comes from South Africa:

The vacuum-cleaner salesman was illustrating his sales talk by repeatedly sprinkling sand on a piece of carpet and removing the sand very deftly with his vacuum cleaner.

"Now, madam," he wound up, turning to one woman in the crowd around him, "can I interest you in buying one of our vacuum cleaners?"

"No good to us," was the reply. "We never sprinkle sand on our carpet."   —*Outspan* (SOUTH AFRICA)

Even a simple act like handing a dollar bill to a prospect can be showmanship. For example, here is part of a talk a life insurance salesman uses:

If some drunken driver smashes head-on into your car on the way home tonight and you never see your wife and children again, what are the three most important things that you would want your wife to have?

(Wait for his answer.)

(Then I hand him a dollar bill.) How many of these dollar bills would she need to provide herself with those three items?

2. Use action. Do something. Make something happen. For example, R. G. Sanderson, the Dale Carnegie Sales Course sponsor in Dallas, Texas, writes:

I was a retail salesman for General Foods in Enid, Oklahoma. In March of 1938, my immediate supervisor told me that Joe Bateman, the district sales manager, would soon be out to work with me for a day. I learned that I was supposed to make a drive on Certo, which is used in making jams and jellies.

The product managers in New York had not bothered to consider that in northern Oklahoma March is not the month for making jams. It is the month for shoveling snow.

That week, when I noticed a grocery store throwing into the trash some black-colored, fully ripe bananas, I started trying to find a way that such bananas could be used in making a jam. On looking into our Certo recipe booklet, I found a recipe for pineapple-banana jam. I made up some of the jam and found it to be rather tasty.

Then I got an idea. Here is how I worked it:

I would walk into a grocery store, go up to the banana stalk, pick up several black, fully ripe bananas, and ask the grocer what he was going to do with them. He usually answered, "Throw 'em away." Then I would ask, "Aren't you throwing away your profit?" He of course would admit it.

I would then say, "If you had a merchandising plan that would not only sell those black bananas for you but also sell Certo, sugar, paraffin, and jelly glasses, you would like to try it, wouldn't you?" The answer was always "Yes."

Salesmanship sold jam

By the time Mr. Bateman came out to work with me, I had made up jam for the grocer to taste and I had worked up a demonstration.

What were the results? When the big boss came out, I was ready. He worked with me in a snow-covered country territory on a day the temperature was around 15 above.

In spite of the snow and cold, we sold every account we called on that day. For my two weeks' assignment on this product, I sold more than all the men in my sales group put together.

When the first promotion from the retail ranks was made from the Oklahoma City District, I got it!

A new idea in showmanship has been developed by Standard Oil Co. of California for use by its salesmen. This was written up in *Printers' Ink*. A summary of the article follows:

Problem: How the salesman can create an unforgettable impression in the prospect's mind of the high melting point of Calol industrial grease.

Solution: The Calol salesman places a metal plate about the size of a half dollar in front of the prospect. In the center of the plate is a crater. On the side there is a small hole. The salesman sticks a match or toothpick in the hole (to form a handle). He then places a sample of Calol industrial grease in the crater, lights a match and holds it under the metal plate.

Result: Calol does not melt.

Comparison: Next the salesman places conventional grease in the crater and heats it with a match. Soon the grease breaks down into a semiliquid.

3. Use a striking exhibit or demonstration.

For example:

Remington Rand salesmen use showmanship in selling their razor by shaving the fuzz off a peach.

Corning Glass salesmen, to show the strength of Pyrex dinnerware, hammer a 3-inch nail through a 2-inch board with a cup.

Johnson & Johnson salesmen, to demonstrate their Band-Aid "Super-Stick" Plastic Strips, stick one end of a bandage to an egg. Then they pick up the egg by the bandage, drop it into boiling water, then pull it out.

4. Turn your demonstration into a contest.

A dozen years or more ago Electrolux salesmen used to be faced often with this statement from prospects: "Oh, dear, I couldn't get all my stuff in that refrigerator." The salesman used showmanship by making a contest out of it. So he answered, "Let's see if we can."

Then he spread out on the kitchen table a paper printed with spaces equal to the various shelf areas of his refrigerator.

Next he took everything out of the prospect's icebox and placed it on the imaginary shelves.

It was a contest—and contests are a form of showmanship.

5. Do something unexpected.

A salesman named Payson, who used to work for me in Portland, Maine, about a third of a century ago, wanted to sell his old car.

It was January. The first question the prospect asked was, "Will it start?" That's important in Maine, where the temperature goes down to 30 or 40 below and where it sometimes takes more juice to turn over the engine than to run a rock crusher.

The average salesman would have turned the question off with some such answer as, "It always has." Not Payson—he did something unexpected.

"Well," said Payson, "I left the car out this winter—the snow gives it a lot of protection. To show how well this car starts, let's go try it. I say it will start instantly."

He drove the man to his home, got a snow shovel, dug through a drift to the car door, opened it, stepped in, stepped on the starter.

What happened?

You'd never guess it—but the car started—and the prospect bought.

Anything unexpected is
likely to be showmanship

Another example of doing the unexpected I clipped from a magazine. Here it is:

Twenty years ago in Flint, Michigan, a brawny, 6-foot-3-inch Dane with a tough face and bristling black walrus mustache walked into the office of a parts buyer at the Chevrolet plant, toting a long steel exhaust pipe under his arm. He was an executive of a small auto-parts company, and he wanted an order from Chevrolet. After listening to a few minutes of thickly accented sales talk, the buyer raised a question about the pipe's durability.

William S. Knudsen did not argue the matter. Instead he raised the pipe high over his head, hurled it crashing to the concrete floor of the buyer's office, whence it bounced up and knocked a piece of plaster out of the wall.

Two months later, the buyer again met Knudsen walking down a Chevrolet corridor. "Well," he joshed, "back to sell some more exhaust pipes, are you?"

"No," replied Knudsen in his husky half-whisper, "I'm the new general manager here."

6. Arouse curiosity—dramatically.

A salesman for a gadget that took just under three minutes to perform its function always asked permission to give a demonstration. As he made the request he produced a three-minute sand glass, holding it in view of the prospect. It was rarely the case that anyone was able to resist feeling curious about what was coming. The sand glass was laid in front of the buyer and the salesman said: "I'll be through before the sand runs down." He was always as good as his word.   —*National Sales Executives Bulletin*

A mere piece of paper may be showmanship

Showmanship stunts do not necessarily call for elaborate equipment. For example:

A vending-machine salesman unfolds a heavy piece of paper, about 2 by 3 feet in size, spreads it out on the floor in front of the dealer and opens with: "If I could show you how to make that space worth $250 a year to you, you'd be interested, wouldn't you?"
          —*Printers' Ink*

While I can't tell you exactly how to become a good show-man, I can at least make some suggestions, as follows:

1. Get "showmanship-conscious." Be on the lookout for ways you can put drama into your sales talks and your demonstrations.

2. Be alert to see if you can't use some of these elements of showmanship in your selling: action, color, conflict, curiosity, magic, motion, sound, sex. (See *Showmanship in Business.*)

3. Study the methods used by other salesmen to get showmanship. Then see if you can't adapt their ideas to your sales talk.

4. Don't do anything so undignified that it will embarrass you or the prospect. Standing on your head isn't showmanship —it's show-off-manship. It would not sell anything but a course in How to Stand on Your Head.

*   *   *

Here ends the section on Convincing Your Prospect. Now let's ask ourselves what we want our prospect to be thinking at this point in our sales talk.

The answer is, "I want my prospect to be thinking, 'I am convinced that this product is all right and that it will do what the salesman claims.' "

NINE

To make them buy it

make them want it

Step 4: * How to arouse desire

——————————————————— CHAPTER 30

How to arouse desire

*The salesman's job: to persuade people to want what
they already need.* —F. ST. ELMO LEWIS

* Great Rule 4: To arouse desire:
1. Remind your prospect that he lacks the benefits your
product will give him and get his agreement.
2. Remind him that your product will supply that lack.
3. Paint a word picture of your prospect using your product,
enjoying it and benefiting from it.

NOTE: The first two steps are merely reminders of something you
have already told the prospect. Hence, in this desire step, they
should be presented briefly but forcefully.

*　　*　　*

You have finished the conviction part of your sales talk. You
have done well thus far. You have won attention; you have
gained interest; you have satisfied your prospect that your
goods will do all you claim for them.

"What do I do next?" you ask—or maybe you don't ask
at all, but pull out your order blank instead—and then wonder
why you do not get the order!

I know that salesmen commonly make this mistake because,

139

in sales meetings, I often ask salesmen, "Why do people buy your product?"

The answer usually given is, in substance: "Because it is a good product."

The correct answer is: "Because they *want* it."

Naturally, people would not buy your product if they thought it was a poor product—price considered. But they do not buy it merely because they think it is well made, durable, and worth the price.

You might, for example, convince me that the hearing aid you sell is the best hearing aid made—still I wouldn't buy it. I don't need or *want* a hearing aid.

Since people buy a product not exclusively because it is a good product but because they *want* it, you will certainly make more sales if you know how to make people *want* what you sell. In this section we shall tell you how to do it.

In a recent book on selling I found this not too helpful suggestion for arousing desire: "Create desire with a few well-chosen words."

Yes—*but what words?*

In *The Art of Persuading People*, James A. Worsham gives this principle for arousing desire: "Find out what people *want* (not merely what they *need*); be in a position to convince them that what you offer will satisfy that want, then place your proposition within their reach."

When you and I make most of our important purchases we are moved not by *logic*, but by *desire*. That is true of most of the important decisions that all of us make.

"I like to think of how wisely man fails to be moved by the logic of so-called compelling facts. Consider kissing—surely one of life's rare delights. Now all the compelling facts of science, of hygiene, and of bacteriology frown upon, if not condemn outright, the act of kissing. . . . Fortunately the average man is not moved by the compelling knowledge or logic of the scientist—so, he kisses.
                              —DR. IAGO GALDSTON,
                              Journal of American Dietetic Association

If you don't sell your prospect, somebody else may

Salesmen skip the desire step of their sales talk more often than any other.

"Yet they sell," you object.

True. People, fortunately for poor salesmen, sometimes develop their own desire.

When I bought my first car, I walked into a showroom, pointed out the one I wanted, and said, "I'll take this one." The salesman did not appear in the transaction at all. I bought my first television set, my first vacuum cleaner, my first washing machine, and my first dictating machine the same way. Advertising had developed my desire.

W. J. Cameron, speaking on the *Ford Hour*, said: "About 65 per cent of the motor cars sold today are bought by people who walk unsolicited into dealers' places of business."

This explains how salesmen can make sales without bothering to arouse desire. How many more sales could they make, however, if they did bother? Vastly more! I have known many salesmen who have more than doubled their earnings by applying the rule for arousing desire.

Follow the formula until it becomes automatic

Knowing salesmen, I know that the next question most of you will ask is this: "Do you mean to tell me that, toward the end of a sales talk, I should say to myself, 'Now then, I must arouse the desire of this man'—and then start off deliberately to do it?"

That is just what I do mean!

Yes, and you keep on doing it consciously and painstakingly until you learn to do it automatically—until your subconscious mind has taken over the job.

The salesman who knows how to appeal to the dominant

buying motive of his prospect soon becomes an expert in "motivational selling."

Here is how you start to arouse desire

Before you start on the desire step you should have clearly in mind your prospect's dominant buying motive.

Any *buying motive* is an inner drive, impulse, or intention that moves us to buy. A *dominant* motive is the one that has the controlling influence in moving us.

Other motives besides the dominant one may play some part in influencing the decision, but the dominant motive is the one which most interests the salesman because it most affects the sale.

Dominant buying motives are no new invention. Baltasar Gracian, in *The Art of Worldly Wisdom*, published in 1653, wrote:

First guess a man's ruling passion, appeal to it by word, set it in motion by temptation, and you will infallibly give checkmate to his freedom of will. Find out each man's thumbscrew. You must know where to get at anyone. All men are idolaters, some of fame, others of self-interest, most of pleasure. Skill consists in knowing these idols in order to bring them into play. Knowing any man's mainspring of motive, you have, as it were, the key to his will.

Gracian listed some of the common buying motives—the desire for fame, self-interest, pleasure. What are the other buying motives?

I've seen as many as fifty buying motives listed by various writers. I think the important ones are:

1. The desire to stay alive and well. (Self-preservation.)

2. The desire to make money. (Perhaps greed, perhaps ambition.)

3. The desire for a feeling of importance. (Pride, prestige.)

4. Love of family. (The desire to provide for and to protect your wife, children, parents.)

5. Sex attraction. (Which includes the desire to appear well to persons of the other sex.)

6. The desire to get ahead—to be somebody. (Ambition.)

7. The bargain instinct. (Economy, the desire to make a profit.)

Perhaps we should have included among the motives "The desire to gamble," since a Gallup Poll a while back indicated that fifty out of every hundred people in this country gamble.

Another motive that dominates many sales is illustrated by the story which follows:

A man had been looking at a car in a motor showroom, but did not make a decision on the spot.

The following day he turned up again and stated that he had decided to buy the car.

"That's fine," said the salesman, pleased at having satisfied his customer. "Now tell me, what was the one *dominating thing* that made you buy the car?"

The man grinned and replied: "My wife."

—*Tid Bits*, LONDON

Why are buying motives important?

Why is it so important to know the prospect's dominant buying motive?

Let's take an example: A bachelor saves his first $100. The motive that prompted him to do it was probably fear—fear of hunger in his old age, fear of the poorhouse, fear of the high cost of sickness. Ten years later he is worth, let us say, $500,000 (he must have struck oil!), but he continues to save. The motive, however, is different. He no longer fears starvation. Possibly his dominant motive now is love of ease and luxury. He wants, for his old age, not merely enough food—he wants golf, fishing, travel.

If you were soliciting savings accounts, and if you went to that man when he was dominated by fear of a penniless old age and talked to him about saving enough money so he could spend his winters in Florida, you would waste your talk—you would be appealing to the wrong motive. When he is worth $500,000, however, his dominant buying motive has changed. If you talked to him about putting enough money away to keep him out of the poorhouse—you would waste your breath.

Be sure you know the prospect's dominant buying motive before you try to arouse desire.

An important—and obvious—point about buying motives was brought out by Ivey and Horvath in their book *Successful Salesmanship* as follows: "Behind every sale there is always a buying motive. Curiously enough, the motive that impels the customer to make the purchase is, however, *never* a desire to *own* the purchased article itself, but is always concerned with what the buyer believes the article will *do* for him."

How to learn the prospect's dominant buying motive

How do you find out the dominant buying motive of your prospect?

If you are selling something that costs a considerable amount of money, you will try to learn, before you call on your prospect, his dominant buying motive.

If you cannot find out the dominant buying motive before you call, then try to learn it, as the sale progresses, by asking questions and by listening.

How a half-million-dollar sale was made by locating a prospect's dominant buying motive and playing on it comes from the pen of Adrian Anderson. He wrote:

George S. Hellman, a book dealer, once offered the elder J. P. Morgan the famous Wakefield collection of manuscripts of great American authors.

Because its price ran into hundreds of thousands of dollars, Mr. Morgan found it extremely difficult to make up his mind to purchase it.

One day, after many fruitless calls on the great financier, Hell-

man took one of the manuscripts out of the collection, put it in
his pocket, and again went to see his distinguished patron. Mr.
Morgan was still unable to make up his mind.

"Here's one of the poems in the collection," said the dealer;
"and if you will excuse me for being personal, whenever I read it I
think of you and your grandchildren."

Mr. Morgan put on his spectacles and read:

> Between the dark and the daylight
> When the night is beginning to lower
> Comes a pause in the day's occupations
> That is known as the children's hour.

When Mr. Morgan had finished reading the poem, he looked
up, and in an enthusiastic voice exclaimed, "I'll take the collection."

The buying motive that closed that sale was *love of family*.
Mr. Hellman played on that motive—and made the sale.

_____ CHAPTER 31

Desire starts with a want

Recipe for selling: Find out what'll make 'em happy,
then talk about it.   —MURRAY, DERBY FOOD CO.

All right, you now have the information you need to start
arousing desire, so let's consider the first of the three steps.

STEP ONE: *Remind your prospect that he lacks the benefits
your product will give him and get his agreement.*

Before you start on this step be sure that: (*a*) you have
given the prospect all the facts and benefits needed to convince him that he would make no mistake in buying it, and
also that (*b*) you have answered *all his objections.*

If you don't do that, the prospect may, in the middle of your desire step, say, "Yes, but ..." or "Explain to me about ..." Then you are in a bad spot. You can avoid this calamity by doing a thorough job in the conviction step.

Some salesmen, at this point, ask, "Suppose I can't convince the prospect that he should buy my product—though I've done my best—how can I arouse desire?"

The answer: You can't—so go back and start talking benefits again.

Assuming that you have thoroughly convinced the prospect that your product is okay, then you naturally start the desire step by reminding the prospect that he lacks your product.

You are not bringing up anything new. In the interest and conviction steps you talked about "benefits"—about how your product would do something for the prospect that should be done. Now, in the desire step, you remind him tactfully of something he has already admitted.

You say, for example, "As you told me, Mr. Blank, the way things are handled now, your secretary is always behind in transcribing your letters" or "We agree that looking at color television is a lot more fun than looking at black-and-white pictures."

In other words, you get the prospect to admit—or at least not to deny—that he lacks the benefits he will gain if he owns and uses your product. You observe the important part of Step One—you secure his agreement.

Of course you will have sense enough not to insult the prospect by saying, "Your secretary is always behind in her work" or "Your financial reports are usually three or four weeks late." Surely I don't have to tell you to cushion this *reminder* of the prospect's lack. You do it with "cushions" like: "As you have told me ..." or "Your bookkeeper reports ..." or "I judge from what you have said ..." or "We're agreed, I'm sure that. ..."

We don't want what we don't lack

Does this first step—this step of reminding the prospect of his lack—make sense?

Hobbes, writing over 300 years ago, said, "Desire is the craving for something not possessed."

Look back to some purchase you have made recently—a purchase that ran into money—a color television set, an air-conditioning unit, an oil-burning furnace, or a home—and ask yourself if your desire for that article did not begin when you realized that you lacked it. Didn't you say to yourself, "Other people have this—I haven't"?

Never forget this fact: All desire is built on a feeling of lack or want or longing.

The salesman's job may be merely to point out the lack—or it may be to intensify the feeling of lack. I hardly have to tell you that, all the way through the interest and conviction steps, the efficient salesman is pointing out the prospect's lack.

A writer in *Manager's Magazine* said:

One of the best salesmen I know has this motto hanging over his desk: "The best way to make a sale is first to find out what problem a man is worrying about, and then to show him how what you have to sell will solve his problem."

We can go a step further and say that frequently it helps to call to a man's attention something about which he should be worrying, but isn't.

If they're cold, turn on the heat

George H. Harris, a successful life underwriter, is quoted by Maxwell Droke as follows:

I never hesitate to employ emotional appeal. When the situation demands it, I bear down with a good deal of force. Sometimes the picture I am obliged to paint is not a pleasant one.

"Go 'way," one prospect said to me, "You make me miserable."
"Good," I replied. "When you are so miserable you can't sleep
at night, call me up and I'll write your policy."

What was Harris doing? He was taking the first step of
arousing desire—he was reminding the prospect of his lack of
life insurance.

As E. St. Elmo Lewis says, "Salesmanship is the ability to
persuade people to want what they need." (And, apparently,
sometimes what they don't need.) For example, a third of a
century ago practically nobody desired radios. Nobody felt the
lack of them. Popular-priced radios didn't exist, so nobody
called your attention to your lack of a radio. Naturally, you
didn't feel any lack.

Finally, however, radios became practical. In my own case,
my family found that our neighbors owned them, so we began
to feel our lack—and finally we bought. In most cases, however, people bought because a salesman pointed out the lack.

Make him shiver and he'll buy

Let's take another example of pointing out a want. Suppose
you are selling oil-burning furnaces. You might say:

"With your present equipment, in order to have the house
warm when the children get up, you have to get up at five
o'clock in the morning and open up the furnace and put on
coal. Your wife sometimes has to shovel on coal in the afternoon. When you are away on trips, either your wife has to take
over the whole job of tending to the furnace—shoveling on
coal, shoveling out ashes—or you have to hire somebody to do
it. The temperature of your house, of course, is uneven. You
are too hot in the forenoon, too cold in the afternoon. Getting
out ashes is a dirty job—one that you don't enjoy."

In other words, you were pointing out what is wrong with
his present situation. You were trying to dissatisfy him with
his present heating equipment. You were pointing out his
lack. You were taking the first step toward arousing desire.

"What's in it for us?" they ask

If you have trouble with this step, it may help you to ask yourself:

1. After my prospect owns it, what use will he make of the item I am trying to sell him?

2. What satisfaction or pleasure or gratification will he get as a result of using it?

A retail grocer, for example, buys your new, highly advertised soap powder with the idea of reselling it at a profit. That, for him, is the *end use* of that product. The satisfaction he will get will arise from seeing a lot of customers buy it—and hearing the cash register ring.

So, when you take Step One with this grocer and point out his lack, you remind him (you *told* him earlier in the sales talk, so you merely *remind* him now) that he has no soap powder which is as heavily advertised and hence as easily sold.

How can your product supply that lack?

The second step almost takes care of itself!

STEP TWO: *Remind your prospect that your product will supply his lack.*

The next, or second step, is quite natural if you will only ask yourself, "What is my prospect thinking?"

If you have carried him through the first step, he now thinks, "Yes, that's right. I don't stock a fast-moving soap" or "I don't like to get up at five o'clock to start a furnace" or "Both my cars are falling to pieces" or "I hate to ask my secretary to work overtime every day."

If you have made your prospect feel his lack, then your next step is an entirely obvious one: you remind him that your goods or service will supply this lack.

You say, for example, "Buy this house and you have a bedroom for every member of your family."

You have taken the second step—you have shown how your article or service will supply the prospect's lack. This is a simple, easy, obvious step.

──────────────────────────────────── CHAPTER 32

What is concreteness—
and why talk about it now?

Make 'em see it, hear it, feel it, taste it,
smell it—that's concreteness in selling.

You will recall that the third step of arousing desire is to paint a word picture of your prospect using your product and benefiting from it.

Before we consider how to apply this third step, it is important that you know what *concreteness* is and why the ability to talk in concrete language is important in every step of a sales talk—but especially important in the desire step.

Probably, unless you are most exceptional, you don't know just exactly what the word *concrete* means, as it is used in this chapter. If you are like most salesmen who have worked for me, you think that *specific* and *concrete* mean about the same thing. They don't.

Just for fun—please stop right now and see if you can define the word *concrete*—not the roadbuilding kind but the sales-talk kind.

The Thorndike-Barnhart Dictionary defines "concrete" as "naming ... something *perceived by the senses.*"

A salesman has achieved concreteness in his sales talk if the prospect can see, in his mind's eye, your product in action.

Or if the prospect can hear it in his mind's ear.

Or if he can taste it with his mind's tongue.

Or if he can smell it with his mind's nose.

Or if he can feel it with his mind's finger tips.

Let me stop right here to straighten out a wrong idea that has arisen in every sales school I have conducted since I wrote the previous edition of this book. This wrong idea (and I must have produced it by stupid writing) is that, in order to be concrete, you must appeal to *all five senses.*

Of course that isn't true.

Use such sense appeals as are appropriate for the article you are describing—and no more. Don't drag in any sense appeals that don't make sense.

If you are describing an apple or a potato chip or a summer resort, you could quite appropriately appeal to all five senses. But when a salesman tries to appeal to the prospect's sense of taste in selling an automobile—and I've heard them do it—or the sense of smell in selling a portable radio, he is underrating his prospect's mind and overworking his own imagination.

So, I say again, you should not try to appeal to all senses. Appeal to as many as "make sense"—and no more.

You say, "This frame is strong," and your statement is not concrete. But say instead, "You balance this frame on a beam, load a ton of sandbags on each end, sight down the top, and see that it has not even bent." This statement is concrete because it brings a picture to your mind's eye—a picture of yourself squinting down the frame.

What about appealing to other senses? Well, here are examples which might be used in selling a summer resort:

Sound—"When you step off the boat you hear the lapping of the water on the shore, the song of birds."

Smell—"You smell the aroma of pine needles and of new-mown hay."

Taste—"You stop at the country store. Strawberries! You slip one into your mouth and get the sweet, tangy taste of sun-ripened berries."

Feeling—"You pick up a canoe paddle and feel the smooth grain of the wood and the nicely formed handle that fits so well into your hand."

Paper salesmen appeal to the senses, as follows:

Hearing—The salesman tears the paper.

Sight—He asks the prospect to note the fibers.

Feeling—The salesman hands the prospect a piece of the paper to feel.

Smell—The salesman says, "Good paper has a clean smell —note this," and he asks the prospect to smell the paper.

Taste—Lastly he asks the prospect to taste the paper just to demonstrate to himself that it tastes, as well as smells, clean.

Let's take an abstract word—for example, the word "sympathy." It does not bring up any picture in my mind. Suppose, instead, I give you a little section out of a verse by Elizabeth Barrett Browning.

> A red-haired child
> Sick of a fever, if you touch him once,
> Though but so little as a finger tip,
> Will set you weeping; but a million sick . . .
> You could as soon weep for the "rule of three"
> Or compound fractions.

That language is concrete—it appeals to the senses of sight and touch.

Ben Sweetland, in his book *I Can*, expressed it well when he wrote:

Man has progressed in his mastery over the elements and germs. And, through the invention of labor-saving devices, has greatly simplified the art of living. And now, as we pass the halfway mark in the twentieth century, we are learning one of the most important secrets of life—the potency of *mental pictures.*

The mind does not think in terms of words—but pictures. Everything we see, hear, or read, we translate into mental pictures. In other words, we "see" what we hear and read.

How the senses are appealed to by salesmen was discussed by Charles Fitz-Patrick in an article in *The American Salesman*. He tells of a salesman who has had great success in selling a pressure cooker at $14.75. He would say to the prospect, "Will you just run your hand around the inside of this cooker? Isn't that a smooth finish? Nothing to chip or flake off into your food."

Almost always the prospect would take the cooker in her hands. Then the salesman would continue, "Notice the looking-glass shine on the outside. Glance at your reflection in it. You'll be able to clean it in seconds."

Another example given in the same article is of a toy salesman who says to the customer, "There's nothing in the finish of this toy to hurt a child. If you wish, I'll remove the wrapper so you can run your tongue across it!"

A good example of the effectiveness of concreteness is this heading of a recent advertisement: "No bald head ever feels the thrill of a woman's fingers running through his hair."

Concreteness in language is of great value to salesmen, so practice using language that appeals to the senses. Drill yourself in doing it. It will help you increase sales.

Please note this point: There are degrees of concreteness— as we use the word in this book. If you say, "The truck rumbles by," you have painted—in rather faint colors—a word picture. It is more concrete if you say, "I hear the rumble of the truck, I see a flash of red body and chrome trimmings, I feel the tremble of the sidewalk, I smell the sickening fumes—yes, and taste them too."

Try to make your word pictures as concrete as practicable. A salesman in one of our sales classes once summed up the rule succinctly thus: "The concreter the better!"

The third step of arousing desire is all concreteness—all the painting of word pictures. In this third step you aren't appealing primarily to the prospect's mind; you are appealing to his *feelings*. And what a prospect *feels* about your product is

vastly more important in arousing desire than what he *thinks!*
So be concrete—appeal to as many of the *prospect's five
senses* as is practical.

CHAPTER 33

Can you paint word pictures? If not, it will pay you to learn how

*Selling is more than persuasion . . . It is skill in helping
people visualize the results and benefits of products and
services.*   —ELECTRICAL INSTITUTE OF WASHINGTON

NOW FOR THE THIRD STEP: *Paint a word picture of your prospect using your product, enjoying it, and benefiting from it.*

Alas, most salesmen, when they are asked to use word pictures in their sales talks, are cowering cowards!

"I can't do it," they say. "Word pictures sound 'corny.' I'll
give my prospects facts—but no pictures! I can appeal to their
brains but not to their emotions."

That's too bad because people buy on emotions more than
on reasoning. Facts appeal to the brain, emotions appeal to
the heart—and most buying results from heart appeal.

Yes, *you* can do it—*you*—any salesman—any time

Let's kill off this idea that "word pictures" of the prospect
using a product and enjoying it are necessarily long, "corny,"
difficult, hard to produce.

The shortest word picture I ever heard was produced by a
friend of mine who said, "I've got a new secretary . . . [pause]
. . . *Wow!*"

That one word "wow" brought up a mind picture of that new
secretary.

Suppose you are trying to sell a man a hammer. You might say, "When you pick up this hammer, heft it, then whack in a nail—you know you have bought a *hammer!*" (That is a word picture because the prospect can, in his mind's eye, see himself using that hammer.)

Nothing hard about that word picture, is there?

Or suppose the salesman is selling you a vase as a gift for your wife and he says, "When your wife unwraps that vase she'll step back, smile, and say, 'Honey, it's lovely.'"

A word picture in seventeen words! Surely, that's easy.

If you still think that word pictures are hard to produce, read the following:

1. "When you clamp this Stillson wrench on a pipe and give it a pull, you feel the pipe turn."

2. "What happens when you own this power mower? You come home tired at night, dreading that grass-cutting job. When you get home you look around that big yard. The grass is cut—your boy did it!"

3. "You write your lecture notes with this felt-point pen. You prop them up on a stand. Walk to the other end of the room—and read them easily."

4. "You hit that ball a good clean swipe and watch it sail down the middle of the fairway. You glance at the distance marker—about 275 yards!"

Why go on? Surely you must realize by now that a word picture can be effective—even though it is brief—and that brief word pictures are easy to produce.

This example of an effective eight-second word "picture" appeared in the magazine *Specialty Salesman:*

One hot Saturday morning in August, a handyman rang a doorbell. A gentleman answered.

"That's a lovely yard you have out there, but I see the grass needs cutting," the caller said. "It's awfully hot today. So why don't you just sit down in the shade and enjoy a cool lemonade while I cut it for you?"

"Fine," said the homeowner.

The sale was made—that easy. Yet the price wasn't even mentioned. The seller of the grass-cutting service didn't have to worry about closing the sale. The prospect wanted the beautiful picture the salesman had painted.

In eight seconds the salesman closed the sale. The prospect could see himself enjoying the benefits so temptingly pictured by the handyman.

The lesson is clear. Paint a picture, in terms of customer-benefit, and you'll sell.

Long "word pictures" work, too

Let's turn now to a longer and more flowery—but highly effective—word picture.

This example was given me by William J. Mulvehill, of Stowe, Ohio. Mr. Mulvehill wrote:

One morning, a man called me long-distance from Cleveland, Ohio. He said, "Mr. Mulvehill, I have the car you want. I have a beautiful red Mercury station wagon sitting in my lot right now.

"When you buy this car, Mr. Mulvehill," he continued, "here's what's going to happen to you: you walk out your front door and see, shining in your driveway, a beautiful station wagon. The sun glistens on the red paint, and shines on the paneling. You walk slowly across the driveway and stop for just a moment as you run your hand over this 'wood' paneling. It feels as smooth as glass. It should feel that way—it *is* glass—Fiberglas.

"You open the door of this car," the salesman continued, "and slide in over the soft rubber seats. You stop to admire the beautiful snowy-white and red leather. You reach down and turn the ignition key. A soft purr responds. You move your gear selector lever into *drive* and step gently on the accelerator. You glide down the driveway.

"As you drive up the road, your neighbors stare, because you have the most beautiful station wagon they have ever seen."

Mushy? Yes, but I bought the car!

I bought it without ever seeing the man who sold it. I bought it without even seeing the automobile. That's what word pictures can do!

That word picture may sound a bit flowery—yet it sold a car to a hardheaded, practical, down-to-hardpan engineer!

What did this salesman do? He did more than paint a word picture of that station wagon. He pictured the prospect looking at it, admiring it, driving it—yes, and he pictured the prospect winning the admiration of his neighbors.

A word picture sold that car—and it will sell your product, too, if you will give it a chance.

"People buy images," says Wally Powell of the Hoover Company. "The sharper you can make that image, the sooner you're going to get that name on the dotted line.

"When a woman buys a hat, she doesn't buy just so much cloth. She buys a mental image of herself wearing that hat."

John Cooper, assistant managing director of the Dale Carnegie Sales Courses, expressed the idea well when he said, "Tell the prospect not what the *product* looks like, but what the *prospect* looks like, using and enjoying the product."

The fact that word pictures sell other things besides products was demonstrated in the book *The Last Hurrah*, by Edwin O'Connor, published by Little, Brown & Company. In this part of the novel, one character, Frank Skeffington, was attempting to sell another, Norman Cass, Jr., on becoming fire commissioner. To do it, he painted this word picture:

"First of all, I'm afraid you'd be extremely conspicuous. At every major conflagration you'd be present, in a position of command, a recognizable figure in a Commissioner's uniform of pure white. I have to admit to you that you'd be a cynosure of all eyes. And then, in your day-by-day activities, you'd ride in the long maroon Commissioner's car, equipped with a siren and two uniformed firemen to attend you; you'd be traveling at top speed at all times along our city streets; other cars would necessarily pull over to the curb to let you pass."

Word pictures sell when facts fail

Word pictures not only sell individual prospects, they sell groups of prospects as well. At a Bale-Whiting Sales School

in Winston-Salem, North Carolina, an excellent example of
the effectiveness of word pictures in group selling was given
by Charles F. Moester, then a traveling sales representative of
the Winston-Salem *Journal-Sentinel.* He said:

Once I went to Mt. Airy, North Carolina, to try to sell a group
of thirty-two boys on getting going in a prize contest.

At the start of my pitch, I talked as hard as I could but I didn't
get a spark of interest.

Then I got smart—and started to paint a word picture of the
boys enjoying the prize—which was a trip to the shore. I pictured
the bus ride to the resort, the meals in the hotel, the games on the
beach, the dip in the Atlantic. I made them feel the rush of the
bus . . . taste the meals . . . smell the salt air . . . feel the salt water.

Before I had finished carrying the boys, in their minds, on this
prize trip, I saw their eyes begin to shine. They steamed up fast.

Never before did the doors in Mt. Airy get such a knocking! We
got forty subscriptions in two days—which was an all-time record
for the *Journal-Sentinel.*

And one word picture did it.

This step calls for a little imagination

"Why should I paint this word picture of the prospect's
benefit?" you ask.

Because the best way to arouse desire is to pick up the prospect mentally and carry him into the future and let him see
himself enjoying what you are trying to sell him. It is an
appeal to the heart.

Sir John Lubbock said: "You are more likely to carry men
with you by enlisting their feelings than by convincing their
reason." Surely this is true in the semifinal step of your sales
talk.

Think of your own case. Before you bought your first automobile, didn't you have in your mind a picture of yourself driving the car around—on business or pleasure? Before you
bought your first television, didn't you have a picture of your-

self and your family sitting in front of a television set, watching and listening? Couldn't you, in your mind, see the wonderful programs coming right into your own living room?

Perhaps the prospect at this point in your sales talk will paint his own mind pictures—but the wise salesman does not take a chance. He does the painting himself.

Here's another example of the miracles a word picture can perform. It was told by Oral T. Carter, then a salesman for a trucking company, now president of Oral T. Carter and Associates, Inc., Cincinnati, at a meeting of a Dale Carnegie Sales School Class in Cleveland in 1939:

One day we were given in this class the rule for arousing desire. The next day the boss called me into his office and said, "O.T., do you want to go out on a forlorn hope?" I answered, "No, I don't want to, but I will."

"Here's the problem," he went on. "A man living here in Cleveland has been transferred by his company to Los Angeles. The expenses are being paid by the company for which this man works. They have already closed with one of our competitors to do the hauling—at a price lower than we can quote. Go out and see if you can do anything to get the job for us."

I went out, talked with the woman of the family, and persuaded her to switch the job to us and to pay, out of her own pocket, the difference between our price and our competitor's.

I was so astonished at my success that, after the order was signed, I asked this woman what had influenced her to make the change.

She answered, "When you told me how your truck would back up in front of my new home in Los Angeles, and how your men would carry those containers with my dresses in them up into my room, and when you pictured how nice and fresh my dresses would look when they came out of the special containers—well, that was when I decided I just had to ship by your trucks."

Only a word picture! But it closed an "impossible" sale.

CHAPTER 34

Salesmen who have sense appeal to the senses. It's easy; why not do it!

*People think in mind pictures—
let's sell them with word pictures.*

How do you paint word pictures? Before we answer that question, let's ask ourselves another: What do we want our prospect to think as a result of the "pictures" we paint in the desire step of the selling process? Don't we want him to see himself using and enjoying this product we are trying to sell him?

"All right," you say, "you might possibly be correct about how to arouse desire. So I'll try word pictures just once, if you'll tell me how to produce them."

This I will gladly do.

It's simple—you take just two steps.

First: Determine the "end use" of your product for this particular prospect. That is, what will the prospect use it for? Why will he buy it? What does he want with it?

Some examples of "end uses" follow, as they might apply to individual prospects:

Public-speaking course—The end use might be to get the prospect ready to make a speech at a convention.

Dictating machine—The end use might be to finish each day's work in time to play a little golf before dinner.

Portable television—The end use could be to enable the prospect to watch shows even when he is on the road.

The end use of a hammer is normally to drive nails, of a saw to saw wood, of a putter to sink putts, of a bat to hit the ball.

All right, you know what we mean by "end use."

When you have determined the end use of your product for the particular prospect, you then ask yourself:

Second: What will the prospect look like, using this product? Picture it in your mind. Throw the picture into words. Difficult? Nonsense!

Let's reduce this painting of word pictures to kindergarten proportions. Let's assume you want to paint a word picture of a prospect using a hammer.

To make it really simple, let's start with you painting a word picture of yourself using a hammer.

It might run like this: "I walk up to the work bench with two sticks of wood in my hand. I put them on the bench, one on top of the other. I reach up and take down the hammer. I reach in a tin box and take out a nail. I hold the nail upright with one hand and tap the nail gently, to start it. Then I hit it a few whacks and the job is done."

Now then, to paint a word picture of *your prospect* using a hammer you change the "I's" to "you's," thus: "*You* walk— *you* put them—*you* take down—*you* take out—"

Of course, after you get a little practice, you start thinking through the picture without bringing yourself into it.

I don't blame you for saying, "Look here, Whiting, you don't have to make it quite *that* simple." But after you have seen intelligent men flounder and fuss, sweat and swear, grunt, groan, and grimace as I have over painting word pictures, you will realize that this explanation can't be made too simple!

All right, let's try again.

What do you sell?

Let's say it's a gasoline lawn mower. What does your prospect look like as he drives this machine over his lawn?

Or perhaps you sell color television sets. Can't you see your prospect and his family sitting in front of the set and enjoying a picture presented in color? And since you can see it with your mind's eye, can't you describe it?

Let's take a more difficult picture. Let's ask, "What does a salesman look like making a successful speech at a sales convention? What does a man look like as he turns a dictating-machine belt over to his secretary and departs for the golf course?" Surely you could describe a man driving up in front of his room in a motel, unloading his portable television, plugging it in, and then settling down to enjoy the TV shows.

First, you see it in your mind; second, you tell what you see —and you have a word picture!

So let's stop saying it is difficult to paint word pictures— that it can't be done. Stop excusing yourself, and instead give word pictures a whirl. They are miracle workers for salesmen —so why deprive yourself of such an efficient helper!

Again I say, painting word pictures is easy—will be easy *for you.*

Suppose you were trying to sell a man a fly rod. Ask yourself these questions, and answer yourself thus:

What would he use it for? For catching brook trout.

Where would he use it? Chiefly in Green River.

When would he use it? Any Saturday.

How would he use it? He would put it in his car, drive to the bridge on the Egremont Road, walk upstream a half mile or so, string up his rod, select a fly, and start casting.

All right, you've thought it through—now put it into words. For example, you say to your prospect, "It's Saturday afternoon. You get up from the lunch table, put on your fishing clothes, grab your rod and reel, step into the car—and in five minutes you are at the bridge. You park the car and walk upstream a half mile. Then you string up your rod. . . ."

No need to take your time to finish the picture, but surely you would carry the prospect through the excitement of landing his first fish with the new rod.

Your prospect, if he is a fisherman, will listen avidly to this long word picture—and his desire will certainly be aroused by it.

What do purchasing agents "long for"?

Maybe you say, "I sell to purchasing agents—they don't *long* for anything but low prices."

If you think this, you are overlooking the fact that the goods which purchasing agents buy must be either used by somebody in his organization or resold. The people who use the article he has bought, or who resell it, must be pleased, or the purchasing agent will hear about it!

Remember, when he is buying typewriters the purchasing agent has somebody to please besides himself and the treasurer. He has to please the people who use the typewriters, or he will be in hot trouble! So when you paint a word picture of the stenographers using those typewriters efficiently and enjoying them and turning out more work, you arouse the purchasing agent's desire to buy them for his company.

The picture you paint for a purchasing agent should show employees of his company using the product you sell and getting efficient service and long wear and pleasure and satisfaction from using it—a picture perhaps of employees congratulating him and thanking him for his wise purchase!

Oh, it can be overdone, but it shouldn't be overlooked.

If you are going to make a routine sale of a routine item—a few thousand sheets of carbon paper or a few gross of blotters —you probably don't need a word picture, or much selling. But when you are trying to sell a purchasing agent some expensive piece of equipment, you should use the desire rule, complete with word picture, just as you would on any other prospect.

Only, in cases of this kind, the person who is using the product and enjoying it and benefiting from it in your word picture is not the purchasing agent but a company employee.

I beg of you, try word pictures. Use them just a few times, by way of satisfying yourself that they work. Watch your prospect when you begin to project him into the future—when you bring before his mind's eye a picture of himself doing what he wants to do. Note his intense interest.

Once, when Bob Bale and I were putting on a sales school in Earle, Arkansas, we picked up an excellent example of how a word picture helps to close. The story was told me by Ed McCormick, who then sold cars for H. K. Barwick, the Ford dealer in Earle. Here it is:

I was trying to sell a secondhand car to a colored boy. He wanted it to take him to the river, where he fished for "cat." After I had talked to the boy awhile, I saw I was about to lose him. He was beginning to look around for the door.

He was just fixing to say, "I'll come in tomorrow and talk about it" when I decided to try a word picture.

I was showing him a Model A—a car with small wheels and high off the ground—just the thing for muddy roads. Lots of men who drive Lincolns and Cadillacs have an old Model A to go fishing in. So I said to this boy, "You hop into this car and go fishing. You sail right along like a packet on the Mississippi. When you hit a mud hole, you go through like you were riding a catfish. When you use this car to go fishing, you'll be sitting on the river bank, hauling in the catfish and laughing to yourself, while the boys who have regular cars will be wallowing around in the first mud hole."

That picture of him, sitting on the bank hauling in the fish, got him. He bought the car.

Now, to summarize, to paint word pictures:

1. Ask yourself, "How will the prospect use this product?"

2. Next, ask yourself, "How will he *look* when he is using this product and enjoying it and benefiting from it?"

3. Then tell him!

I wouldn't want to hurt the feelings of any reader, unless I thought it was for his own good, but I can't refrain from saying that I think any salesman who knows how to use word pictures in his selling—and doesn't—is just stupid.

It works miracles for all salesmen

All right, you now have a tested, workable rule for arousing desire. Will you use it? Will you at least *try* it? Will you take all three steps—not just the first two? Will you persist in using this rule until it becomes second nature to use it? If you will, I can guarantee that, other things being equal, you will increase sales and earnings.

CHAPTER 35

These rules may help you paint effective word pictures

Making word pictures is as easy as making mud pies—once you learn how.

To paint effective word pictures—the kind that arouse real desire—please observe these rules:

1. Keep your word picture in the present tense: Not: "You *picked* up the mouthpiece," but: "You *pick* up the mouthpiece."

2. Make the prospect the hero. You should say, "*You* take the steering wheel of your car" or "*You* walk down the gangplank of your new boat."

3. Paint a word picture of your prospect doing something he wants to do (like making a cruise to Hawaii) or getting some result he wants to get (like increasing the output of his plant.)

4. Your word picture must be sincere, honest, and believable. The desire step will not work for you unless you believe the prospect will benefit if he buys your product.

To build a word picture: (*a*) feel *yourself* living the experience you are going to describe, then (*b*) convert it into a picture of the prospect living it.

5. Don't make the mistake of thinking you must appeal every time to all five senses. Appeal only to those which are appropriate to the prospect and the product. (Yes, I know I have said this before—but it needs repeating!)

6. Tell the prospect what happens!

You have pointed out the prospect's lack; you have told him how your product will supply that lack. Then introduce the word picture by saying, "Now that you own this television set, here's what happens. You turn it on. . . ."

In other words, introduce your word picture with some such phrase as "Here's what happens," or "This is what you do."

Scare them, if necessary!

7. Don't be afraid to put some "scare" into the first step— when you point out the prospect's lack or want or need. The following example of how it can be done was given by Alfred DeStefano at a meeting of the Dale Carnegie Sales Course in New York. Mr. DeStefano said:

I'd been selling rather successfully for a period of seven years. When my company, the Costa Ice Cream Company of Woodbridge, New Jersey, asked me to take the Dale Carnegie Sales Course, I said to myself, "What on earth can they teach me that I don't already know?"

Well, I found out!

It was in the seventh session (on a hot August night) I was taught something that made it possible for me to make sales where I never could make sales before.

The very next day I called on an account I had been soliciting for six solid months. Previously, I tried everything I knew on that account—and failed. I guess I just didn't know everything!

But that day I applied one of the rules that I had been taught the night before—the rule for arousing desire. I painted a word picture.

This is what happened. I called on Mrs. Edward Wilson. Mr. Wilson worked full time at Westinghouse, and Mrs. Wilson operated a store full-time with what little help Mr. Wilson could give her.

I went through the first three steps of the selling process. Next I pointed out that Mrs. Wilson was losing $1,000 a year by not stocking our product. Then I said, "Look what might happen. You are surprised one day when Mr. Wilson comes home a lot earlier than normal. 'What's wrong?' you ask. 'The plant has just laid off 300 workers,' your husband answers. Your thoughts immediately turn to the children and their needs. Then your fears seem to vanish because you still have the store.

"Here's what happens: Every morning your husband opens the store early and tidies up. By nine o'clock customers begin to drift in. When you enter the store you hear the glad sound of the cash register. When the afternoon rush comes, you and your husband are both behind the counter—dishing out Costa ice cream with both hands.

"At last closing time comes—you open the cash register and glance at the total for the day. You turn to your husband and say, 'We've made more today than we did when you were working full time.' "

When I ended this word picture, Mrs. Wilson said, "I believe I'll give it a try. When do you want to start deliveries?"

In other words, salesman DeStefano used "scare copy" in the first step—in pointing out the lack. It worked. Then he painted a word picture—and it worked, too.

8. Try the "before-and-after-taking" technique.

This technique fits neatly into our three-step method of arousing desire. It is legitimate and effective. For example:

STEP ONE (before taking): "You tell me, Mrs. Blank, that getting rid of garbage is a real problem. You have to keep a garbage strainer in your sink. When it is full, you put it in a garbage-bag which is in a holder on the floor. When the garbage bag is full you have to lift it out of the container and put it into the garbage pail at the back door. It's a messy job."

STEP TWO: "As soon as our garbage-disposal unit is in your sink, your garbage troubles are over."

STEP THREE (after taking): "You throw the garbage into the sink, sweep it into a hole, and turn on the power. You hear a little whirring noise—and your garbage is gone—and your garbage troubles are gone, too."

When you use this before-and-after method you can use word pictures effectively in the first step as well as in the third step.

9. Word pictures can be used effectively in retail selling.

Dr. Charles F. Walker of Portland, Oregon, gave me this example of a brief word picture—a forty-two-word word picture. Here is the story as Dr. Walker dictated it.

I decided forty years ago that I would buy an inexpensive tuxedo.

To pay for it, I had saved $25. I went to a clothing store and asked the salesman to show me a $25 tuxedo. Within a minute or two he showed me one. Before I realized it, he had another, which he placed beside it; but it cost $35. I had only $25. While I was in the process of deciding I couldn't afford the $35 suit, the salesman brought a third suit at $50. I allowed myself the merest glance and recognized it immediately as the best suit—but I had only $25. Summoning all my courage, I told the clerk that I would take the $25 suit.

The salesman did not retreat, nor did he offer any argument. Instead he said, "You are making a good purchase. As soon as you can, I am sure you will want to buy one of these better suits because you know, Mr. Walker, a tuxedo is not just a covering for your body. The first time you wear this suit [and he held up the $25 suit] you will be attending some social function, probably a dance. The first time the delicate touch of your lady's finger falls upon this fabric, she knows a story that the greatest eloquence cannot refute."

That salesman knew better than I what I wanted, and he knew how to help me reach the decision that was best for me, by an appeal to sentiment rather than sense. I recall that I bought the

$50 suit, though I no longer remember how I paid the difference. I have always considered that he did me a great service.

The retail clerk who sells like a professional uses word pictures. Here are some examples:

(*a*) "If you buy this necktie to go with your blue suit, people will say to you, 'My, what a becoming necktie!' "

(*b*) "When you wear this dress down the street, the boys whistle as you pass by."

(*c*) "In this car you whiz past virtually every car on the road."

(*d*) The route salesman says, "You put in a big display of this bread. Then look what happens: Customers look at the display. They walk up and grab the bread. The old cash register rings until the bearings get hot."

Word pictures are easy—and they work

All right, to sum it up, use word pictures because they help you to arouse the prospect's desire to own what you are selling.

Do it! It's easy. Maybe you will stumble over it a bit, at the start. With practice you will rattle off word pictures as easily as you deal out product knowledge.

You know your product—you know what the prospect will use it for. So surely it should be easy to paint a picture of him using the product.

Not many salesmen know how to use word pictures—how to arouse desire by the method we recommend. If you use it, it will give you a real advantage over your competitors.

And remember: now that you have finished reading about how to arouse desire in the hearts of your prospects, ask yourself, "What do I want my prospects to be thinking when I finish this step of the selling process?"

You want your prospect to be thinking, "I want what he is offering."

Step 5:* How to close the sale

and get the order

CHAPTER 36

How to close at the right time

Psychological moments are like ghosts—everybody talks about them but nobody ever saw one.

Probably the oldest joke about selling is this (the salesman is right in the middle of his pitch):

Prospect: "All right, I'll take it."

Salesman: "No you won't—not till I finish my sales talk."

This brings up the question, "When should I ask for the order?"

Some of the old-time books on selling would have answered that question by saying, "Ask for the order at the 'psychological moment.'"

The inference was that, at one certain moment, if you asked for the order you got it; if you didn't ask, you lost it!

The truth is that the so-called "psychological moment" is rarely a *moment* and not exactly *psychological.*

A right and a wrong time to try to close

Undoubtedly, however, a period comes in every successful sales talk when the prospect is ready to buy. This period may be a short second—or a long month.

When I lived in Augusta, Maine, I found a house I wanted to own. For some reason—I think because the owner was out

171

of the city—I could not buy it for a full three weeks after my mind was made up to take it. The "psychological moment," in that case, lasted three weeks! If, at any time in those twenty-one days, the owner had said, "Is it a deal?," I would have said, "Yes." At the end of three weeks, I bought it.

Salesmen should bear in mind, also, that they don't necessarily lose the sale if they miss the "psychological moment." If they try to close at the wrong time, instead of at the right time, they find it harder—but not necessarily impossible.

So, don't be one of those salesmen who spend so much time trying to detect the psychological moment that they forget to make a good presentation. In fact, you don't have to guess at the psychological moment at all—you don't have to worry over the right time to close—if you follow the suggestions which are presented in the next two chapters.

──────────────────────────────── CHAPTER 37

Watch for buying signals

The fact that the prospect is not conscious that he is giving buying signals is no reason for you to be unconscious.

Suppose the prospect gets ahead of you and is ready to close before you realize it; how can you avoid the danger of talking past the buying period—of missing the so-called "psychological moment"?

By watching for "buying signals" (which we discuss in this chapter) and by using "trial closes" (which we take up in the next chapter).

If you will watch for buying signals and if you will use trial closes, you will rarely be puzzled as to when to ask for the order. As a result, you will eliminate one of your great worries. You will shorten your presentations, and you should make more sales, and hence more money.

What are the buying signals—what should the salesman watch for? He should note:

(*a*) what the prospect *does*

(*b*) what the prospect *says*

"What is the prospect likely to *do*," you ask, "that will serve as a warning?"

If he does any of the acts listed below, he may be signaling you, unconsciously, that he is ready to close. So, watch to see if your prospect—

(*a*) relaxes—and especially if he opens his hands

(*b*) leans toward you

(*c*) assumes a more pleasant expression

(*d*) shows his agreement with points you are making by nodding his head

(*e*) steps back to admire your product

(*f*) uncrosses his legs

(*g*) re-examines a sample

(*h*) picks up the order blank

(*i*) has an unusual sparkle in his eye

(*j*) picks up the literature and reads it

Your common sense tells you that such actions may be buying signals or they may not. But here is almost invariably a safe and sure buying signal:

(*k*) If your prospect does something which indicates that, in his mind, he has already bought the product.

This last is the red traffic light—and it stops your pitch and starts your close. Your prospect may, for instance, ask permission to drive the car around the block again; he may dictate a letter on the dictating machine; he may brush some dust off the television set; he may inspect the item more critically.

So, I say again, if the prospect *does* anything that indicates that, in his mind, he already owns your product—waste no time, ask for the order!

Listen intently for "Buying Questions"

An even better signal than something the prospect *does* is
something he *says*—particularly any questions he may ask. If
those questions indicate that mentally he has already bought
your product, then waste no time—the order undoubtedly is
yours for the asking.

What is the prospect likely to say?

The real estate prospect might say, "We could put the
piano in that corner and the TV right here."

The prospect who has decided to buy may ask:

"Does it get out of order easily?"

"Can I buy it on time?"

"Do I have to have a pilot's license?"

"Can they get in and out without spoiling my lawn?"

"Do you install it?"

"Do you have a repair department?"

"Can I turn in my old machine?"

Or he may say, "I wasn't planning to spend that much for a
car," or, "I assume the price includes the batteries to start the
motor."

If you are selling to both a husband and wife at the same
time and "Poppa" says to his wife, "Well, Momma, what do
you think?" you can be fairly sure that one of them is sold. If
"Momma's" reply is favorable, ask for the order.

Vincent F. Sullivan, in the book *How to Sell Your Way
into the Big Money*, lists these signals:

"Supposing I do buy this . . ."

"If I should take this . . ."

"I really should wait" (or "ask," or "shop," etc.) . . .

"How about delivery?"

Ralph Peck of the Auto Exchange of Roanoke, Virginia,
told me of a buying signal they watch for in the secondhand
car business. He said, "It's a buying signal when the prospect
comes to the lot with his license plates in a paper bag!"

The best buying signal of all is when the prospect reaches for the order blank. Aggressive salesmen sometimes pick up the order blank and appear to be handing it to the prospect. If he reaches for it, the deal is closed; if he doesn't, the salesman keeps right on selling.

If you get the signal, don't wait—close!

If you get a buying signal, don't stop to make another point; don't stop to finish a sentence; don't stop—just close. Close as though it were the most natural thing in the world, at just that point, to ask for the order.

Vincent F. Sullivan gives this warning about buying signals: "Don't let the customer know that you know he has just about made up his mind. The minute you do, the customer begins to feel either that he has been rushed into buying or that he is being played for a sucker."

CHAPTER **38**

The trial close can work miracles for you

Salesmen who talk past the buying point, in effect, sell their product—then buy it back again.

Have you ever seen a paragraph like this in a newspaper?

Thomas F. Jones, salesman, was shot and critically wounded by a prospect whom he had just asked for an order.

You never saw an item like that. My prediction is that you never will.

Yet beginning salesmen fear to ask for the order as they fear to face a sawed-off shotgun!

That is why it is so difficult to get them to use one of the strongest weapons of the professional salesman—the trial close.

What are trial closes? They are questions asked (or suggestions made) by the salesman at various times in his sales talk to determine whether or not his prospect is ready to close. The Frigidaire manual calls them "closing feelers."

Trial closes have this great advantage over buying signals— they are under the control of the salesman. The prospect may or may not give a buying signal—but the salesman can always try a trial close.

Here are some sample closing questions

In general, a trial close is some question on a minor point or an alternative decision, such as:

"Do you have your securities delivered at the house or the office?"

"The factory is rushed and deliveries are uncertain—so quick action is important, don't you think?"

"Do you have items like this shipped direct or through a jobber?"

"Can you spare the time, this morning, to go over to the doctor's office for an examination?"

"Would you wash your clothes this afternoon if we could deliver the washer then, or would Monday be better?"

Trial closes help you to know when to close

Why are trial closes necessary?

1. Because they tell you when to ask for the order.

For example: Suppose a man phones your office and makes some vague inquiry about the article you are selling. You follow up the inquiry with a call. Maybe your prospect is ready to buy. In that case, if you push off into a long sales talk you may talk yourself out of the order. On the other hand, you may develop the fact that the prospect is only mildly interested. In that case, you want to shoot the whole selling process at him.

2. Because trial closes usually shorten the sales talk. In addition to the obvious advantages of shortening the talk, there is this one: it is less likely that some unhappy slip or some serious interruption will upset the sale.

The shorter the talk, the safer—provided it is just long enough to get the order.

Norman Krisbury of Patrick and Heddon, Scotch Plains, New Jersey, found that trial closings saved him time. Here is the example he told in a Dale Carnegie Sales Course session:

I sold Ted Eliades a home on Carsam Street in Fanwood, New Jersey, with the help of trial closings. I started using them at the very beginning of our talk and I kept it up.

The first few trial closings showed no results. Finally I hit on the right one, when I said, "When we make Mr. Paul an offer for his house, shall we request that he repair the three or four defective clapboards?"

He answered, "Yes"—and I brought out the contract.

Mr. Paul agreed to fix the clapboards, and accepted the offer.

I honestly feel that, if I had not used trial closings, I might still be showing houses to Mr. Eliades.

To sum it up: you learn whether or not your prospect is ready to sign the order blank by using trial closes.

After you have talked a few minutes you ask, "Do you like the larger size or the smaller?" If he expresses a preference, you ask, "Is Monday soon enough?"

If the answer is, "I'd like it this afternoon," you fill out the order blank. If he says, "Oh, I'm not going to buy," you are no worse off than you were before you used the trial close, and you start right back in your sales talk, just as though he had not answered you at all.

Especially use a trial close immediately after you have answered an objection. As Charles Roth points out, "When the buyer throws you a resistance, he is like a boxer who has thrown a hard punch—he is temporarily off balance. The last thing he expects is a closing action." So surprise him with a trial close.

"How soon will you need it?"

A paint salesman, quoted by J. C. Aspley, used to fire this question at his prospect, virtually without warning: "How soon will you need the paint?"

If the answer was, "Maybe in a couple of weeks," the salesman started to write out the order. If the answer was vague or even negative, the salesman went right on with his sales talk as though the prospect hadn't spoken.

Remember, the trial close leaves you no worse off if you get a turndown; and vastly better off if you get an acceptance.

Do the thing you fear to do

One of the sins of beginners is the failure to ask for the order. Because they are afraid to try to close, they talk on and on. Usually they get farther and farther away from the order the longer and longer they talk.

In fact, one great advantage in learning to use trial closes is that it forces you to do, again and again in each sales talk, the thing that most salesmen fear to do—ask for the order. After you have done it often enough, you stop being afraid of it.

You would think, from watching some salesmen, that a "no" was like an electrocution—once the switch is pulled you're dead. Fortunately, a "no" in a sales talk is no more serious, as a rule, than a fleabite.

Some salesmen seem to think that they must wait until they get a buying signal before they use a trial close. Please don't *you* make that mistake. Don't wait for anything—start using them early and often.

I noted, in reading a sample sales talk put out by Air-Way,

that they suggested using repeated trial closes. Here is part of their canned talk:

Five trial closings in nine sentences!

Considering all this work that the Air-Way Vacuum Cleaner will save you, don't you agree that it is dirt cheap at 15 cents a day?

This sand and dirt which your old machine leaves in the rugs, and which the Air-Way cleans out, causes your rugs to wear out long before they should. Wouldn't you like to save that money with an Air-Way?

Your Air-Way floor-waxing unit weighs only a few ounces, but the suction from the motor pulls it to the floor with a 7-pound pressure. Wouldn't you like to save strain and backache with an Air-Way?

As you have seen, this universal joint on your Air-Way will make it unnecessary to lift or move heavy furniture while cleaning. You would like to avoid moving heavy furniture, wouldn't you?

This dirt here that the Air-Way removed from your rug after your old machine had already been over it contains, on the average, five million germs for every thimblefull of dirt. The question that we have to answer is: "Do you want this dirt in your rug, or safe in the dustproof bag of your Air-Way?"

My friend and associate, John Cooper, makes this point about trial closes.

The time to ask for an order is when the prospect is ready to buy—the time to ask for an opinion is any time. For years I have trained salesmen to recognize the basic difference that I have arbitrarily chosen to make between a trial close and an order-taking question. I tell them to remember these three points:

1. A trial close asks for an opinion.

2. An order-asking question asks for a decision.

3. An order-asking question can be made into a trial close by prefacing it with some such statement as, "If you were to buy now."

EXAMPLES: "In your opinion, which is a more convenient delivery date, Monday or Wednesday?" The salesman asks for an opinion.

If the salesman were asking for a decision, he might say, "We can have this delivered next Monday. Is Monday satisfactory?"

So much for trial closes.

Let us assume that, in any given sales talk, (1) you have used trial closes and that they have not produced the desired response, (2) that you have now answered all the prospect's objections, and (3) that you have taken the three "desire" steps. How should you ask for the order?

You will find out by reading the next chapter.

CHAPTER 39

The secrets of closing

A good sales talk is a good thing, but the signed order is the thing.

Great Rule 5: Get a decision in your favor by weighing the ideas opposed to buying against those in favor of buying. Then ask for the order.

Note that there are two distinct parts to the act of closing:

1. Getting the decision.
2. Getting the signature.

The closing of the selling process is not some great, amazing astounding, separate act. It is merely one step in a process. If you have taken the other steps effectively, you have a right to expect an order, not every time, but often enough to qualify you as a professional salesman.

Closing is just part of the sale

Henry Simler, president of American Writing Machine Company, told Burton Bigelow, "I don't believe that salesmen should consider closing as a separate part of the sale." He added, "I don't believe I ever closed a sale for a typewriter. I always let the customer buy—and I have disposed of a lot of typewriters!"

A man who has sold an intangible service all his selling life said, "I set myself the task of creating such a compelling desire for my service that the buyer will ask, 'Well, how do I get it?' or 'When can we get started?' "

Wilkinson, in his book *Selling*, says something that a lot of salesmen who get "fluttery" at closing should memorize: "Remember that your sale has been made or lost before you arrive at the time for the signing of the order. This final step is merely a formality."

To tell you that closing is the one big step in selling is like telling a golfer that putting is the one big step in golf. If, in a golf match, you have already taken eleven strokes to get on the first green, there's no use in saying to yourself, "Now for a good putt!" It's too late. The putt, in that case, is utterly unimportant, just as a close is utterly unimportant if you have messed up the other four steps. In that case, a "good close" will not do it!

The beginner usually looks upon closing as a private miracle that experienced salesmen know how to perform. The beginners want to know how they, too, can perform this miracle.

Donald A. Laird, in an article in *The Management Review*, said: "Listening to evidence is easy enough (on the jurors); but it tries men's souls when they are locked in a room with nothing to do but decide." Dr. Laird then pointed out that a sale should not be made by piling up facts and then asking for a decision, but rather by getting a series of agreements throughout the sales talk—then letting the decision "creep up on the customer as his other decisions do."

"Good closers" are just "good salesmen"

You've heard about "good closers" all your selling life, haven't you? You've heard about fairies, pixies, space men, and leprechauns, too!

Well, they're all in the same classification!

The "good closer" does not exist. He is merely a good salesman. When a man says, "I have trouble *closing*," he really means, "I have trouble *selling*."

Do you want evidence? Here's how to get it: Invite a so-called "good closer" to make a sales call with you. Go through the first four steps of the selling process—and butcher them. Then dare the "closer" to step in and get the order with a "few well-chosen *closing* remarks."

If you have built up a willingness to buy in the previous steps, closing is easy. If you haven't, it matters little how you close, because you are not going to get the order anyway.

Did you ever try to drive a pig (or preferably a disagreeable old boar) into a pen? If not, you have missed one of life's great experiences! The pig may go peaceably along the road for a hundred yards or so. He does this to fool you! Then the pig comes to the pen—and refuses to go in! If the refusal is firm, and if the pig is a boar—and a large one—it will probably take ten men and a vast amount of perspiration, profanity, and persuasion to get the pig into the pen. I've seen it happen.

In this case the preliminary steps have not been properly taken. You haven't built up the pig's desire to go in. If you had kept him on short rations for a couple of days, then laid a trail of shelled corn into the pen, you would not have had to make the "close" by force.

"I'm ready to close—what do I say?"

Let's now assume you feel that you have carried the sales talk successfully through the steps of attention, interest, conviction, and desire. You then face the problem, "What must I say to get the order? How is it done?"

I went around for years asking people, "How do you close?" I wrote a book on selling before I was any too sure. Up to that time I had nothing but the old, reliable rule, "Ask for the order." That isn't the worst rule in the world, either! Millions of sales fizzle out each year because so-called salesmen don't ask for the order. So, if you can't remember the right way to close, just ask for the order anyway. However, there's a better way.

The most interesting example I ever read of asking for the order—and getting it—appeared in Westbrook Pegler's column, "Fair Enough," which appeared in the *World-Telegram and Sun*. Here it is:

Many years ago when the world was young and Theodore Roosevelt was president and a reporter could feed a family on $25 a week, my old man landed a job on the *Chicago American* by a feat of bland originality which has become historic in our stately profession. Landing in Chicago, broke, my pop entered the hyena room of the *American* in an old loft building with concave floors and infested with roaches which could be broken to the saddle, singled out the majestic Moe Koenigsberg as managing editor, asked for an assignment and was handed a terrible turkey on which, for 48 hours, all the veteran safe-blowers, porch-climbers and impersonators of gas-meter inspectors on the staff had exhausted their arts and strategems to no avail.

The clipping was a cheerful item about a toothsome female of some social standing in her neighborhood who had broken her engagement or perhaps an ankle. My old gent's mission was to get a picture of the subject, by fair means if all others failed. Otherwise he was to keep on going.

My pop got the picture in an hour or so, and only a few weeks ago at the publisher's convention in New York, in recalling his awe, Mr. Koenigsberg wattled that bosomy double chin of his which, when oscillated, emits a faintly bluppy sound as of a hot-water bottle gurgling on a bed, and said that my old man was always one to do the unique and unexpected.

When my pop came in and dropped the picture down, Mr. K. called out the guard and inquired, in his soft and wheedling way, just how Mr. What-did-you-say-your-name-was had wrought this triumph and would the management, perhaps, be subject to indictment as accessory to one or more murders for its share in the coup?

"I went out to her house and rang the doorbell and she came to the door and I asked her for a picture and she gave it to me," my old man said, "so I came right back and here it is and, by the way, what are my hours?"

How I learned the right way

In my early days as a sales manager, I could not find in any book or anywhere else a procedure for closing that made sense. Finally, one day, I chanced on Norval A. Hawkins' book, *The Selling Process* (long out of print). In it I found a rule for closing. It seemed a reasonable rule—it squared with common sense. The next day I took it out and tried it on my prospects. It did not close them all, but it closed more than any other plan I had ever tried. I have used it ever since. Tens of thousands of men under my direction have used it. It makes sense. It works.

In the next chapter I shall give you the substance of Hawkins' rule for closing.

CHAPTER 40

How to use the weighing close

*A false balance is an abomination to the Lord; but a
just weight is his delight.* Proverbs 11:1

Norval A. Hawkins' book, *The Selling Process,* was the first
one I ever read to point out to salesmen that the decision to
buy or not to buy is a *weighing process.* "When he [the pros-
pect] weighs the ideas in favor of buying," says Hawkins, "in
contrast with the lesser weight of the ideas opposed to buying,
he decides to buy. . . . If the balance tips the other way, he says,
'No.' "

Salesmen blunder in closing because they disregard the fact
that the prospect must make a sacrifice when he buys anything
that costs money. So, as he considers the deal, he is weighing
in his mind the advantages of the course you advocate against
the advantages of pursuing the course he had in mind when
you began your pitch—the course of not buying your product.

Once, years ago, a Buick salesman and a Chrysler salesman
were both working on me. Every time the Buick salesman told
me the good points of the Buick, I was thinking of the advantages of owning a Chrysler. Every time the Chrysler salesman
told me what I would miss if I didn't buy a Chrysler, I was
thinking of all the good things I had been told about the
Buick. So I bought a Studebaker.

Many salesmen adopt the policy of presenting, at the close,
only the advantages of the proposition. They seem to feel that,
by the time they are ready to ask for the order, they have hyp-
notized the prospect into forgetting his reasons for not wanting to buy.

Keep your head out of the sand

Some salesmen say, "It is dangerous at the time of closing to bring up any reasons why the prospect should not buy."

How can it possibly be "dangerous"? You have nothing to lose, *because the prospect is thinking of the disadvantages anyway.*

Since it is unsafe to let the prospect do his own weighing, you take over the job for him. You balance the advantages against the disadvantages and show that the advantages of buying weigh far more than the disadvantages.

Suppose, for example, you were trying to sell a public-speaking course. You could say:

"Mr. Prospect, before you make a decision, let's weigh the ideas opposed to buying against the reasons for buying. Let's consider first the ideas opposed to buying. What are they? Well, first the course will cost you money—$125. Next, it takes time—one or two nights a week for fourteen weeks. Third, it requires a bit of courage, at first, to stand up in front of a group of people and talk. Fourth, it requires effort—not much, but some. It's lots less trouble *not* to take the course. Now, Mr. Prospect, can you think of any other sound reasons why you should not take the course?"

Generally he can't, so you go on. "Let's look now at the advantages of taking our public-speaking course. You will overcome fear. You will gain poise and self-confidence. You will learn how to think on your feet. You will develop the qualities of leadership. You will put yourself in a position to earn more money. You will prepare yourself for advancement."

"Which weighs more, Mr. Prospect: the reasons for buying or the reasons for not buying?"

This is a "close by contrast" or a "weighing close." I don't know whether or not it is a *good* close by contrast. I know, however, that it works, because I have used it successfully on many thousands of prospects.

Give this method of closing a sincere, intelligent, persistent trial. When you do, it will become your standard method of closing.

This method of closing-by-weighing works on bosses, too. Evidence that it does was given me by Sherman A. Hawley, 217 North Orange Street, Peoria, Illinois. He wrote me:

My partner and I are licensed photographers for a studio in the highly competitive field of school photography. We learned that our largest competitor was going to put in equipment to manufacture a new picture process. Though it was new in this field, its popularity was assured.

We asked the head of our studio to purchase the necessary equipment for making something similar. It cost $15,000. He refused.

In this bad situation we decided to use the "weighing close" on our boss. So we drew up a document. It had two columns. On one side we put all the ideas against buying the equipment. In the other column, all the reasons in favor of buying. Anybody who read it could see that the ideas *for* vastly outweighed the ideas *against*.

We presented it to the boss.

Three weeks later we received his promise that he would do more for us than we had proposed. After only four months, we have increased our own business by 15 per cent.

The weighing close worked for these men. It will work for you.

—————————————————————————— CHAPTER 41

It takes courage, but it works

*If you would win a man to your cause, first convince
him that you are his sincere friend.*   —LINCOLN

Some of the reasons why I believe that it is good sales policy
to summarize, just before you ask for the order, all the reasons
against buying, as well as those *for* buying, are as follows:

1. Your prospect is thinking of the reasons for not buying
anyway—so why try to keep them a secret? As evidence, ask
yourself if, in any purchase you ever made that called for a
considerable expenditure, you did not think of the reasons for
not buying right up to the time you signed the order or said,
"I'll take it."

2. Ideas opposed to buying are like steam. Confine them
and they are explosive; let them out in the open and, like released steam, they are only moist vapor.

3. An idea opposed to buying, left to roam around in the
prospect's mind, is fuzzy, vague, and somehow tremendously
important to the prospect. Once the salesman has stated the
idea opposed to buying, this idea becomes clear and usually
not so important.

4. Stating the reasons opposed to buying makes the salesman face the things he fears—which are the reasons for not
buying. He overcomes his fears by doing the thing he fears
to do.

5. By stating the negative reasons, the salesman causes the
prospect to regard the salesman as a friend, an adviser, an
assistant purchasing agent. The prospect says to himself,
"This salesman is fair. I'm glad to do business with a man like
that."

It probably sounds strange to recommend that a mental attitude of "I came to help rather than to sell" will greatly improve a salesman's work, but the experience of scores of leading salesmen proves that it will. The idea is not altruistic—it's simply a practical way of making sales efforts more fruitful and profitable.

From this help habit will stem self-respect, confidence, and the self-assurance which will make our recommendations virtually irresistible. You can't lose!

—HAL BERGDAHL IN *A Bonus Every Month*

6. Remember, we said to mention *all* the reasons against buying. Why? If you fail to mention even one negative idea which the prospect has thought of, he will feel proud of himself for having thought of it. He will give it importance out of all proportion to what it deserves.

7. If the salesman has mentioned all the reasons against buying, he is in no danger that, at the last minute, the prospect will think up a new reason against buying. If he does and if he presents it vigorously he will perhaps wreck the sale.

You reassure the prospect

Charles B. Roth, in his excellent book *The Secret of Closing Sales*, says: "The closing secret is that you must overcome any fears in your prospect's mind. Before you press for the close, you must reassure him. You must restore his confidence and courage."

This is exactly what you do in the weighing close method. You reassure him; you restore his confidence in his own judgment; you make it easier for him to sign.

Put the prospect out of his suffering

Testimony as to the mental unhappiness of people who have to make buying decisions was given by *Exide News* as follows:

In helping a customer to make up his mind, it probably will be good salesmanship to recognize his mental discomfort. For instance, if Mr. Smith knows he needs a new battery, the thoughts passing through his mind may be like this:

"I didn't expect to have to buy a new battery this week—wanted to buy that new fishing reel, confound it! My insurance is due and Sarah wants those new drapes—what would happen if I bought a cheap battery?—better not—maybe it wouldn't stand up—wonder if this fellow's telling me the truth?"

And on and on the stream of thought flows through the customer's mind until something happens to break it off and force a decision. And what a relief when the decision is made!

Let your prospect deflate himself

Just the other day I was trying to sell a sales manager a course in selling for his men. He started in on what he assumed was a strong argument. As so often happens, the longer he talked the weaker the argument became. Finally he said ruefully, "I guess I'd better stop. Now that I get my argument out in the open, it's more in your favor than it is in mine."

CHAPTER 42

It's worth your while to learn to weigh efficiently

Your customer wants to buy. He may deny it—but, anyway, you keep on thinking so.

Here are some rules for weighing effectively that I learned through my years of selling and sales management:

1. Take a few words to connect the end of the desire step with the beginning of the weighing step. Say, for example,

"All right, Mr. Blank, I am sure you are now ready to decide about buying this ... The sensible way to make the decision is for you to consider both the ideas *for* buying and those *against* buying. After we do that, you be the judge and determine which weighs the heavier and decide accordingly. Let's start with the ideas you have mentioned which you feel are unfavorable to buying."

2. Remember, before you have reached this step you have, in the earlier part of your pitch, given the prospect all the important facts about the product, with the related buyer's benefits, and that you have answered all his objections. So do not, at this point, start in giving the conviction part all over again and don't give any of the answers to his "ideas for not buying." Keep in mind that, if you have done an efficient job, you have already covered these points.

In the weighing step, just *summarize* the points *for* and *against*—just tick them off.

3. Don't slur over this summary of the advantages of your product on the ground that you have already been over them in detail. Don't forget any of them. All you do at this point is to *list* the advantages—but list them with force, sincerity, enthusiasm, and brevity.

4. Let your attitude be that of a friend who is going to present the prospect with the ideas for and against buying, *so that he can make up his own mind.*

Give yourself a break!

Hawkins gives ten suggestions for making the points in your favor seem heavier than the points against you, which I have boiled down, as follows:

(*a*) Make the ideas against buying seem trivial by using tones and gestures that suggest lightness. "Of course, this is the most expensive washer on the market." "Yes, it calls for quite an expenditure to put in this installation." The words are against you; the tones and gestures can be *for* you!

(*b*) Naturally, in the same way, you try to make the ideas in your favor seem important by tone and gestures that suggest weight and importance. "It pays for itself through savings" can be said in a tone and with gestures that make it weigh an ounce—or a ton!

(*c*) Show that there are many more ideas in favor of buying than against it.

"Yes," you say, "but suppose there *are* more ideas *against* buying."

Well, we know that a 2-pound bag of sugar looks lighter than two 1-pound bags. So, if a salesman must deal with too many *no* ideas, he puts two or three in one package. In other words, he combines them.

"Of course, I know your secretary will not like to give up her shorthand, and it will be hard on her if any of the belts are crushed in transit, and at first she may object to wearing the headpiece." Three objections combined into one. Certainly they do not sound as weighty as though the three had been presented separately.

(*d*) Make the ideas in favor of buying attractive, those against buying unattractive. How? For example: "Perhaps your secretary will object, but then, you are paying her $125 a week to do what you ask—not what she likes." You have tried to make that objection unattractive. Now for the other side: "This machine will actually save you an hour a day. You have every right to spend that saved hour on the golf course, piling up health for yourself." Note that you have painted this in bright colors.

(*e*) Don't hurry the summing up of the advantages of your product. Pause after each one, to let it sink in. Some salesmen end each important point with a question that calls for an answer of "yes." "Earnings like that ought to assure you regular dividends on this stock, oughtn't they?" "Twenty-five thousand dollars should be enough to pay for the education of your children, shouldn't it?"

Keep away now from the word "objection"

(*f*) When you start to give your list of ideas unfavorable to buying, don't say, "Your objections to buying are..." or "Your reasons for not buying are..." (In fact, avoid the word *objection* in the closing part of your talk.)

Instead, introduce the reasons against buying by saying something like this:

"You may have felt that the price is too high and the demand..."

"You have pointed out that..."

"Other people I have talked to have felt..."

In that way, you are not admitting that there are any disadvantages to buying your product.

Also, I like "*ideas* opposed to buying" better than "*reasons* for not buying."

(*g*) Some salesmen write down the ideas for and against their product on their pad. A better way: get the prospect to do it.

Whether or not to *write* the points for and against—rather than to *speak* them—depends on several factors, notably these:

1. *The prospect.* If he is the slow, plodding type, who is willing to take lots of time to decide, write out the ideas for and against. If he is the kind who will be impatient at this slow method, don't use it.

2. *The product.* If it is an inexpensive item, don't waste the time. If it is an item that costs lots of money, it may pay to take the time to do it.

(*h*) Before you start presenting the negative side, it is an advantage to find out the chief reason in the prospect's mind against buying—to find out what the prospect considers the largest sacrifice he must make to buy your goods.

If you have asked plenty of questions and if you have thought of this problem all along from your prospect's view-

point, you probably know already your highest hurdle. If you
don't, then ask, pointblank, "What is your chief reason for
not wanting to buy today?"

_____ CHAPTER 43

Get the order on a "minor point"

No smart salesman ever forces the prospect to an-
swer the question, "Will you buy it or won't you?"

All right, you have finished the weighing process. Your prospect sees that the advantages of buying your product vastly
outweigh the disadvantages.

But the prospect probably does not say, "All right, wrap
it up."

No, he probably sits there, awaiting your next move.

You could ask him, "Well, will you buy or won't you?" Such
a challenge would be better than to say nothing. But better
still, close on a minor point or an alternative proposal.

Why? Because any man hates to say, "I'm whipped—I
give up."

Your prospect probably struggled against being interested.
He put up objection after objection through the conviction
part of your sales talk. He fought against desire. He hated to
admit that the reasons in favor of buying weighed more than
those against buying. He gave ground reluctantly, fighting
every step of the way.

Do you expect him now to wave the white flag voluntarily?
Perhaps he's whipped and maybe he knows it. But even so, he
hates to admit defeat.

If you are wise you will let him save face.

You will do it by assuming that of course he has decided

for himself that he is going to buy and that the only decision now is on some minor point—or between two proposals. By assuming that *he* has decided to buy, you dodge the idea that you forced the decision.

Here are some questions that get the orders

So you ask, "Which carriage do you prefer, the wide or the narrow?" You assume that of course he is going to buy the machine and that the only question is as to the width of the carriage. If he says, "Narrow," or if he says, "Wide," you hand him the order blank.

Here are some suggested minor points or double questions that you can use in closing:

"Which base do you like better—the high or the low?"

"Would you rather take the cash discount, or do you like the payment plan better?"

"In just what amount shall I write your policy?"

"Which of these do you prefer, this one or that one?"

"How do you prefer paying, weekly or monthly?"

"What color do you like better?"

"Where do you plan using it, here or there?"

Carl Arnsworth, in the magazine *Men's Clothing*, gave this advice to retail salesmen, which, by the way, might give a useful hint to any salesman:

How do we close? We do it first by finding out what the customer really wants and showing suitable merchandise. The next thing we do is to eliminate items the customer is not interested in, so that you have as few items as possible in front of him.

Finally, when you find that the customer is genuinely interested in one or two things, suggest to him, "I think this is the one you are really going to like," or, "I think you have passed by the best one," or "Which of these two do you prefer, Mr. Jones?"

It is up to you to help the customer decide—without forcing him in any way. That is a main feature of successful selling.

How the British do it

Here are some examples of "minor point" questions given by an English writer, Alfred Tack, in his book *Professional Salesmanship*.

1. "Do you sell more of the small size or the large?"
2. "My experience has been that demand is in the ratio of three of black and two of brown to one of yellow. How does that fit in with your trade, Mr. Trader?"
3. "This product is packed ready for display. I think you will find that it will pay you to put it on your counter just as soon as it arrives."

Negative or "scare" questions are often effective. For example:

"Suppose your house burned down tonight—are you insured for enough to replace it at present prices?"

"More people are killed by automobiles than by war—are you sure you will always be lucky?"

"Aren't you afraid people will notice that your shoes are run down at the heels and get a wrong idea about you?"

The technique of assuming that of course the prospect is going to buy is not new. Ben Franklin used it in a pamphlet he wrote to help Robert Grace sell the stoves that Grace manufactured on Franklin's model.

In this pamplet Franklin pointed out (not too truthfully— I'm afraid) that open fireplaces caused many women to lose their teeth, ". . . and do also very much contribute to damage the eyes, shrivel the skin, and bring on early the appearances of old age." Carl Van Doren, in his *Benjamin Franklin*, goes on to say, "Having artfully appealed to women, Franklin went on to explain . . . how Pennsylvania fireplaces were constructed. Then, one by one, he gave fourteen advantages and answered the objections that had been raised. After this, as his argument was complete and unanswerable, he directed workmen how to install the new stoves."

Make it easy for them to say "yes"

John Wilson, in his excellent book *Open the Mind and Close the Sale*, gives this advice about closing questions:

If you want a prospect to answer "yes" to your questions, then word the question in such a way that *it is easy for the prospect to say "yes."* An example of how *not* to ask a question might be, "Do you think the first of the month would be a good time to install this equipment?" And the prospect may think of a dozen reasons why that particular date is not satisfactory.

The prospect certainly would not give a negative reply if you said, "You want to receive the benefits from this equipment as soon as possible, don't you?"

An excellent suggestion was made by Wilfred D. Galpin of the General Electric Company in his pamphlet "Twenty-five Ways to Close the Sale."

Here are some of his and some of mine:

(*a*) The Subtle Question. Ask a question that will enable the prospect to indicate by his answer that already, in his own mind, he is enjoying the ownership of the article. For example, "Can't you picture yourself, after you have finished this course in public speaking, standing up at a company convention and holding your fellow workers breathless with your talk?"

If he can see himself doing this he will be likely to enroll.

(*b*) The Instruction Close. In this case, you ask the prospect if he would like to know how to use the article—then start in, at once, giving him instructions. For example, "Let me show you how to put the belt on and start the machine." If he says, "Okay," he is ready for the order blank. Some typical instruction closes might be:

Golf club: "If you like this putter, I'll go out on the practice green with you and show you how to sink putts with it."

Residence Property: "As soon as you move in, I'll be glad to help you find a yard man and a cleaning woman."

Salesmen who sell intangibles can use this close, for example:

Public-speaking Course: "Let me give you a couple of tips about your first talk."

If the prospect accepts your offer of help, bring out the order blank!

(c) The Order-blank Close. When your order blank is out, ask the prospect what his initials are, or what his street address is. If he lets you write these facts on the order blank, he is probably sold.

(d) The Action Close. (This close was designed for selling refrigerators. Maybe it could be adapted to fit your product.) The salesman says something like this: "This refrigerator is strong as a safe." Then he slams the door as hard as he can three or four times. If the prospect tells the salesman not to slam the door so hard, she is sold. She already considers that it is *her* refrigerator which the salesman is abusing—and the signing of the order follows easily.

(e) The Service Close. Offer some service to the prospect in connection with the product you are selling. This is known as the "screwdriver" close. For example: "The touch of this machine seems too heavy. Let me adjust it to suit you."

(f) The Suggestion Close. The clothing salesman picks up the suit the prospect likes and starts for the fitting room. The retail salesman lays the merchandise aside, thus suggesting that the customer has decided to take it.

(g) The Last Resort. If all other closings have failed and yet you are convinced that the prospect ought to buy, just hand him the order blank and a pen and say, "Please put your name right here." My friend Bill Stover, who, before he became a Dale Carnegie sponsor, was a top salesman for Remington Rand, suggests a better wording: "Do you wish to sign now, or have I failed to explain something to you?"

Bell Telephone used to recommend this wording to its salesmen, "Well, in this case, Mrs. Blank, you want the tele· phone—so let's go ahead and arrange for it now."

The company assumes that the salesman expects to get the order—as he should.

Why shouldn't you expect to get the order? If you have handled the sales talk well, if you have nailed down each point of importance you made, if you have satisfactorily answered all objections, if you know in your heart that buying your product will really benefit the prospect, then, in heaven's name, why shouldn't you expect the prospect to sign? And, since you expect to get the order, why not ask for it? Maybe that's all the prospect is waiting for!

CHAPTER **44**

Some general rules for closing

You believe easily what you hope for earnestly.
—TERENCE

Rule 1: Ask for the order.

I have heard successful sales managers express the opinion that more sales are lost because men don't ask for the order than for all other reasons combined!

A salesman for a key-making machine entered a hardware store and gave the shopkeeper a demonstration.

"Isn't it a wonderful machine?" he asked.

"Yes, it is."

"It would be a marvelous investment and a great timesaver, wouldn't it?"

"Yes."

"Well, why don't you buy it?"

"Well," said the shopkeeper, "why don't you ask me to?"

—DR. DAVID A. MACLENNAN, ..
Priming the Preacher's Pump

In *The Salesman's Refrigerator Primer* of the General Electric Company, Wilfred D. Galpin says:

About noon one day, one of my best salesmen came into the showroom, proudly waving an order for a washing machine. He had gone out to see one of his prospects, Mrs. Johnson, and said, "I've been out here four or five times to see you and I've told you all about the proposition, so I've come out this morning to ask you for the order."

"I know," Mrs. Johnson replied. "I've been trying to give you the order, but you wanted me to have a demonstration. My sister has one of your washers and I know all about it. I'll take one."

Why shouldn't he buy!

Rule 2: You should always expect the prospect is going to buy from you.

From J. C. Aspley's excellent *Closing the Sale* I take this incident:

A highly successful sales manager, a man who is now general manager of his company, was asked by a beginner how he could tell when it was time to close. . . .

The old-timer's reply was a classic. Said he, "Don't wait until you get to him; sell him on the way. Simply go to get the order signed."

Some salesmen carry to an alarming extent this matter of expecting the prospect to buy!

Perry Holdogle, owner of a big telephone property with main offices in Rockwell City, Iowa, related this experience. "About six months ago I was in urgent need of 200 telephones and decided to order them from the manufacturer who would make the quickest delivery. I sent a wire to four manufacturers as follows: "How soon can you ship me 200 five-bar sixteen-hundred-ohm bridging telephones?"

The Kellogg Company wired, "Can ship at once." The Stromberg-Carlson Company wired, "Can ship within twenty-four hours." The American Electric wired, "Can ship as soon as order is received," and Overshiner of the Swedish-American Company wired, "Shipping you the 200 telephones today." And by golly, he did.

In other words, he assumed that the prospect was going to buy. (P.S.—I should hesitate to recommend this method for general use.)

I know the technique of assuming that of course the prospect is going to buy is effective—because I've had it worked on me. Once when we were conducting a securities-selling campaign for a power company in the South, we stopped at a small-town hotel for several days. And every day I ate eggs for breakfast—though I don't especially like eggs for breakfast.

I did it because every morning the waiter asked, "How'll you have your eggs fixed?" He assumed I was going to have eggs—so I had eggs!

If your thinking is right, your poise will be right

Rule 3: Don't wobble! What are you afraid of? Few salesmen were ever thrown out for asking for the order. If the salesman sways mentally at the time of closing, he shouldn't be surprised if the prospect sways too. Be poised, calm, and decisive. How? It's easy! Think not about yourself but about your prospect, and how your goods will satisfy his lack.

Rule 4: Keep one strong point about your product in reserve for use in case your prospect balks just at the point of closing.

This is important. The expert salesman is never caught at the close of his talk without one major advantage of his product, held in reserve—ready to use to clinch the deal.

For example:

(*a*) Oh, I forgot to tell you—we pay the freight.

(*b*) Another thing—we supply the reinforced envelopes, for safe mailing.

(c) Oh, yes, here's another big advantage—the starter goes on automatically if a power interruption occurs.

(d) Another thing—with this model you get tubeless tires free.

Rule 5: Use any honest "hook" or "hurry-upper" (that is, any honest, legitimate reason why the prospect should buy *now*, rather than *later*).

If the price is going up, if the offer will soon be withdrawn, if the supply is running low, you will hardly fail to mention this. However, be sure you stick to the exact truth. A lie may close one order but it doesn't build business.

Here's a hurry-up that I know has been worked on me:

After wearing myself out for years turning the pages of the heavy wallpaper sample books, I discovered how to hurry the final choice when the customer had narrowed it to two or three patterns. I would point to one and say, "I'm sorry, but I'll have to see if we have enough of that one in stock." Immediately this pattern became the choice.

I would then go to the back room, where I knew there was plenty. When I returned with it a look of relief would spread over the customer's face and the sale would be made in no time.

—MRS. R. E. MUTCH IN *Rotarian*

It's too bad that that one isn't strictly honest and exactly ethical. I hate not to recommend it—but I don't!

Here are some suggested "hooks" that I do recommend, assuming, of course, that they are true.

"If you buy this set of clubs today, you get this box of balls free."

"Stock prices have been going up for a long time. If you wait a week you may have to pay more for this mutual fund stock."

"You can undoubtedly get insurance now, but what about a few years from now, even a few months from now—who knows?"

The automobile salesman says, "Up to midnight tonight I can let you have white-walled tires without extra cost."

The jobber's salesman says, "If you place the order today, I can give you a dozen free."

Once, in a Dallas, Texas, car lot, the "wash boy" said, "Let me wash your car."

I tried to turn him down by saying, "No, it looks like rain."

He got the job with this "clincher": "If it is raining when you take your car out, the wash is free."

Rule 6: Save up one good, strong question for the final push. The Equitable recommends these questions to its agents:

"You realize that you ought to have this protection, don't you?"

"Wouldn't you do better by settling this matter now than by worrying over it a few weeks longer?"

"Why delay in doing now what you admit is a duty to your loved ones?"

"If you knew you couldn't get this protection next month, you would take it now, wouldn't you?" (Wait until he answers, "Yes.") "Then why run the risk of not getting it at all?"

Car salesmen sometimes use this one: "You realize, of course, that while you're standing here dickering, your car is depreciating!" This is good only if the prospect has a sense of humor.

Rule 7: Never leave a prospect until he has said "no" at least *seven* times!

If salesmen could only get clearly in mind that *no* is not final and irrevocable—that many sales are made after the prospect has said "no" at least once, often many times—they would sell more goods and waste less time.

So, adopt this slogan: "Don't quit—keep selling." Or maybe you will like Jean Cocteau's better: "Always get up one more time than you have fallen."

On the rock near the top of Mt. Washington there is a marker on the trail to show the spot where a woman climber lay down and died. One hundred steps more and she would have reached the hut at the summit—the shelter she sought.

A battle, so the strategists say, is won by the army which can hold out minutes longer than the foe.

A man cannot do everything, but he can keep going. He has energy for one step more. He has a bit of resource left, even when he thinks all is spent.   —A. K. CHALMERS, *The Constant Fire*

How many times have you "died" in a sales talk, when a few more "benefits" would have carried you to your goal?

Christopher Columbus got *no* for eighteen years before he got his yes. "I can't wait eighteen years," you say. True—and equally you are not likely to discover another America. Admire and emulate Christopher's courage and persistency, and regret only that he was not a better salesman!

I picked up, in Detroit, a good example of what can be accomplished by a man who pays no attention to a *no*. The man with the bad hearing for *noes* was Bill Wischman.

Bill's brother worked for the Michigan Consolidated Gas Co.—so Bill decided *he* would work for them, too.

Bill applied for the job—and was promptly turned down.

Why? Because he had a double-barreled speech impediment—he stuttered and he talked with "word whiskers."

Bill applied again and again—only to be turned down.

He applied nineteen times before he was hired.

Why did the company finally take him—in spite of his stutter? Because Bill did not hear the first eighteen *noes*.

The important rule, "Don't quit too easily," was well summed up in that ancient classic (published exactly fifty years ago), *Ginger Talks*, by W. C. Holman, when he said, "The fact that a man has repeatedly said *no* to you is no sign that he won't say *yes* if you go back at him once more with a little better aim and ammunition."

An amusing example of the value of persistence was presented in *Printers' Ink* in an article by Bernard L. Salesky, president of Champ Hats, Inc. He said that, in his early days as a salesman, he called on the owner of a men's-wear store—who ultimately picked him up and threw him bodily into the street—so hard he rolled into the gutter.

This shook Mr. Salesky's body—but not his determination. He went back to the hotel, bathed, put on a new suit, and went back to the scene of his first repulse.

His opening words were, "Now that you've had your fun, let's get down to business." The merchant first scowled, then broke into a big smile and said, "All right, let's see what you got that's so blankety-blank good."

As you might expect, the salesman walked out with a good order.

The moral is: don't be disturbed by a *no* even if it lands you in the gutter!

One of the most useful pieces of advice about closing I ever read appeared in the magazine *Salesman's Opportunity*. It was written by John D. Murphy, contributing editor. Mr. Murphy's point, in brief, was this:

Every time a salesman and a prospect get together, a sale is made. Either the salesman sells the prospect on buying, or the prospect sells the salesman the idea that he is not going to buy.

Did you ever stop and ask yourself just how a prospect can win the sale?

Every salesman knows about the "assumptive close." At a certain point in the sale you merely assume that the sale is made and act accordingly.

In using the assumptive close, the salesman *takes it for granted* that the prospect has already decided to say "yes."

Few salesmen realize that the same psychology can be used by the prospect on the salesman. There is such a thing as an "assumptive no," just as there is an "assumptive yes."

Go back mentally over the last five sales you lost. Be honest with your answers. Did the prospect actually come out and say "no"— or did he say something that you "took" for "no?"

Prospects dread saying, "I am not going to buy from you."

Instead they say, "Well, I'll think it over," or "I can't afford it."

In too many cases, when a salesman hears these words or something similar, he *assumes* that the prospect has said, "No, I am not going to buy today," so he quits. The prospect used the salesman's favorite tool against him—the assumptive close.

The outstanding salesman never takes an *assumptive* "no" for an answer.

The point where the one salesman picks up his bag and leaves, thinking he has heard a "no," is the very point where the *star* salesman starts selling.

Rule 8: Don't be too tense in this step of the sale.

Act as though signing the order were a rather routine part of the day's work. Vincent F. Sullivan, in his book *How to Sell Your Way into the Big Money*, says, "Most people will sign anything that is shoved in front of them if they believe signing is a normal routine matter."

Rule 9: Never agree to call back on a prospect until you have tried every known way of closing on the spot—and failed. Every time you let a prospect put you off, you are weaker in the eyes of two important people—the prospect and yourself. If a prospect promises to buy later and has no good reason for the postponement, either he is not telling the truth or he could be sold *now*.

Don't be put off—it costs time and orders.

Remember also that between your call and your call-back, your competitor may slip in and get the order.

You can close with an example

Rule 10: Try using an example, a "for instance," to give the final push. In other words, cite a case that is analogous to the case of your prospect.

For example, a young man came up to me at a Dale Carnegie public-speaking class promotion meeting and said that he could not decide whether or not to take the course. I asked him a few questions. Then I said, "Let me tell you the case of a young man who faced about the same problem that you now face. Like yourself, he was trying to become a good salesman and, like yourself, he was having no great success." Then I told him in considerable detail how this man had taken the course—and that while it was in progress he had forced his way into the lead of his sales force. I told how, within two years, he was made district manager of his organization. That example gave the necessary push and the man enrolled.

Get the order blank out early

Rule 11: Even after you have your prospect's agreement to buy, you have, in some forms of selling, the additional hurdle of getting the order blank signed.

I never could believe very enthusiastically in the necessity of using suggestion, hypnotism, or force in getting the pen into the prospect's hands. If he has practically agreed to buy he is not likely to back away from signing.

Here are some practical suggestions about using the order blank:

(*a*) If you use an order blank, bring it out early—and bring out only one. It often pays to have terms or conditions printed on it. If you do, you can hand it to the prospect even before you expect him to sign it and ask him to read something printed on it.

Some vacuum-cleaner salesmen use a novel plan to get the order blank into the hands of the prospect: After they have demonstrated the cleaner, they empty dirt on an order blank. They then ask the prospect to hold the order blank and to pour the dirt into an envelope, which the salesman holds. By this method the prospect is left holding the order blank! (I'm not recommending it—I'm just telling you about it.)

(*b*) Once you have the order blank out in front of you, *leave it out*—so that the prospect will get used to seeing it. Ditto your fountain pen—maybe you can use it as a pointer.

(*c*) Write something on the order blank before you hand it to your customer—your own name or the prospect's address. If you have done this, the prospect is, perhaps, more likely to sign.

Don't say, "Sign here." Men have for years built up a resistance to "signing here." Instead say, as security salesmen

and insurance salesmen do, "Please put your name here just
as you wish it to appear on the ... [certificate or policy]." Or
"Please write your name here as I have written it above," or
"Please sign your name as you usually do."

Other possible ways of asking for the signature are, "Just
your name and address, please," or "Now, if you will just
initial this, please."

(*d*) While the prospect is signing, *you talk*. Don't say anything important—but don't sit in total silence. Talk steadily
about the advantages of your product or service—so your prospect will not have time to think up any new reason for not
buying. (This rule is important.)

"How do you ask for the money?"

Rule 12: Maybe you have to get the check with the order.
Literally hundreds of salesmen have asked me, "How do you
ask for the money?"

The best way I know to ask for the money is to *ask for it*.
At this late stage in the sale, why hesitate? You might say, as
we did in the securities business, "Give me your check now
and I'll attach it to the order and see that it goes through
promptly." Or you could say, "I'll fill out the order while you
write your check." Or, "Please make the check out to the company. The amount is. ..."

Rule 13: Make it harder for your prospect to refuse to buy
than it is to go ahead and buy.

Bob Bale and I were once the victims of this closing technique. We were trying out a new sales school in a little town
in Arkansas—Osceola, perhaps—I've forgotten. Anyway, this
town had only two restaurants. The first morning we were in
Osceola, we ate at one of them. This café did not serve fresh
fruit. So the next morning we tried the other one. It did. We
went back to the first restaurant for lunch the second day.

When the only waitress in the first restaurant (who was

probably part owner as well) came for our lunch order, she asked accusingly, "Why weren't you here for breakfast?"

We explained that we liked grapefruit for breakfast and that we could get them at the other place.

The waitress said not a word, but walked to the telephone, called the grocer, and said, "Please send us a half-dozen grapefruit."

We ate the rest of our breakfasts at her restaurant! She had made it hard for us to refuse.

Usually, as in the above case, the principle involved is to do something which, unless the prospect stops you, amounts to a tacit agreement to buy. For example, the salesman pulls out his order blank and says, "You'll want delivery of one gross next week and another about December 1." It isn't a question —it is a statement. As he speaks, he writes this down on his order blank. He doesn't stop, he doesn't look up. He just fills out the rest of the order blank. As the salesman talks, the prospect knows that he must stop the salesman or else he has ordered the two gross. If the prospect does stop him, the salesman is no worse off; if the prospect does not, the salesman has the order.

Roth calls this "the physical-action technique." He says, in brief, that you should do something, like filling out an order blank—something that the customer must either stop you from doing or else leave himself in a position where he has almost a moral obligation to sign.

High pressure in Kansas

Miss Zelda Gordon of Augusta, Kansas, who acted as a temporary secretary for me in Oklahoma City while this book was being revised for the third time, told me this story:

A magazine salesman approached me one day with a deal for three monthly magazines. He pulled out a contract and asked my name and address. When I told him, he filled out the contract.

Before I knew what it was all about or had said that I would accept the offer, he handed the contract over to me to sign. Because I did not know anything about contracts and because I did not know for sure that I could refuse to sign a contract after it was made out, I signed it. The salesman made me feel that, since I had let him fill out one of his contract blanks, I had to sign it.

This, of course, was high-pressure and objectionable—in fact, almost dishonest.

Watch out, if you use any of the suggested methods, that you don't go over the line that separates legitimate selling from high pressure.

Rule 14: Get the order—then get out!

As soon as you have completed the sale, thank the buyer, say something good about the product, congratulate him on his good judgment, predict that he will be pleased with his purchase—then *get out.*

After a prospect has agreed to buy, a reaction almost always sets in. He asks himself, "I wonder if I have made a mistake?"

"Aren't you the fellow who sold me this car a few weeks ago?" inquired a man who stopped at a used-car lot.

"I sure am," smiled the salesman.

"Well, tell me about it again," said the buyer. "I get so discouraged."   —NEAL O'HARA, MCNAUGHT SYNDICATE

Don't be around when the prospect "gets discouraged" or you may get an on-the-spot cancellation. Usually this reaction soon passes—but don't you be around at the exact moment when it grips the buyer.

CHAPTER 45

A sum-up of the closing rules

Cultivate deafness—when the prospect is saying "no."

Now, to sum up: which of the rules for closing are vitally important?

These:

1. Expect to close. If you don't expect to close, you won't close very often. (Virgil once said something like this: "They are able to close because they think they are able to close." Those were not his exact words, of course, but are what he might have said if he had been a sales trainer.)

2. Use trial closes all the way through your talk and watch for buying signals. Then you will be sure to start closing in time.

3. Close by comparing the ideas opposed to buying with the ideas in favor of buying. The prospect will do it anyway —you can do it better.

4. Ask for the order on a minor point or an alternative proposal. Don't ask the prospect whether or not he is going to buy. Assume that of course he is going to buy and ask him if he wants the green or the brown, if he wants it delivered today or next week.

5. Always save one strong point for the final push at the end.

6. Don't quit until the prospect has said *no* at least seven times—or has thrown you out!

7. If you are knocked down, pop up.

Do you float or sink? Are you buoyant or waterlogged? When you are knocked underwater by an objection or a refusal, do you bob up as a cork bobs up when it is pushed underwater? You should!

8. Ask for the order immediately after you answer a serious objection—it is a favorable time to get a yes.

9. When you have made the sale—get out fast!

        *   *   *

I don't care how experienced and successful you are; I'll bet ten thousand to one that you don't use all of these closing rules.

Don't just read these rules—act on them.

Pick out just one closing method suggested here that seems to fit into your selling and try it for a week. If it works, keep on using it until you do so automatically.

Then try another one—and another. When you do this, you will be astonished at the increase in your effectiveness in closing.

§ELEVEN

You may never learn
to welcome objections
but you can learn
not to fear them

--- CHAPTER 46

How to answer objections

> *A man who will not kick on price is not very much in-*
> *terested in your proposition.* —JOSEPH E. ROGERS

When the average man thinks seriously about buying some
article or service that costs real money, he thinks at once also
of reasons for not buying it. This is true even if he has the
desire to buy and has practically made up his mind to buy.

To understand objections and why they are raised, just look
at yourself: Suppose you have been getting along with a slightly
battered Chevrolet, and suppose your earnings are good and
you have the money to buy a better car. Then suppose a Buick
salesman calls, demonstrates his car, and starts his sales talk.

Your mind is seething. You say to yourself, "Shucks, I don't
need a new car. I'm getting along all right with the old one.
It's foolish to spend this money right now—I might need it
sometime. . . . On the other hand, my car is getting pretty
old. It may not be safe. . . .

"Then again, why should I buy a Buick? The Chrysler looks
pretty good to me . . . Of course, I like to stick along with

213

General Motors ... still, Chrysler has a mighty live organization ... Then there's the Mercury. ... I wonder what my
wife will think about my buying a car? She's not so hot for
spending money. ..."

With such thoughts seething in your mind, naturally you
raise objections to whatever the salesman is trying to sell you
—you try to put off making the decision, even though you
really want to buy.

If you are willing to admit that most objections are the result of indecision on the part of the prospect you are ready to
think about the kinds of objections and how to overcome
them.

The same words may have different meanings

Objections fall into four general classes, as follows:

1. *The trivial objection* which is normally a remark thrown
in just to make conversation.

(For example, "I'm too busy." "I don't really need it." Or,
"I think they'll be cheaper next year.")

2. *A half-baked objection*—something the prospect read or
heard somewhere and does not fully understand—something
brought up largely to impress the salesman that the prospect
is a pretty smart buyer.

Selling Magazine says: "In a good many of your sales calls,
there is an even chance that your prospect doesn't believe a
single thing he says against your proposition. He simply has
elected to match his wits with yours, and he doesn't care who
wins, so long as a good scrap is enjoyed by all."

An excellent example of this type of objection was the experience of Eugene Stevens, president of the Continental Illinois
Bank of Chicago, who in his early days sold bonds in Minne-
apolis.

One day he was trying to sell bonds to an extremely rich
and influential prospect but was finding the going heavy.

The prospect raised one half-baked objection after another.

Mr. Stevens says of the interview, "I saw I was not getting anywhere with him. So, suddenly I leaned forward across his desk and said, 'You know yourself these objections are of no importance. They do not in any way affect the value of these securities.'

"A smile broke on the prospect's face. 'You're right,' he said. From that moment on it was easy sailing," concluded Mr. Stevens, "and I made an important sale."

The prospect admitted afterward that his real objection was that he thought Mr. Stevens didn't know bonds.

3. *The genuine objection*—something that the prospect considers as a valid reason for not buying.

Are sincere objections unavoidable? Some of them are. However, you can lessen their number. How? (*a*) By telling the complete story; (*b*) by being sure that your story has been told clearly, and (*c*) if desirable, by answering objections before they are raised.

4. *An objection which is an indication of indecision on the part of your prospect.* If the prospect finds it hard to make the decision—if, as in many cases, he is actually *afraid* to make the decision—he does something easy: He raises an objection.

What is your prospect thinking?

Here is a good general rule for handling objections: *Try to understand what is going on in your prospect's mind.*

If you can make a good guess as to what he is thinking and why he is thinking it, you are in a better position to answer objections and to close the sale. And the way to know what he is thinking is to ask a lot of questions—and then listen to the answers.

Once, when I was making sales calls with a securities salesman, we called on a man we both knew. The salesman made a sales talk. When the salesman had finished his pitch, the prospect said, "I have no money."

The salesman fortunately was paying more attention to

what the prospect was *thinking* than to what he was *saying,* so he answered, "How would it be, Mr. Blank, if I came to your house tonight and sold your wife on this stock?"

The prospect agreed and the sale was made that night—after the wife was sold.

The prospect wanted to buy but wanted his wife's approval —and he was ashamed to admit it. If the salesman had not guessed what was going on in the prospect's mind, he would probably not have made the sale.

Objections will not terrify you when you recognize that many of them are the result of mental uncertainty.

As D. R. Freeman, once director of sales training for Henry L. Doherty and Company, used to put it: "Objections are as much a part of the selling process as hurdles are part of a hurdle race. When you go into a hurdle race you expect to jump hurdles; when you attempt to make a sale you expect to answer objections."

To the experienced salesman objections are ... well, not exactly *welcome* ... maybe it would be fairer to say they are regarded as a *necessary evil.* When you get one, it is no fun; when you don't, there is no sale.

It is as though you had, by accident, taken poison! The emetic you take is no treat, but it's a lot better than letting the poison finish its job!

Objections indicate interest on the part of the prospect. Who ever heard of an interested prospect who didn't put up some resistance?

To the happy salesman, who regards selling as a game, objections add spice and excitement to the contest with the prospect. Just as golf without traps would be monotonous, so, to this type of salesman, selling without objections would be dull.

No matter how much you fear objections, you should fear still more the man who does not offer any objections—who "yes-yesses" you all the way through your sales talk. You know he is doing it to avoid unpleasantness. He will, at the end of your talk, almost invariably turn you down, pleasantly but firmly. If he does not think of any objections, he is probably not seriously thinking of your offer at all.

As Kin Hubbard stated it, "The chronic grumbler is a church social compared to the feller that agrees with everything you say!"

A tip: if a prospect starts "yes-yessing" you, stop right in the middle of your pitch and ask, "Mr. Blank, why have you decided against buying?" This question may startle him into telling you his real objection to buying. And, depend upon it, *he has one*—maybe *several!*

Note another encouraging point: an objection is often an indirect request for information. When a prospect says, "I don't believe I could ever learn to use a dictating machine," he may really be asking, "Do you think I could learn to use a dictating machine?"

Therefore—to sum it up—treat most objections not as invitations to argue, but (1) as requests for more information, or (2) as evidences of indecision.

What you must know to answer objections

To answer objections effectively you must:

1. Know how to get in the right mental attitude toward both the objection and the objector.

2. Know *why* prospects raise objections.

3. Know *the various kinds of objections*, since different sorts of objections must be answered in different ways.

4. Know *when* to answer them.

5. Know *how* to answer them—what to say.

Some you can answer—some you can't

Objections may be broadly classified as follows:

I. Hopeless objections—those that *cannot*, as a matter of practical selling, be answered.

II. Objections that can be satisfactorily answered.
Let's first consider the unanswerable objection.

It's a hopeless objection if the intended victim of an automobile salesman says, "Well, I'll tell you, I'm still paying installments on the car I swapped for the car I traded in as part payment on the car I am two payments behind on now!" Such an objection is, for the moment at least, unanswerable.

Another example of a hopeless objection that really was hopeless—for the moment—was given me by Tom Brooks in Charlotte, North Carolina, in April, 1955. He said, "I gave my pitch to a buyer here in Charlotte. When I had finished he said, 'I'm not interested,' and walked into the next room and locked the door."

Another example of an objection which is unanswerable I clipped somewhere. It was a Westerner talking about New York. "New York," he said, "is some town, all right. Cars scootin' like lightnin' overhead, dash-burned long trains a-divin' underground, buildin's so blamed high you can't see the top of 'em. It'll never be a success, though—too fur away."

The answerable objections, which make up the great body of all objections, can be divided into two general classes:

A. Objections that *are not* stated.

B. Objections that *are* stated.

Objections that are not stated. One of the most difficult situations in selling arises when a prospect has in his mind an objection which he considers valid but which he will not express. Possibly he is a bit ashamed of it.

Often he masks his real objection by using a "put-off," such as, "I want to think it over." Since you cannot answer objections until you know what they are, your one hope is to smoke 'em out.

How to smoke out objections

Here are some suggestions for getting prospects to state their objections:

1. Give the prospect a chance to talk and to state his objections.

2. Ask questions designed to bring the objection out into the open. Ask your prospect, "Why don't you want to buy?" This question may be asked either in the middle of the sales talk or near the end of it.

If at the end of your talk the prospect declines to buy, it often pays to say, "Something is holding you back, Mr. Prospect. Please tell me the real reason why you are not willing to buy now."

The experienced salesman ought often to be able to guess what the prospect is thinking when he brings up an objection. The inexperienced salesman need not feel, however, that he must be a mind reader to handle objections successfully. Fortunately, in most cases, if you answer an objection according to rule, you will soon learn the prospect's state of mind and will know how to proceed. Of course, if you do not learn you just keep going anyway.

Objections that are stated. The most common form of objection is the objection that the prospect voluntarily states. The methods we recommend for answering normal objections will be given in a later chapter.

Beware the prejudiced objection

Prejudice: weighing the facts with your thumb on the scale.   —IVERN BOYETT

One of the most difficult problems a salesman can face is to answer an objection which arises from *prejudice.* A prejudice, according to *Webster,* is "an opinion adverse to anything that *is not based on just grounds.*" Frequently a prejudice does not seem to be based on any grounds! As the Duchess de Abrantes stated it, "Prejudice squints when it looks and lies when it talks."

Liberty Hyde Bailey said, "I once asked a farmer why he

didn't blast out a certain rock. His answer was, 'I'm not going to because it's always been there,' " which was surely an adverse opinion not based on good grounds. Salesmen frequently meet objections based on prejudices no more valid than that one.

How to handle prejudiced prospects

A prejudice can be handled in only one way. The trouble is, nobody knows what it is.

Prospects are full of prejudices—and from these prejudices objections often grow. Such objections as "I never buy stocks that are not listed" or "I hate dictating machines" are often adverse opinions based on insufficient or incorrect evidence. Usually they are vastly harder to handle than objections based on sound reasoning. Most prejudiced prospects would rather keep on believing what they believe than to believe what is true.

H. K. Nixon says, in his *Principles of Selling*, "You cannot smash a prejudice. You cannot overcome it by sneers or jeers or pitying smiles." That tells you how you can't do it. Now for some rules for handling prejudices:

1. Treat a prejudice with respect. Show the prospect that you understand how he arrived at his opinion—even if you don't agree with him. Make him feel that you are sympathetic.

Remember, a prospect's beliefs are vastly important to him —important out of all proportion to their value. Men will rarely fight over facts, but often over prejudices.

2. Do not try to overcome a prejudice by argument. The prospect didn't arrive at his prejudice by reasoning—he will not give it up as a result of reasoning.

"Reasoning against a prejudice," said Charles Mildmay, "is like fighting a shadow; it exhausts the reasoner, without visibly affecting the prejudice."

3. The best way to overcome a prejudice is to suggest tactfully and indirectly that the prejudice is inconsistent with something else that the prospect believes.

An excellent example of meeting an objection based on prejudice by pointing out the inconsistency of the prospect's position was given in *Printers' Ink* in an article by Herbert L. Stephen.

The objection was given to Joseph Luchs when he was a salesman for the Philadelphia *Inquirer*. The prospect, a retail druggist, said the reason he didn't advertise in the *Inquirer* was because he didn't like its politics (independent-Republican).

Mr. Luchs met this prejudiced objection by saying:

I sincerely appreciate your frankness, and I understand your attitude. However, it is obvious that you don't have anyone at the front door of your store checking the politics of the customers before you let them in.

You appear to have no objection to selling your merchandise to people with whose politics you don't agree. There are 175,000 independent-Republicans who might like to buy your cut-rate drugs, but who don't have a chance to see worthwhile weekly offerings in your newspaper advertisements.

Mr. Luchs showed the druggist that his attitude in not using an independent-Republican paper was inconsistent with his practice of selling goods to independent-Republican voters.

He got the order!

─────────────────────────────────── CHAPTER 47

It is helpful to know
when to answer objections

The best time to tackle a growing problem is before it grows up. —RAY FREEMAN

One question that faces the salesman when an objection is raised is, "*When* shall I answer it?"

You can answer an objection: (*a*) before it is raised; (*b*) when it is raised; (*c*) later, or (*d*) never.

(*a*) *Answering objections before they are expressed.* Occasionally it pays to answer an objection *before* it is brought up.

The only time you should answer an objection in advance is when you feel reasonably certain that it will be raised.

Mrs. E. K. Pollard, president of Southern Institute in Birmingham, Alabama, gave me this example of successfully answering an objection before it was raised:

When the late Senator Oscar W. Underwood of Alabama purchased a Virginia estate across the Potomac River from Washington, D.C., I sold his town house to the Washington College of Law.

I knew the location of the Underwood property was desirable for a law school. The building was substantial and the price was reasonable. But undoubtedly my prospect would object to the floor plan. With our architect, I studied their present quarters and then the Underwood property. The architect made a sketch to scale showing the Underwood house as it would appear when remodeled—from reception room and business office to the last classroom. I presented the drawing to the president of the college and to its founder, Mrs. Ellen Spencer Mussey. That was it!

Without the drawing and the authority of the architect on structural changes to meet the objections before they were expressed, I never could have closed the sale, which actually was one of the easiest I ever made.

I learned the rule, "Answer unavoidable objections in advance," not out of a book but out of experience.

I was trying to sell the preferred stock of a power and light company. On one of the first sales calls I made, the prospect let me flounder through my entire pitch. Then he said, "What's the price of this stock?" "One hundred and seven dollars and fifty cents," I told him.

"You forgot to tell me," said the prospect with a bit of a sneer, "that I can buy it for considerably less from Portland brokers."

"Forgot!" I didn't even *know* it then!

I learned it fast enough. Just about everybody I called on mentioned it. Our other salesmen were always meeting the same objection.

For a while, in our ignorance, we didn't know how to overcome the objection. One salesman, for example, was calling on a lady who lived just outside Portland to sell her this preferred stock. After he had finished his presentation, the lady said, "Please tell me why you charge $107.50 per share for your stock when I can buy it in Portland for less than a hundred?"

"Well, madam," said the salesman, "it's this way: the stock we sell is new stock; the stock the Portland brokers sell is *used* or *secondhand* stock!"

That wasn't the right answer. It showed too much imagination—so we fired him.

The rest of us soon learned that since we were almost certain to have that objection shoved at us, we were better off to answer it in advance. As a result, before the prospect had a chance to ask about price, we would explain that if he needed to get his money out of the stock, we would resell it for him for at least $105 a share. The Portland brokers would not make any such guarantee. Our resale service justified the price differential and answered the objection.

We followed that practice successfully for five years and sold a lot of preferred stock—so we know it works.

The practice of answering an objection before it is raised gives sincerity to your talk—it shows the prospect that you are willing to give consideration to the bad points as well as the good points of your product.

A rather extreme case of answering objections before they are raised was given by R. A. Stevens in the house organ *The Howe Salesman* as follows:

Not so long ago a wholesale flour company put a new salesman in a territory where he had a few mediocre accounts and a big list of tough prospects.

After several weeks of almost complete failure the salesman reached a thriving small city where his company hadn't sold a barrel of flour in more than thirty years. The first store he entered, he burst out with:

"Look here, I know you haven't any wish to talk to a flour salesman. After all you don't make enough out of flour to pay for handling it. You'd be better off if you didn't have to carry a stock and could keep your investment down."

The grocer stared at him with open mouth.

The salesman went on:

"But you do have to carry a certain stock; so you should get a profit from selling flour in some other way."

Then he explained a display plan built around his flour, which would help the grocer sell more butter, eggs, table syrup, and baking powder.

The salesman walked out of that store with an order.

If you state an objection which you feel sure the prospect will raise, the prospect does not feel that he must defend it. If the prospect brings it up, he feels that it is his personal objection and that he must fight for it.

Just because you feel it advisable to answer an objection in advance, you do not necessarily state it in the form of an objection. That is, you do *not* say, "Now, Mr. Jones, of course you are going to say, 'I don't like XYZ Common Stock because it is not listed.'" Instead of stating it as an objection, you turn it around into an advantage. You could say, for instance, "One point you will like about XYZ Common Stock, I feel sure, is that it is not listed. You know why some of the largest banks in New York once took their stocks off the Big Board. . . ."

Elma Easley wrote in *The Insurance Salesman* this good example of answering an objection before it was raised:

After I have finished talking with my prospect about his insurance program, I feel he will raise the stock objection, "I just can't afford it at the present time." So I take the initiative by saying, "If you are like most people, Mr. Jones, meeting the premiums on this policy won't be easy, it will entail a real sacrifice on your part. There really isn't much left over at the end of the month, is there?"

At this point he thinks I am very understanding and that he is probably pretty safe. He knows that I know it wouldn't be easy for him to pay the premium on the policy; so we are in agreement on that great big objection.

However, when we have talked for a little while about the roughness of his present financial situation, I say, "Well, at least you do have a steady income now, and unless we can start this plan, that is more than you will have when you are older." Then I go back into my talk.

Now for the normal time to answer objections:

(*b*) *Answering objections as soon as they are stated.* The best time to answer objections, as a rule, is as soon as they are stated. How they should be answered will be treated later.

(*c*) *The answering of some objections should be postponed.* Under certain circumstances it is advisable to put off answering objections. Instead of taking them up as they are given, you say, perhaps, "I shall come to that in a minute."

Listed below are some of the circumstances in which it is advisable to postpone the answer to an objection:

1. If the objection is immaterial.

2. When the answer will be so long and involved that it will interfere with the orderly progress of your sales talk.

3. A third reason for postponing an answer is that you are not equipped with the facts necessary to make a truthful and convincing answer. In that case, the answer has to be postponed until you get the facts.

Salesmen should never guess at answers to objections. If you do not know the answer, admit it frankly and state that you will, at some later time, supply the prospect with the true and authentic facts. Then be sure that you do supply them.

(*d*) *Some objections should never be answered.* The objections which should not be answered at all are (1) the unanswerable objection, such as "Oil royalties are not a perma-

nent investment," and (2) the petty, trival, unimportant objection, such as "Dictating machines get out of order." If you
can't answer it or if it is not worth answering, why bother!
Either pass along and forget it or wave it aside as unworthy of
notice.

George Biggs gave, in *Printers' Ink*, an excellent example of
the good results of ignoring objections:

I was calling with a salesman who had been on the job only a
few weeks. After two calls we visited a dealer who had the reputation of being hard to sell. This dealer started telling us what was
wrong with our line. He gave objections 4, 16, and 22 in almost the
exact words we have them in the sales manual.

To my surprise the salesman virtually ignored the objections. He
fished in his pocket and brought up an order blank. "Yes," he re-
marked casually, "I knew that was the way you felt about it. You
told me when I was here three weeks ago. I have been thinking
over what you said and I believe you could start out with an initial
stock about like this and make some money."

With that he handed over the order blank on which a suggested
order had been written. The dealer signed it!

My friend W. A. Gayle, Jr., of Montgomery, Alabama, told
me, "I have a standard way of answering ridiculous objections.
For example, today I was talking to a wealthy man about en-
rolling in a $125 sales course.

"He said, 'I can't afford it.'

"I looked at him, smiled, and said, 'It sure is a pretty day
outside,' and then I went right back into my sales talk.

"He smiled and said no more about his poverty-stricken
condition!"

CHAPTER **48**

Five ways to answer objections

The salesman who expects to sell without meeting objections is the same one who expects to live without meeting trouble.

You have your choice of five standard ways of answering objections. Those in common use by professional salesmen are:

1. Turn the objection around into a reason for buying. I have heard one sales manager repeatedly issue this challenge: "No matter what the objection is, I can start my answer by saying, 'Why, Mr. Blank, that is the very reason you should buy.'"

Every salesman should perfect himself in this particular technique of answering objections. It is not just a showy stunt; it is based on sound common sense.

This policy was taught, many years ago, to National Cash Register salesmen. The N.C.R. theory was that, when a man states his objection, he reveals his principal reason for not buying. If the salesman can turn that objection into a reason for buying, he will have an excellent chance to get the sale.

It happens again and again that the reason why the prospect has decided not to buy is actually the very reason why he should buy.

For example, the prospect for an automobile says, "I don't need a new car—I don't drive very much." The salesman can answer, "That's the very reason why you should buy a new car. You don't drive that old car because you aren't proud of it, because you are afraid it will break down. Now if you buy a new car...."

For another example, the prospect for a public-speaking course says, "I don't need a course—I am rarely called on to speak." The salesman replies, "That's the very reason you ought to take the course. You are rarely called on to speak because, as you admit, you don't make a good speech. After you take the course and become a good speaker, you will be called on more often."

This method of turning the objection around into a reason for buying is an effective way to answer objections. We recommend that you try it—but only once or twice in any one sales talk.

2. Let the prospect answer his own objection. Often the salesman can get the prospect to answer his own objection or to admit that it is not a valid objection. This method should be used when the prospect raises an objection on a subject he obviously knows little about.

To let the prospect answer his own objection you just let the objector talk. Perhaps this is all he wants to do anyway. As some philosopher put it, "Many a man would rather you heard his story than granted his request." So ask your prospect questions about his objections and let him talk. Maybe he will answer his own argument. In any event, he will lower his steam pressure and cool off.

You may say, for example, "I am interested in this point, Mr. Blank. I wish you would explain it to me more fully." You may merely ask him, "Why do you believe this?"

If, as so often happens, the objection is not a valid one and the prospect has at best only a half-baked idea of what he is talking about, he will usually flounder around a while and end by admitting that the matter is of no importance.

"The best way of answering a bad argument," said Sydney Smith, "is to let it go on."

To let a man answer his own objection takes a lot of patience and a lot of questions, but it is a method that really works.

Ronald W. Forsythe, 29 Canaan Avenue, Kentville, Nova Scotia, Canada, who represents the Imperial Life Assurance

Company of Canada, sent me this example of how he allowed
a prospect to answer his own objection:

Back in 1951, I went to see a life insurance prospect, Roy A.
Shepard, and presented the insurance plan which I thought best
suited his needs. When I said good night, Mr. Shepard said to me
rather flatly, "I do not need more life insurance."

Two nights later, my wife, Verna, and I called on Mr. Shepard
on other business. We arrived at his house about 7:30 P.M. At
eight o'clock we had finished our business. We discussed the
weather and everything else we could think of. I suggested a game
of cards—but they did not play cards!

Finally I said to him, "Why do you not need more life insurance?" Frankly, at that time I had not even heard of the "why"
technique. I just stumbled on it that night by accident.

So Mr. Shepard set out to answer that question. Between eight
o'clock and eleven Mr. Shepard answered my question—fully. At
eleven o'clock he began to talk about what life insurance *might* do
for him and soon was talking himself out of his objection. Then I
woke up.

At twelve o'clock I handed him the application, which he signed.

That was the longest sales talk I ever gave without saying a word.

What did I learn from that experience? To ask "Why?"—then
wait for the answer if it takes all night!

A great man invented this method
of answering objections

This method of establishing the truth by asking questions
is not new. Socrates invented it a few hundred years before the
birth of Christ. It still works well today.

For example, suppose I was talking to a prospect who might
buy a hundred copies of this book to supply his salesmen. The
conversation might go as follows:

Prospect: I wouldn't give this book to my salesmen.

Whiting: Why?

Prospect: Because I don't believe in your teaching that a

salesman should state not only the reasons for buying but also the reasons for *not buying.*

Whiting: Why?

Prospect: Because I don't want prospects thinking about reasons for not buying at the time I am leading up to the close.

Whiting: Why not?

Prospect: It would lessen our chances of closing successfully.

Whiting: Wouldn't he be thinking of these negative reasons anyway?

Prospect: Maybe not.

Whiting: Why wouldn't he?

I am not going to carry this to the conclusion. This method takes time—sometimes lots of it. However, when you have helped a prospect to talk himself out of an important objection, you can ask immediately for the order—and usually get it.

3. *The third way to answer objections is to explain them away.* You explain to the prospect the true situation—you give him the facts. You assume that he has not really raised an objection but that he has asked for information. For example, when the prospect says, "Your price is too high," just assume that he asked, "Why is your price higher than that of some of your competitors?" Then tell him why it is higher.

Sometimes you can answer objections with analogies

Sometimes the best way to answer an objection is by citing an analogous case.

Suppose, for example, a prospect said to a man who is selling subscriptions to a magazine, "I haven't time to read more magazines." The salesman could answer, "A few years ago, before you bought your first television set, you didn't dream that you could find time to spend an hour—or two—or three a day in front of it, did you? But when you began to get so much enjoyment out of it, you just made opportunities, didn't you? It's the same with this magazine. When you find how much information and enjoyment and stimulation you will get from it, you will easily find time to read it."

Be alert to discover ways of answering objections by citing analogous cases. They are effective.

Some objections can be laughed off

Another handy method of meeting objections is by telling an appropriate joke. This is useful when the objection is unimportant or when it is obviously a "put-off."

Thus, to a put-off like "Come around April 1 and perhaps I can do something then," a salesman might reply, "That reminds me of the excited would-be passenger who ran up to the information man in the station and said, 'Can I catch the five o'clock express for Jonesville?' The information man answered, 'That depends on how fast you can run. It started three minutes ago.' "

The salesman would then switch back to his sales talk and perhaps say, "We can't offer this item after the fifteenth, and therefore, if you are planning to buy. . . ."

When you answer an objection by telling a joke, bear in mind that (1) certain people are practically devoid of a sense of humor, (2) you may not be another Bob Hope, and (3) the prospect has probably heard it before.

Moral: Be cautious with humor in selling.

Try answering objections with examples

A still better way to answer an objection is with an example. Instead of saying, "You're mistaken," you say, "John Jones thought just what you think—let me tell you what he found out." Then tell him.

Be on the lookout for interesting examples you can use to answer objections.

Now for the fourth method of answering objections:

4. Admit it. Certain objections to buying cannot be overcome—because they are valid, true, and unanswerable. So admit them and drive on!

Don't waste time trying to convince the prospect that he is
wrong—especially if he isn't! If the prospect says, "I'm overstocked now"—and you know that is the truth—don't get into
an argument with him as to whether or not he *is* overstocked.
Instead say, for example, "I know how things are at this time
of year. However, I have a couple of items you will want to
look at because nobody else in this town is offering them and
they have proved to be fast sellers."

Nothing is perfect—not even your product—or, darn it,
even this book!

A U.S. government bond may be nearly 100 per cent safe,
but the yield is low. Some uranium companies hint at enor-
mous "dividends" but their stock may not be safe. People
who buy anything buy it almost always in spite of certain
valid objections.

If the objection is valid, the best course is to admit it—and
then point out how the objection is outweighed by the other
advantages of the article or service you are selling.

One advantage of admitting an objection is that it impresses
the prospect with your sincerity and fairness.

Here's an example as evidence that people buy things in
spite of the fact that they aren't perfect. Sidney Edlund says
that he was fired from his first job. He felt that his life was
ruined, that nobody would ever give him another job. The
next time he was interviewed about a job, naturally he was
asked, "Why did you leave your last job?"

Edlund shuddered. Here was the unanswerable objection
to hiring him. He met it head-on. He said, "I was fired for calling the boss a skunk."

"Was he a skunk?" asked the employer.

"Yes, he was."

"I believe you," said the employer, "and you can start work
Monday."

5. Deny the objection. To answer an objection by denying it is rarely good practice. A denial is justified, however:

(*a*) If the objection is obviously untrue. If a wealthy prospect says, "I have no money," you could smile and, without giving offense, say, "Of course, I don't believe that."

(*b*) If you feel reasonably sure that the objector does not mean, or only half means, the objection. For example, once when a life insurance salesman called on me I said, quite pleasantly, "Of course this life insurance game is pretty much of a racket." To which he replied, "Of course you don't mean that, Mr. Whiting." I didn't—and that settled it.

Always enter a denial if the prospect questions your own honesty or integrity or that of your company or any of its officers. In such a case you have no alternative but to deny it firmly, since a salesman cannot answer that sort of an objection with arguments, reasons, or talk. As Emerson said, "The louder he talked of his honor, the faster we counted our spoons."

A salesman can usually enter his denial without using physical violence and without losing his dignity or his courtesy.

Charles W. Mears, in his book *Salesmanship for the New Era*, recommends this course:

Let the salesman take a deep breath or two, look directly at the prospect, and say slowly and clearly, "I don't believe I quite understand what you say." That gives the prospect a chance to cool down and soften what he says.

If the prospect repeats the obnoxious statement, even then there are better ways of responding than to blurt out, "That's just a plain, malicious lie, and you know it, you human boll weevil."

If the salesman says, "Well, fortunately for me that doesn't happen to be the real story," or "I have some facts that do not altogether agree with what you say," he makes it clear to his prospect that he is not intimidated and is ready to proceed with his presentation.

Denial is sometimes necessary, even at the loss of a sale. Some salesmen have won respect with their trade by becoming known as men who couldn't be intimidated.

A good, safe technique in answering an insult is to ask politely but seriously, "Would you mind repeating that?" A lot of blustering prospects will back down when they hear that request.

_____ CHAPTER 49

Some general rules for answering objections

Good manners and soft words
have answered many objections.

Here are some useful rules for answering objections:

Rule 1: Smoke out all important objections. (I mentioned this point earlier but I bring it into this chapter too—it's that important!)

If you feel that the prospect has some reason for not buying that he hasn't stated, ask him what it is. Say, "What is the reason you are not willing to buy?"

Norman Krisbury of Scotch Plains, New Jersey, told me how he found and answered a prospect's main objection:

One day I was working on Earl Smith to sell him a house at 4 Tuttle Street, Greenbrook, New Jersey.

He said, "I like the house, but it needs to be painted." I sensed from what he said and the way he said it that that was the key objection. So I said, "Is that the only objection you have to this house?"

"Yes, it is," he admitted. "The expense and work involved in repainting it is more than I care to tackle."

I wrote a contract which provided that the house was to be painted at the seller's expense. Mr. Smith signed it.

Always be on the lookout for the prospect who must con-

sult wife or husband before making a decision. This is likely
to be a hidden resistance. People hate to admit that they
must consult their partners before they commit themselves to
spend anything more than a few dollars. For example:

My wife is the type who finds it hard to say no to door-to-door
salesmen, and it was after she had inescapably committed us to
one such unnecessary but major expense that we had our first
heated argument in two years of married bliss. Our tempers soon
cooled down, however, and I thought all was forgiven and forgotten until I returned from work the following day and found
this sign posted on our door:
      Salesmen: Beware of vicious husband!
                                    —WILLIAM D. JOHNSON

Rule 2: To answer objections successfully, get into the right
mental attitude—and stay in it. You are there to persuade the
prospect to buy something he needs—something that will
benefit him. You are there to render a service. If the prospect
raises a string of objections, he's not to blame—you are. He
raises objections, in all probability, because he does not know
the facts—you have failed to give them to him, clearly and
forcibly enough to erase objections from his mind.

If a purchasing agent raises an objection which is strong but
not valid, don't say to yourself, "He's a dumb purchasing
agent." Say instead, "I'm a dumb salesman or I would have
made him see that that objection is silly." Then jump back
into your pitch and convince him. Don't quarrel with him—
teach him.

F. W. Nichol, vice-president and general manager of the
International Business Machines Corporation, said, "Selling
is not conquest. It is cooperation. Businessmen do not want to
be fought. They want to be taught. People would rather buy
than be sold."

If you will always bear in mind that you are on a mission of
service, you will never become disturbed by an objection. If
you are obviously unsettled by an objection, your prospect is

likely to think, "Ah, I've caught him now." Immediately the prospect is on the offensive and the salesman on the defensive.

Rule 3: Never argue with a prospect.

Of the 2,461 recognized ways of losing a sale, arguing with the prospect stands near the top. Salesmen for a hundred years have been familiar with the venerable saying, "Win the argument and lose the sale"—yet they go on arguing. Don't *you* make that mistake.

Crack a joke and avoid an argument

Occasionally a timely joke will keep you out of an argument that might cost you a sale. Accompany it with a smile, use it on prospects with a sense of humor and it sometimes works miracles. For example:

When Calvin Coolidge was presiding over the Massachusetts Senate, two senators tangled in ill-tempered argument. One of them had been making a pompous, dreary speech which ran on interminably. A fellow lawmaker whispered to him, "Wind up your talk before your audience goes to sleep."

The orator wheeled furiously and grunted, "You go to hell."

The senator so advised turned red and stuffily marched up to Coolidge's bench.

"Did you hear what Senator Blank just said to me?" he demanded.

Calvin Coolidge saved the faces of both parties and turned an embarrassing situation into an amusing one. These were his words:

"Yes. But I've looked up the law and you don't have to go."

Rule 4: Restate your prospect's objection in your own words before you answer it. If an objection is worth answering at all, it is worth restating. This restatement tends to make your prospect feel important.

F. Alexander Magoun of the Massachusetts Institute of Technology said:

I have found in my work that it is a very good technique, when you disagree with another man, to listen to his statement and then to say to him, "Now, as I understand it, your position is so and so." And then you proceed to explain his position in your own words and do a better job at it than he can do. Then he knows you understand. Once he knows you understand, he is willing to listen to you. But up to that point, all he is trying to do is hit you over the head.

Then you say, "Well, now, I see that your position is so and so. Have you thought of this?" And then you can tell him your story and he will listen to you.

Agree with him about something

Rule 5: Find some point of agreement with your prospect before you start to answer an objection. This is just about the best-known way to "cushion" your answer and to render it unobjectionable.

This is one of the most important of all rules for answering objections. Therefore be sure to remember: in answering an objection *try to find some point of agreement with the prospect.*

Why? Well, consider the state of mind of the prospect. He believes he has discovered some good reason for not buying. He states that reason. Suppose you answer by saying, "Why, Mr. Blank, that's not so. You are crazy to think a thing like that." What happens? Mr. Blank's feelings are hurt. You are giving no consideration to a pet idea of his. At once he goes to the defense of his objection. And what happens then? You are launched into an argument—a dispute.

Soften it, brother, soften it!

Instead you say, for example, "I quite understand how you feel, Mr. Blank. I had the same feeling when this was first presented to me...," or, "I am glad you brought up that point, Mr. Blank." Look glad! You ought to—your prospect is interested.

The natural way, after you have agreed with the prospect about something, is to say "but" and then tear into your answer. Don't do it, my friend! Don't. The man who invented the "yes, but" technique of cushioning objections was neither a good psychologist nor a good salesman.

Many books on selling recommend the "yes, but" method— but not this one. That word *but* is loaded like an H-bomb. The word may not explode but the prospect will. Bulwer expressed it well when he said, "*But* is a word that cools many a warm impulse, stifles many a kindly thought, puts a dead stop to many a brotherly deed."

Why let your prospect hear that fighting word? A safer word than *but* is *and*.

Don't say, "Yes, the price is high, *but* it will outwear any other dingbat on the market." How much less likely you are to start a fight if you say, "Yes, it is high in price *and* it will outwear..."

Or, to take another example:

Prospect: "It costs a lot of money."

The **yes-but** method salesman: "Yes, *but* it makes you a lot of money."

The **yes-and** method salesman: "Yes—*and* it makes you a lot of money."

Don't skim over this idea. It is important. *Yes, but* leads right into an argument. *Yes, and* ... or *yes, period* leads right into a sale.

Often it is hard to use the word *and* in this connection because it does not make good sense. For example, if your prospect says, "The price is too high," it doesn't sound exactly logical to say, "Yes, the price is high and look at the quality." So you use the yes-pause method. After you have presented the "cushion" you pause, then start a new sentence.

For example, the prospect says, "The price is too high."

You reply, "I understand how you feel about price, Mr. Jones."
Then pause, smile, and say, "The quality is even higher than
the price, Mr. Jones." Then go on and justify the price.

Or suppose the prospect says, "My secretary doesn't like
dictating machines." You could answer, "I don't blame your
secretary for not wanting to lose practice on her shorthand."
Pause, smile, then resume, "Let me tell you how Mr. Jones
across the street met that situation."

Remember this "yes-pause" technique. It is effective.

Some useful "cushions" are:

(a) "Generally speaking, what you believe is sound and
right, and ..."

(b) "Because you are a reasonable man, I am sure you will
be interested when I tell you the facts. They are ..."

(c) "There's a lot to be said for your viewpoint and ..."

(d) "We differ in our views. Now, the question is, can we
get together? Let's look at the facts ..."

(e) "You are a fair man and have taken a fair attitude,
based on the facts at your disposal. Let's review all the facts
that bear on this. ..."

(f) "Let's think this matter through together."

Do you know why most salesmen, in answering an objection, say "yes, but," rather than "yes, and"? It's because it is
easier. The wrong way usually is. You can start with "yes, but"
and then trample all over the prospect. It's fun for the salesman but death to the prospect's pride—and the sale!

Suppose your prospect says, "It's complicated. I don't believe I could ever learn to use it." Then you say, "Yes, and ..."
Where do you go then? Well, you might say, "Yes, and I
know a lot of people who thought that. Let's look at the facts
and find the truth."

For another example, your prospect may say, "I don't believe in insurance" (or whatever it is you are selling). You can
weaken his position by saying, "Neither do I." Then pause before you go on with, "Unless you consider. ..."

This "Neither do I, unless ..." is an effective way to start answering an objection that starts off with "I don't believe." It tends to disarm the prospect.

Note that you have greatly lessened the danger of getting into an argument by agreeing with your prospect—on some immaterial point. His first feeling is that you are going to agree with him all the way through. By the time he finds out that you have merely agreed on some minor point, perhaps you have given him enough facts to swing him around to your point of view.

Mark Twain expressed this idea humorously when he said, "We like a man to come right out and say what he thinks—if we agree with him." Since you can't agree with him all the way, you do the best you can—you agree with him partway.

John Alford Stevenson says in his book *Constructive Salesmanship—Principles and Practice:* "You will find it a good plan to memorize a number of opening phrases for meeting objections which will serve to make your replies less blunt."

This is good advice.

Act as if it were a real objection—even if it isn't

Rule 6: Never treat a prospect's objection with contempt.

Maybe you find it hard to reconcile two such seemingly contradictory pieces of advice as, "Ignore trivial objections" and "Never treat a prospect's objection with contempt."

Before you decide which way to answer a trivial objection you have to guess how the prospect regards it.

If the prospect knows that the objection is trivial and immaterial, if he just threw it in to see what you would say— you can safely ignore it. If, on the other hand, the prospect thinks that it's a sound objection—even though it isn't—you will probably lose a sale if you sneer at it.

I remember, when we were selling preferred stock to Maine farmers, we occasionally traded them out of some other stock. To complete the deal we had to get them to sign a stock

power which contained the words "in these premises." To a
Maine farmer his "premises" meant his house and farm, his
property. The farmer's objection was that he wouldn't sign any
stock power that mentioned his "premises." It was a trivial and
silly objection. If, however, we had treated it with contempt
—if we had sneered at it (which it deserved)—we would
never have completed the deal. We found out because one
of our salesmen tried it!

I borrowed the good advice which follows from an Ad-
dressograph-Multigraph Corporation sales manual:

> If you shoot your answers back too fast it makes the buyer feel
> he is "up against" a clever salesman, and nobody likes to have
> business dealings with clever people. They much prefer people
> who are not so nimble-witted. Being slow-minded seems to fit in
> with the popular conception of honesty.

Don't waste too much time on objections

Rule 7: Answer briefly.

I have already told you not to treat your prospect's objection
with contempt. Now I tell you also not to treat it too seriously. Try to find a middle ground between too much and too
little. Use as few words as possible. Don't spin out answers.

Don't feel that you have to bury objections in graves 10 feet
deep. People don't buy because you have answered objections
but because they want what you are selling. Get back as
quickly as you can to talking about the prospect and his wants
and how your goods will supply these wants.

Rule 8: In answering an objection, don't wrangle.

The prospect states his objection. You answer it. If the
prospect then shows signs of entering into a lengthy disputa-
tion, it is generally best to say something to this effect: "I
thoroughly understand your point, Mr. Blank, and I appreciate your explaining your feelings to me. This point, of course,
is not an essential one." Then rapidly pick up the thread of
your sales talk and move along.

You hear people ask, "Who won the argument?" They might as well ask, "Who won the eruption of Vesuvius?" or "Who won the 1955 floods?"

The magazine *Supervision* gives this excellent advice about arguing: "When you are arguing with a fool, make certain that he is not similarly occupied."

Rule 9: Never appear to doubt that you have answered the objection completely.

After some salesmen have answered an objection at great length, they have the bad habit of saying, for example, "Now, Mr. Blank, have I made this point clear—do you agree with me that the machine is all right in this respect?"

Some sales experts recommend this course. I do not, however.

Why do I think that this is a bad practice?

First, because you are asking your prospect to admit that he is wrong—which is an idiotic thing for a salesman to do. Let your prospect save face.

Second, you don't want to give your prospect a chance to spin out the discussion of that point or to raise another objection. Try never to let a prospect pile one objection on another. Always try to sandwich in a bit of sales talk between objections!

Rule 10: Don't become sorry for your prospect! When that happens, you're not selling him; he's selling you!

Rule 11: Don't guess. A poor answer is usually worse than no answer. For example:

A man, much the worse for wear, was standing before the court. The judge eyed him menacingly. "You are accused by your landlord of being drunk and setting fire to the bed."

"It's a lie, Judge," cried the man indignantly. "That bed was on fire when I got in it!"   —ETHEL KENYON, *American Weekly*

Then there was the salesman who met the objection, "I don't want any more of your shrubs because every time I plant one I have a lot of dirt left over I have to get rid of." The salesman answered that objection with this stirring statement: "The way to solve this problem is to dig the holes a little deeper!"

I've heard salesmen come up with answers little better than these two!

Rule 12: Answer a lot of objections by asking "Why?" John Wilson, in *Open the Mind and Close the Sale*, says that *why* is the most important word in answering objections. He points out that whatever the objection is, the salesman can counter it with this one word. He gives ten common objections that can be answered that way, among them: "I think prices are coming down." ["Why?"] "I want to think it over." ["Why?"] "My business is different." ["Why?"]

Perhaps the greatest advantage of sprinkling *"whys"* through your sales talk is: that question forces the salesman to listen and the prospect to talk.

Rule 13: Develop standard answers for standard objections, as suggested earlier in this book.

I recommend writing and rewriting these answers until you have them in the most effective form. By that time you will have substantially committed them to memory.

Then, when a prospect pops an objection at you, you know exactly what to say, which saves lots of mental effort.

The *American Boy* tells of a young man who got a job selling milk chocolates to retailers during the depression. In one month of hard work this young man accumulated nothing but a complete assortment of reasons why storekeepers did not want to buy chocolates.

This young man, out of his month's accumulation of experience, evolved a campaign. He bought himself some plain white cards and got out his typewriter.

The next morning, when he called on a storekeeper, he spread thirty-six neatly typed cards on the storekeeper's desk.

"Here," the salesman said, "are thirty-six reasons why you don't want to buy milk chocolates. Pick any one you choose." The storekeeper grinned, selected one.

"Please turn it over," requested the salesman. The storekeeper did so.

On the reverse side of the card, briefly worded, was a convincing answer to the objection. The retailer read both sides of every card. Then he placed a good-sized order.

Philip F. Prince, director of merchandise training, Sears, Roebuck & Company, Chicago, told me that, in selling their encyclopedia, they used a "canned" opener and "canned" answers to objections. Their store salesmen of vacuum cleaners and sewing machines also are supplied with "canned" answers to common objections.

If an organization like Sears, Roebuck finds it desirable to supply its salesmen with standard answers to objections you may find that it will pay you to follow their example.

TWELVE

What to do—how to do it—
if you are turned down

CHAPTER 50

If you are turned down, what then?

"What do I do," you ask, "if I go all the way through my selling talk and then get a clear-cut and emphatic *no?*"

That's a good question, too!

You need not worry about the *noes* you get on your trial closes. You just disregard them. But now, at the end of the last step, your prospect says, "No, I don't want to buy."

What then?

POINT ONE: Don't quit. If you believe that your prospect will really benefit from using your product—and if you have carried him through the five steps of the selling process—you have a right to expect a successful close. So if you get a turndown it is probably a sign not that your prospect does not want your goods, but rather that you have failed in your sales talk.

So you go right on trying to sell him.

"You ought to feel highly honored, young man," said the big businessman to the life insurance agent. "Do you know that today I have refused to see seven insurance men?"

"I know," replied the agent. "I am them."

He refused to accept turndowns—so he ultimately got it!

Six noes in six days—but he got the order

One of the best examples of the miracles that can be worked after a series of turndowns was written by Robert A. Baker for

Printers' Ink. Mr. Baker quoted Ralph Mitchell of the Kelly-Smith Co., the hero of the incident, as follows:

Back in 1918 when I was learning the media business under Arthur Capper, I felt I deserved a raise. Capper's answer was that if I could bring in a sizable block of billing, space that in the normal course of events we wouldn't get, he might consider my request.

I picked out a large oil firm in Kansas City and I worked up an idea that I thought could add a lot of new outlets for this firm.

Monday morning I went out to their office. The manager greeted me cordially. I told him I had a plan for him to use the *Kansas Farmer.* He said thanks, but he wasn't interested. He wouldn't even let me describe my idea. He just said thanks, he wasn't interested.

Tuesday morning I went back again. The manager again greeted me cordially, but said, even more firmly this time, thanks, he wasn't interested.

Wednesday I went back again. The manager smiled, but I don't think he was amused. He still wouldn't let me tell him what I had in mind.

On Thursday he was neither cordial nor courteous. "Listen, son," he snapped, "I'm not interested—period."

On Friday morning even his secretary cringed when she saw me come in. When the manager came out, red in the face, he barked at me, "Heavens, man, how many times do I have to tell you *no* before you get the general idea?"

"But you won't let me tell you what my plan is or what it can do for you," I said. "You can't know what you're not interested in until at least you know what I'm talking about. I'll keep right on coming back until you let me give you just a five-minute outline of my suggestions."

"*Get out,*" he said, and I did.

On Saturday morning I really expected to be removed from the premises bodily, but when the manager saw me, he shook hands and said, "I'd have been darned disappointed if you hadn't come back. Now step into my office and tell me what in blazes this is that you think is so all-fired good."

I told him I'd give him the highlights in five minutes, and I did.

I stayed four hours, though, answering his questions, and after he had bought my idea, helping him figure out the details.

P.S. Mr. Mitchell got the raise!

So, as I said before, keep on selling until your prospect has said *no* at least seven times.

On the other hand, as my friend Bill Stover puts it, "Know when to lay off and do so promptly, abruptly, and dramatically. Then, when your prospect's guard is down, try once more, boldly and courageously."

POINT TWO: *Try to determine why your prospect has said no.* The chances are the product is not to blame—or the prospect. Why do people refuse to buy something they really lack and want and can afford? Often it is the result of indecision, perhaps even more often it is due to fear.

A husband's fear that his wife will not approve is often hard to combat. Once a retired, wealthy, and not overly bright man, who was married to a very determined woman, skidded to town over icy sidewalks and through the bitter cold of an Augusta, Maine, winter. He went to the local meat market, looked over the stock of meat, bought some pork, and departed. In half an hour he came back and threw the pork down on the counter with these words: "She don't like pork."

Naturally, the best way to find out why the prospect has turned you down is to *ask*. The question, "Why have you decided not to buy it, Mr. Blank?" is likely to elicit an answer that will help you to carry on.

POINT THREE: *Disarm your prospect.*

What do I mean by that?

I mean that your prospect has not only said *no*: but, at your request, has also probably told you *why* he has said *no*. If you started in to argue with him, you would meet with a man who has dug in and is prepared to resist forever. How can you get his mind off his refusal? How can you get him into a state of mind where he is willing to listen to some more sales talk?

Here are some effective plans:

Plan A: Pretend that you have given up. Get up, gather up your materials, pick up your hat, talk about the weather or some other harmless subject. Ask the way to your next prospect. Then suddenly, with your hand on the door, fire at your prospect some selling question or some selling point you have held in reserve for that moment. This is jokingly referred to as "the hat trick."

Plan B: Accuse yourself. Say, "I must be a poor salesman. I ought to go back to driving a garbage truck. If I weren't one of the worst salesmen in the world, I could make you see the value to you of this product," etc. Pile it on *thick.* Try to berate yourself so hard that your prospect will come to your rescue.

Then, without warning, go back into a summary of the advantages to the prospect of buying your product.

Get your prospect to help you

Plan C: Use the magic word, "Why?" With a big smile, ask him why you failed, how you could have gone about the talk so that it would have brought in the order, what you might do to improve your sales talk.

Be entirely sincere about this. If you are, your prospect may give you some good ideas. He may change his mind and buy— may actually sell himself.

If the prospect relaxes, attack!

All right, you have so handled the situation that your prospect has let down his fists, relaxed his hands, and is ready to listen again—*if you have something worth saying.*

Yes, but what?

Naturally, what you say will depend on the answer your prospect gave when you asked him why he was not willing to buy. If your prospect has given his real reason for not buying, then you know exactly what to say.

But suppose he refuses, or evades the point. Often this is a good time to ask some more questions. Check each point:

Interest: "Do you feel, Mr. Jones, that this machine really will save you $100 a year?"

Conviction: "Have I satisfied you that this machine will move *xy* cubic yards of earth a day?"

Desire: "Are you dissatisfied with the way your gas oven bakes?"

The answers to such questions are quite likely to tell you what to say next.

The Burroughs Adding Machine Company recommended these sentences for use on the hesitant prospect:

1. A thing worth having is worth having now.

2. The sooner you get it, the sooner it will start saving money for you.

3. Putting it off is like paying more for it. Decide now, when it will cost you least.

4. The facts are clearer now than they will be again. There is every reason why you should decide now.

If you habitually accept *noes* without a battle, you're no salesman—and have no business trying to sell.

§ THIRTEEN

Put habit to work for you.
It is the basis of learning to sell

—————————————————— CHAPTER 51

The secret of learning
how to sell more

*Salesmen acquire a particular selling skill by constantly
acting in a particular way.* —ARISTOTLE, 1956 EDITION

Most salesmen learn to sell by selling. They learn in the so-
called "school of experience"—the one school that doesn't
have any recesses. Nobody tells them the right way to sell.
Then, having started wrong, they practice these wrong ways
until they do them perfectly—wrong!

The salesmen who learn to sell by experience alone pay a
lifetime of misguided effort for what they could have learned
in this book. This volume was written in the belief that ordinary salesmen have extraordinary possibilities—if they will
acquire good selling habits.

The magic method of learning the good selling habits that
enable you to make more sales is presented in this chapter.
You should adopt this method of acquiring the best selling
techniques. Do it and you will drive ahead to become a better
salesman; ignore it and you will probably stay right where you
are now—if you don't slip back!

This method of acquiring good habits is not new. It was
invented before you and I were born—to be exact, 152 years
before *I* was born, which was a long time ago.

251

The man who discovered it was then the best salesman on the American continent. He was a job printer. His name was Franklin—Benjamin Franklin.

Franklin was, as you know, an inventor as well as a printer Most of the things he invented are obsolete now—things like the Franklin stove.

One of his inventions, however—the Franklin method of acquiring good habits—is still in use by smart salesmen. Nobody has improved on Franklin's basic principle in 227 years!

You can use it to become a better salesman—no matter how good a salesman you are now!

Franklin's method, briefly stated, is this:

He forced himself to use, on every possible occasion, one rule he wished to master, and he kept on using it consciously until he acquired the *habit* of using it *unconsciously*. Then he moved on to the next rule.

Please note these two points:

1. He worked on only *one* rule at a time.

2. He kept on using that one rule consciously until he used it automatically from habit.

Here's the formula for getting into the big league

This is the magic formula for becoming a better salesman. Here are the steps you must take:

1. First you list the rules or methods you know you must use to become a professional salesman—rules or methods you are not using now.

2. Next you select one rule to start on.

3. You start using this rule consciously.

4. You keep on using it consciously until you do it automatically from habit.

5. Then you move on to the next rule. You master it in the same way—you acquire the habit of using it correctly.

Directions for applying these rules will be found in the **next chapter.**

After a while you are a professional salesman because you have acquired professional habits—and you are making a lot more sales and a lot more money.

Acquire good selling habits—that's the secret of selling success. As Thomas B. Reed said, "For the ordinary business of life, an ounce of habit is worth a pound of intellect."

You learn good habits by practice

Dr. Henry C. Link, in his book *The Rediscovery of Man*, said:

Psychologists have found that personality consists of definite habits and skills. These habits and skills can be acquired in the same way that people acquired the habits of writing and reading, that is, by practice and training.

"Good selling" amounts to "good selling habits"—and that's what this chapter is about.

Mere practice is not enough—you must practice the right way. As T. E. Cochran said in the magazine *Your Life*:

"No, practice *alone* does not lead to perfection. It must be accompanied by attention, the desire to improve, and the knowledge of what is right and what is wrong."

So, when you are drilling yourself, pay close attention to what you are doing. Do it, as we have pointed out, *consciously.* Don't be like the small boy who, for saying "have went," was required to write, "I have gone" a hundred times on the blackboard after school. He did. The teacher was absent when he finished. When she returned, she found below the hundred "I-have-gones" which the boy had written, this touching message: "Dear Teacher—I have went. Johnny." Mere practice wasn't enough to cure Johnny.

Secondly, as Dr. Cochran pointed out, you must *want* to improve and, as the doctor didn't point out, you must be willing to work to get what you want.

Lastly, according to Dr. Cochran, you must know the right way to do it. And that's what I am trying to tell you in this book.

Make up your mind to follow this plan in learning to sell more—or give up the idea of ever becoming a professional salesman.

Skills are learned by practice—by salesmen—by all of us!

Don't expect that it will be easy at first to use new and better methods. The only easy progress is downhill! It takes concentration, determination, and a *willingness to risk making mistakes.*

Dale Carnegie gave me this example of how he acquired the habit of tipping his hat to ladies:

When I was about thirteen or fourteen, I lived on a farm in Nodaway County in northwestern Missouri. At that time I began to consider the matter of being polite. I couldn't make up my mind whether to be a gentleman or to be a tough and spit between my teeth.

I decided to go fifty-fifty on it.

I figured that gentlemen tipped their hats to ladies. So I made up my mind to do it at the first opportunity. Hat-tipping is hard, strange work for a thirteen-year-old country boy!

The first opportunity wasn't long in coming. I was cutting a hedge with a corn knife at the time, when, as I looked up, I saw a girl I knew coming down the road in a buggy. I was petrified with the thought of what I was going to do—tip my hat to her! The girl was so far away, and moving along at a horse-and-buggy rate—that it was nearly five minutes from the time I first saw her until she had dipped down one hill and come up another and reached where I stood.

By that time I was in such a panic that, when I reached for my hat to tip it like a gentleman, I missed the brim entirely and knocked it off on the ground.

Well, by constant practice for over fifty years, I have now reached a point where I don't knock it off on the ground oftener than once in ten times—which is a real improvement.

How do professional athletes learn the skills that make them champions?

Grover Cleveland Alexander, one of the greatest pitchers of all time, got pitching practice during his farm life. He threw balls, stones, pieces of brick, apples, anything he could find. He nailed a catcher's glove to a chicken coop and would throw at it until he could hit it nine times out of ten. No one knew better than he that back of his amazing pitching was the patient drudgery of pitching at that old catcher's mitt nailed to a chicken coop.

—REV. A. PURNELL BAILEY, *Grit*

Take golf—how did Walter Hagen become good enough to win two U.S. Open Championships, four British Opens, and five Professional Golf Association Championships? Walter explained it in these words: "Until a man has practiced so much that he does the right thing automatically, he can't win his traveling expenses at any game."

That certainly is true of the "game" of selling. First you learn good habits; then you earn good money!

You establish good habits by drill. This is no new discovery. Military leaders apparently knew it long before historians began to record battles and campaigns. It is still true today. Men learn to be soldiers by drill—as many millions of men in the United States will testify. It would be simpler to let draftees stay at home—and to send them a book! But men don't learn how to be soldiers solely by reading—they learn it by doing. And that's the way you learn to be a better salesman.

Your chief problem in learning to become a better salesman is how to force yourself to use the rules and methods you must use to become a professional—and to keep on using them enough times to establish the habit of using them.

In the next chapter I tell you how to do it.

CHAPTER 52

Acquiring good selling habits
is not easy work

We first make our habits and then our habits make us.
—Atlantic Log

It takes a salesman a long spell of hard trying to acquire right selling methods. Why?

Epictetus gave us the answer nearly 2,000 years ago, when he said, "In theory there is nothing to hinder our following what we have been taught; but in life there are many things to draw us aside." And surely, there are more alluring distractions today than there were in Epictetus' day.

I hope I have convinced you that the right way to learn to sell more is to work consciously on one good selling habit at a time until you do it automatically.

Okay, then let's consider exactly how to do it!

Rule 1: Pick the first rule you need to work on and start.

Rule 2: Work on this one rule until you can use it without thinking.

Put away your shotgun—use a rifle

Don't try to learn and put into use several rules at one time.

I don't care how smart you are—you can't do it efficiently. So use a rifle—not a shotgun.

For example, I once heard a student in a Dale Carnegie public-speaking class say this:

I was given a copy of *How to Win Friends and Influence People* at the opening session of a Dale Carnegie class. I finished it before I went to sleep. As a result of what I read in this book, I resolved

to lead a better life. When I woke up, I knew I meant to do something that day—but I had forgotten what.

The next day I had even forgotten that I meant to do anything
about anything.

A week later, I reread the book. Then I tried a new plan. I took
just one rule—and I took pains to remind myself continually that
I was working on that rule. I started off with "Don't criticize." I
worked one solid month on that rule, until it became a part of me
not to criticize. Does that seem a long time? Well, remember, I
had been criticizing for fifty years—so thirty days to learn how
not to criticize was relatively quick work.

Then I moved on to another rule. Then to another.

Like Ben Franklin, I never attained perfection, but I did
improve.

As I pointed out previously, a week is often long enough to
establish the habit of using a rule—sometimes it takes at least
a month.

Don't stop too soon. If you have to think to use it, you have
not established the habit.

Will Rogers once said that a man who wanted to learn to
speak in public should find an oak stump 2 feet high, and
should stand on it and start making practice speeches. Will
added, "When the stump is worn level with the ground, you
quit."

Rule 3: Commit to memory the words of the rule you are
going to master. Know those words so thoroughly that, if a
prospect started shooting at you with a sawed-off shotgun
(which prospects rarely do), you could, as you ran for cover,
recite the rule.

Rule 4: Keep a box score.

Check up on yourself every night. Give yourself an "error"
for every time you failed to use the rule when you should have
used it and for every time you used it incorrectly.

Ben Franklin had a tablet with a space ruled off for each
day of the month. As to the method of scoring, he wrote: "I
marked, by a little black spot, every fault I found upon exam-

ination to have committed respecting that virtue upon that day."

You should do the same.

Rule 5: Use the rule consciously. Think about it before you call. Plan it. Then pay close attention to what you are saying when you use it.

Rule 6: Use affirmation. (See Chapter 55.)

Rule 7: As soon as you have mastered one rule move on to the next rule.

Rule 8: Go through all the rules you want to learn to use. Then take the list and strike out any rules which you now use automatically. Then start back to review the rules you have not yet mastered.

Rule 9: Be patient.

Don't expect rapid progress in acquiring good selling habits. The only habits which you acquire rapidly are the bad ones.

*   *   *

Now you know how. So start, *start!*

Maybe you should start to improve yourself as a salesman with the rule for getting attention. Learn it, use it consciously day after day for a week at least. By that time it ought to be nearly as natural as walking or eating. Then try the rule for arousing interest—and so on through the book.

Don't wait to read the whole book before you start your course in self-improvement. Keep on reading the book but grab Rule 1 and start work on it tomorrow. Work on it a week at least. Then take Rule 2.

Remember, you can't dream yourself into good selling habits; you must hammer and forge them for yourself.

And remember, also, that the method of forming good selling habits which I have outlined here is the best, easiest, and quickest way to become a better salesman. Why use any other way!

The next rule is another one so important that it gets a whole chapter to itself.

—————————————————————————— CHAPTER **53**

Use the rule or miss the mark

*Spend one day trying to persuade one person (yourself,
for instance) to do one thing he knows he ought to do
to improve himself in any one way, and you'll discover
the root of humanity's ills.*

Now comes the hardest rule in the book to put into effect:

Rule 10: Force yourself to use, on every possible occasion
in your selling, the rule you are working on.

It is hard to get salesmen to observe any selling rule. Why?
Because we salesmen are human— all reports to the contrary
notwithstanding!

All too many of us just will not use the rules we learn. To
paraphrase Gilbert K. Chesterton, "Scientific selling, like
Christianity, has not been tried and found wanting; it has
been found difficult and not tried."

An ambitious salesman will do practically anything on earth
to become a better salesman except use the rules which will
make him a better salesman.

Anyone who has spent much of his life, as I have, trying to
teach salesmen how to sell more, is inclined to agree with the
professor of Antioch College who said, "Education is the
only commodity where the customer tries to get as little as he
can for his money."

I once heard a speaker at a sales meeting repeat the following ancient gag:

Book salesman: "This book will teach you how to be a better
salesman."

Another salesman: "What's the use? I'm not half as good a
salesman now as I know how to be."

The speaker told that as a joke. Yet not one of the salesmen laughed. Why should they? That purported joke was about as funny to those salesmen as the sound of earth falling on a newly lowered coffin!

Why? Because most salesmen know how they can increase sales and earnings—by forcing themselves to use the rules they already know, and don't use! They refuse to be as good salesmen as they know how to be.

Salesmen who will use the rules set forth in this book will inevitably increase their sales. By using these rules many salesmen will double their production. Yes, treble it! But can I persuade any salesman—*you* in particular—to use the rules of successful selling? I can only be hopeful—I can't be certain.

Considering that Christ and Moses and Mohammed and Buddha failed in their efforts to get all the people to do, all the time, what they knew they ought to do, I don't know why I should be hopeful of getting all salesmen to do all the time the things *they* know *they ought* to do.

Maybe I can persuade some salesmen to use part of the rules part of the time. For many of us this will be a real improvement.

When I was general retail sales manager of the Securities Department of Henry L. Doherty and Company (Cities Service Company), I noted one day that one of our salesmen had shown a tremendous increase in sales volume. He was selling more Cities Service preferred stock than any other salesman. This thing apparently had been going on for two or three months, so I investigated.

It proved that this salesman had discovered a new idea for selling the stock. When he explained it to me, I was impressed. It was good psychology; it was good selling; it was good ethics —and it sold the stock.

It happened that, at the time, we had a sales convention coming up. I made this new selling idea the keynote of the convention.

At the convention apparently all the salesmen accepted it. Many of them were wildly excited about it. Some of them could hardly wait to get back to their territories and try it out.

Immediately after the convention there was a sales bulge. Then production slipped back to normal. We asked our field managers to check around and see how many of our salesmen were using the new idea. The answer was, "Around 5 per cent."

The salesmen with whom we talked said that they still liked the idea. Further questions brought out the admission that they thought it was good, and that it worked well for them. When we asked them why they were not using it they said that somehow or other they had slipped back into the old rut.

If a man were told by his employer to cut down a tree and if the employer supplied him with a helper, a saw, and an ax, and if then the man insisted on whittling down the tree with a pocket knife, you would feel that he ought to visit a psychiatrist and have something done about it.

Yet lots of salesmen, when they are given new methods which they know will work, insist on whittling away with old, inferior methods.

They disregard Philip Armour's wise advice, "If you pay a man to tell you what to do, you'd better do what he tells you."

Why salesmen don't use rules they know will work

Why don't salesmen sell as they are taught to sell?

We have asked that question of thousands of salesmen who have taken our sales courses. Here are the reasons salesmen give for not using the rules they are taught.

1. "I'm too lazy to apply the rules." (This reason usually leads all the rest in the voting by salesmen! Some salesmen seem afraid they will get more sales education than they can use *without effort*.)

2. "It's too much trouble for me to *break the habit* of selling as I do now. I hate to change."

3. "I forget to use the new rule."

4. "I resist education. I don't enjoy being taught." (It must have been Ben Franklin who said, "Who needs advice most, usually likes it least.")

5. "I'm not sure the rule will work—hence I fear to try it!"

6. "I sell on personality—so why should I bother with rules?"

7. "I am reasonably satisfied with what I am earning now, so I see no reason to try to increase my earnings."

8. "I believe I know more about practical selling than the men who write the books." (NOTE: He may be right at that! However, he should remember Ben Franklin's wise remark: "He who won't be counseled can't be helped.")

9. "Inability to discipline myself. Lack of will power."

10. "I fear the ridicule of prospects and of other salesmen for trying new methods."

What excuses do *you* use?

Just as a test if you don't use the rules of big-league selling, why don't you run through those "reasons" and put a cross mark against the ones that explain why you, yourself, don't use the rules.

(*We have left this little space blank to remind you to go back and check those reasons. Please do it thoughtfully. If you know why you don't use the rules of successful selling, maybe you are on the way to effect a cure.*)

"What must a salesman do to persuade himself to use the rules for successful selling?" you ask.

You will find, in the next chapter, practical directions for accomplishing this.

CHAPTER 54

Will you use the rules you ought to use— and if not, why not?

It isn't what you learn that makes you successful, but what you use of what you learn.

How can I get you to use the methods of professional salesmen?

Truthfully, I don't know.

How do you force yourself to do anything you know you ought to do? Alas, no certain method has ever been invented, but try the following rules:

A. *Determine* to do it. Use your will power. Remember the ungrammatical slogan of the Yankee skipper: "No sail comes off this vessel but what blows off." That's the spirit of determination which is required. So don't haul down the sails of your determination and don't worry—they will not blow off —unless you do!

NOTE: Remember, you are to work on one rule at a time.

B. Get a clear picture in your own mind of yourself using this rule and, as a result, making more sales and more money. Picture yourself enjoying what you will buy with the extra money this rule will help you to earn.

Sell yourself on using the rule by pointing out to yourself the benefits you will gain by doing it.

Fortunately you don't have to keep on exercising your will power indefinitely. As Professor Hugo Münsterberg of Harvard used to say, "Form habits and the will becomes superfluous."

C. Start! Not later, but now. It isn't hard to use a rule— it's only hard to *start* using it.

When will you start, if not *now?*

The most difficult step any man will take will be that first one, when he rises to his feet against all the protests of his inner self, and proceeds to do now something that he knows he ought to do.

His very soul may squirm but he will be acting the part of a man who is going to make more money. —NORMAN VINCENT PEALE

D. Allow no exceptions.

Never argue yourself out of using the rule you are working on, never evade it, never forget it.

You build good habits by using the right method *every time*.

Don't try to ease gradually into using the rule. Jump in all over—even if it seems beyond your depth.

Dr. David Mitchell said, "By acting in the right way, habit systems grow so strong that nothing else can get in their way."

E. Remind yourself.

I remember once several years ago I went out to Dale Carnegie's home in Forest Hills for a talk. On his desk was a disreputable old glove.

I said, "Dale, what's the idea of that?"

His answer was, "Doesn't that look relaxed? Well, I put that there to remind me to relax."

One of the best ways to remind yourself is to write the rule on cards. Put one at the foot of your bed where you will see it when you wake up; put one on your shaving mirror; put one on the dining-room table; put one on your desk; put one where you can see it in your car; put one in your pack of cigarettes; prop one up in front of you as you eat.

Change the location and the appearance of the cards frequently or you will get so accustomed to having them around that you will not notice them.

Give yourself no chance to quit

F. Make it hard to turn back.

Do you know what happens to a lot of good intentions? This: You use the new technique a few times, you find it requires effort. You abhor effort. You find it easier *not* to use the new method—so you quit.

One good way to guard against this failure due to inertia is to make it harder to retreat than to go forward.

Here are some suggestions for making it hard for you to quit:

(*a*) When you start working on a new rule, sign a pledge or make an oath that you will use the new rule instead of the old one on every possible occasion. Do it solemnly and sincerely. Make this vow, if you have the courage, in the presence of your family or your boss.

One of the best ways to make the pledge effective is to stand in front of the mirror each morning, when you finish shaving, and repeat the pledge aloud.

William James wrote, "The memory that an oath or vow has been made will nerve one to ... efforts otherwise impossible."

Prince Pueckler-Muskau wrote his wife: "When things are difficult to perform ... I give my word of honor most solemnly to myself to do ... [this or that]. If I were capable of breaking my word after such mature consideration, I should lose all respect for myself." [I don't know who the Prince was, but I know he had a good idea.]

Notify your wife, your children, your boss, your fellow salesmen, that you are going to use it. Then you will be ashamed not to use it.

William James tells of a man in Australia who ran an advertisement in his local paper saying that he had sworn off drinking. His purpose was obviously to make it hard for himself to retreat.

So, make a vow!

(*b*) Get others to remind you to use the rule—your wife, your children, your boss, your fellow salesmen. Make a game out of it. Pay a reward to anybody who catches you breaking the rule.

This plan of paying a reward is magic. I know—I've made it work.

For example, do you want to know how to swear off smoking? It's simple. Here's the unfailing formula: Get someone

else in your organization to swear off when you do. Draw up
a legally binding agreement which provides that the company
cashier is to deduct a considerable sum—say two weeks' salary
—from the pay of the first man who breaks through and
smokes. Have the agreement provide that a reward, of half
the penalty, will be paid to the person who brings in proof
that either man has smoked since the swear-off.

It works. I know—I have used it again and again! This isn't
as funny as it's supposed to sound because I usually swore
off for a month or two—not forever. The last time, however,
it was "for good." That was nineteen years ago. I'm still off!

Get your bosses to help you

(c) Make a report every day to your wife and to your boss
as to whether or not you are using the rule. Ask them to insist
that you make this report—to remind you if you forget it.

(d) Use affirmation. Tell yourself that you are going to do
it—tell yourself not once but many times. Build up your faith
that you can and will do it.

* * *

Perhaps at this point you will say to yourself, "Shucks, I'm
doing all right with the old methods. Why bother?"

The best answer I know was given by Gene Flack, who said,
"Everything can be improved. When you are through chang-
ing, brother, you are through!"

Good selling habits are a salesman's best friend; bad selling
habits his worst enemy.

Probably some of you who read this book are saying to yourselves by now, "This book is not for me. What I want is a book
—I read it, and bang! I'm a better salesman."

Friend, there ain't no such book!

CHAPTER 55

You have at your call a profound force which you can use to perform selling miracles

If you are going to reach the peak of your possibilities, you must use both pep talks and faith talks. You should do it to give yourself courage, to bolster your morale, and to build in yourself the belief that you can sell more and advance faster.

Let's not make the mistake of assuming that pep talks and faith talks are exactly the same, because they are not.

> *Faith is dead to doubt, dumb to discouragement, blind to impossibilities.*

The faith talk takes longer, lasts longer. The pep talk is like a battle—the faith talk is like a war. The pep talk gives you brisk energy for a short period; the faith talk changes your outlook on selling and on life—it changes your character, your personality.

The pep talk is the "shot in the arm" that salesmen have been talking about for fifty years. It's quick. You give it to yourself quickly; you get results quickly. You lose the effect of it quickly.

In both the faith talks and the pep talks you use *affirmation*. Just what is affirmation?

Strictly, *affirmation* is an assertion, a statement made positively; a protestation; a suggestion to the subconscious mind.

When you say, "I am going to sell this man; I know I am," you have *affirmed*.

A pep talk is a brief inspirational statement, designed to stir you (or somebody) for a brief period into greater animation, greater exertion, greater excitement.

The pep talk may be short—maybe a few words repeated a few times. "I'm going to make this sale, I'm going to make this sale, I'm going to make this sale," is an example.

Faith talks work—
even if you don't have much faith

"Shucks," you say, "maybe I don't believe I am going to make that sale."

Here's sensational news for you: "You don't have to!"

Thirty years ago, talking at a meeting of men who sold investment securities, I said, somewhere in my talk, "To close a sale successfully, you must *believe* that you are going to close it today."

One of my listeners broke in with, "How are you going to believe you will close a sale today when you haven't closed one in seventeen days?"

I have remembered that question for thirty years, but I didn't remember my answer thirty minutes. What I said then doesn't matter. I didn't know the answer.

I do know the answer now.

I know that you can convince yourself that you can sell by affirming, by persuading yourself—by telling yourself that you can do it—by giving yourself a personal faith talk—even if you don't really believe it!

Your natural reply to this suggestion is: "You preach to us that we should tell only the truth to *our prospects.* Do you mean to tell us we should lie to ourselves by telling *ourselves* that we expect to make a sale—when we don't?"

I do, and I'll tell you why I do.

When you sell yourself with a faith talk, you are dealing with a strange and largely unknown part of your mental equipment—your subconscious mind.

Your subconscious mind is what you sell when you tell yourself that you are going to make a sale.

You don't have to understand
your subconscious mind to use it!

I will not tell you a lot about your subconscious mind because nobody knows a lot about it—and I know less!

But this I do know. Your subconscious mind believes what you tell it—even if your conscious mind doesn't. "There is no absurdity so palpable," wrote Arthur Schopenhauer, "but that it may be firmly planted in the human head... by constantly repeating it."

What I should have told that bond salesman who hadn't made a sale in seventeen days was: "Regardless of what you believe, keep telling yourself that you are going to make the next sale. Your subconscious mind believes what you tell it. Keep on doing this and you will soon begin to make sales."

An interesting example of how pep talks worked a miracle for an insurance salesman was given me by Bob Decker of Tuscaloosa, Alabama. Bob said:

Herman Watson of Fort Payne, Alabama, who sold for the Franklin Life Insurance Company of Springfield, Illinois, credits a considerable part of his success to the fact that he used affirmation on himself. When Watson quit school and went to selling insurance, his greatest handicap was the fear of calling on people who could afford big wads of insurance. Watson overcame this fear of wealthy people by this method: when he drove to a man's home, or his place of business, he got out, walked around his car briskly, and as he did so, said to himself, "Herman, this man puts on his pants the same way you do. What are you afraid of? You have a plan he needs. Now go in and sell him. You can do it!"

Partly as a result of this habit of giving himself pep talks, Herman Watson established a world's record. He made a sale a day for eleven years! [Over 4,000 sales without a miss!]

In other words, Herman Watson built up his courage by affirmation.

A faith talk is a pep talk that has grown up

I had been teaching public-speaking students and salesmen, for years, to give themselves pep talks before I realized that affirmation could be used for something vastly more powerful and lasting than the pep talk—that it could be used in a faith talk.

I wasn't smart enough to figure it out for myself—I got the idea when I began to read books like *The Power of Positive Thinking* by Norman Vincent Peale, *The Magic of Believing* by Claude M. Bristol, *TNT—The Power within You,* by Claude M. Bristol and Harold Sherman, *I Can* by Ben Sweetland and *Think and Grow Rich* by Napoleon Hill.

Finally I realized that affirmation was a mighty force—a force that could, if taken seriously, work miracles for salesmen.

What I read in these books convinced me that affirmation can be carried far beyond the pep talk—that it can be used to build up faith. And, as Dr. Peale puts it, "Faith power works miracles."

Faith talks are for the long pull

Let's be sure that we understand the difference between the purpose of the pep talk and the purpose of the faith talk—even if we have to repeat a bit.

You give yourself a pep talk to get up steam to make one sales talk. You probably have to give yourself another before you tackle the next prospect.

You give yourself faith talks to change your attitude toward your product and your job.

The pep talk works—if it does work—almost instantly. The faith talk must be used for weeks—for months—as long as you live—to keep your courage and morale and belief in yourself and your product up to the proper pitch.

A small dose of affirmation gives you the pep, perhaps for

one talk; a steady treatment of affirmation gives you faith
that you can perform selling miracles.

Perhaps you will understand better the miracles of faith if
you will read these brief excerpts from four wonderful books:

From *The Magic of Believing* by Claude M. Bristol:

This subtle force of repeated suggestion (affirmation) overcomes
our reason, acting directly on our emotions and our feelings, and
finally penetrating to the very depths of our subconscious minds.

If you're a salesman and want to increase your sales—tell yourself as frequently as possible that you are going to increase your
sales. Do it with emphasis.

Strange as it may sound, we usually get what we anticipate, and
if we anticipate increasing our sales and believe that we are going
to do it, our sales will mount just as though some invisible friend
were helping us. It's the repeated suggestion that makes you
believe.

From *TNT—The Power within You* by Claude M. Bristol
and Harold Sherman:

Write fear [as, for example, the fear that you can't make a
certain sale] out of your life by writing down affirmations of
courage and faith and self-assurance.

Create your own tomorrows by your own *positive suggestions* as
applied to yourself and your needs. [NOTE: The faith builder is
clearly a form of "positive suggestion."]

From *I Can*, by Ben Sweetland:

Every time you think of it, from the time you wake up in the
morning until you go to sleep at night, say to yourself, several
times, "I'm filled with power—I'm filled with power."

If you repeat a thought often enough, even though you might
have difficulties in accepting it wholeheartedly at first, in time that
thought will become effective.

From *Think and Grow Rich*, by Napoleon Hill:

Faith is a state of mind which may be induced, or created, by
affirmation or repeated instructions to the subconscious mind,
through the principle of auto-suggestion.

It is a well-known fact that one comes, finally, to believe whatever one repeats to one's self, whether the statement be true or false.

William James declared:

The greatest discovery of my generation *is that human beings can alter their lives by altering their attitudes of mind.* As you think, so shall you be.

Surely these great authorities can't all be wrong. If they are right, then you have a powerful weapon to wield against discouragement and failing morale. You have at your call a powerful force. Use it.

Faith talks really work. For example, take the case of Ivan ("Babe") Leonard of the Drennan Motor Company of Birmingham, Alabama.

"Babe" had been a moderately successful salesman for four years. A couple of years ago he started using faith talks.

At the end of six months of using faith talks his earnings had increased 40 per cent. They have continued to increase. "Babe" gives credit to faith talks for much of this increase in sales.

Henry Meade, a Dale Carnegie Sales Course instructor who lives in Syracuse, New York, gave me this example of a salesman who had faith and was rewarded. Here is Henry's story:

When I first knew Maynard De Rei, he was the sales manager of the C. W. Stuart Nursery Company in Newark, New York.

When Maynard was visiting me once he noted that I was reading *The Magic of Believing,* so we started talking about it. I said, "Maynard, do you believe that faith can work miracles for you?"

He answered, "Positively, I do."

I said, "Just why do you believe it?"

He replied, "I started out with Stuart as a clerk, but at that time I knew that I wanted to be president of the company. I wanted it with an intense fervor. I thought about it all the time. There was actually never any doubt in my mind that some day I would be president of that company."

I know some of the things that Maynard went through before

he accomplished this. For a period of time, Maynard was so crippled by arthritis that he couldn't walk.

In spite of this handicap, Maynard still kept this goal in mind and worked for it with an intense desire, and always with the idea in mind that some day he would be president of the C. W. Stuart Company.

The C. W. Stuart Company is one of five nursery companies, all of which are incorporated. In 1953, Maynard moved from general sales manager of the five nursery companies to Chairman of the Board of the five. In other words, he actually skipped over the position that he had worked so hard for, and got a still better job.

To close this chapter with some good advice, I am presenting an excerpt from that amazing inspirational booklet by George S. Clason, "The Richest Man in Babylon." (Read it, if you haven't.) Mr. Clason wrote:

I advise that you take the wisdom of Algamash and say to yourselves, "A part of all I earn is mine to keep." Say it in the morning when you first arise. Say it at noon. Say it at night. Say it each hour of every day. Say it to yourself until the words stand out like letters of fire across the sky.

Impress yourself with the idea. Fill yourself with the thought.

§FOURTEEN

How to organize your day's work
to get more done
with less effort

—————————————————————— CHAPTER 56

You, too, must live on 24 hours a day—
do you know how?

Difficulty is, for the most part, the daughter of idleness.
—SAMUEL JOHNSON

I heard H. M. Nordberg, vice-president in charge of sales of
Pitney-Bowes, Inc., talk a few years ago before the Sales Executives Club of New York. His subject was "The Cause of Sales
Failures." Mr. Nordberg wrote me afterward that his organization gathered the information presented in his talk from a
study they made of their branch operations.

What did the Pitney-Bowes organization find was the prime
cause of failure on the part of their salesmen?

Not lack of product knowledge, not lack of enthusiasm, not
lack of cooperation, not lack of selling skill. "No," said Mr.
Nordberg, "the prime reason for failure was lack of good self-
organization. Salesmen failed because they did not plan and
did not work in an orderly procedure. They wasted valuable
time because of lost motion and poor scheduling. They used
eight hours to do two hours' work."

Just as failure is the penalty when you don't organize your

time, increased production is the reward when you do organize it.

Fred T. Jordan told me of an agency manager who taught one of his salesmen how to use his time. This man had been selling $350,000 to $400,000 of insurance a year. Once he learned to use his time, his production increased to $750,000 —and for years did not fall below that figure.

This agent was no better salesman after he knew how to organize his time; he knew no more about the life insurance business; he called on the same type of prospects. He nearly doubled his business by *organizing his time.*

When your boss prods you about organizing your day's work, his motive is undoubtedly to get you to make more calls and hence more sales.

Money isn't everything—you want happiness too

However, life can contain more for the salesman than merely eating, sleeping, and talking to prospects. The salesman who organizes his time can find opportunities for recreation, for reading, for study, for civic and social activities, for relaxation, for sports, and for religious activities.

I shall try to show you, in this section of the book, how to make better use of the twenty-four hours awarded to you in every day of the year. It is probable that, if you do, you will have time not only to make more calls, more sales and more money, but you will have time, also, for some of the other activities of a well-rounded life.

However, since this is a book on salesmanship, primary emphasis will be put on solving the problem of how to make more sales calls.

How should you go about the job of organizing your day's work in such a way that you will make many more sales with only a little more effort?

To start, sit down sometime and ask yourself what *is* your job—*exactly what are you supposed to do?*

Write down the answer—and you have made a crude job analysis.

Then ask yourself, "Just how shall I organize my time and my work so that I can make more sales?"

The answer is surprisingly simple. You just organize it, that's all. It isn't that you don't know *how* to do it—it's just that you don't do it.

An excellent example of the miracles which a salesman can perform merely by organizing his day's work was told me by Roy Lockhart, of Birmingham, Alabama. Roy is general agent for the Aetna Life Insurance Company. He said:

Back in 1948, I found myself selling about $400,000 of insurance a year, and from year to year, showing no great gain.

I wanted to earn more money. So I sat down and analyzed my problem. My conclusion was that I was not organizing my time.

I not only decided what was wrong, but I also did something about it. First, I worked out a schedule of mailings, phone calls, and personal calls. Then I started keeping records.

I kept records of the number of phone calls I made to get an interview—the number of interviews to get a sale.

I kept records of the average volume per sale, the average premium per sale, the kind of people I was doing business with, i.e., salesmen, doctors, etc., so I could determine what kinds of prospects brought me the most sales per one hundred calls.

I confined my activities to one community effort (Community Chest) and tried to do a good job on it instead of attempting to work on a number of community drives. I got my wife, Vivian, to help on prospecting by covering the local papers for prospects. She helped further in listening to my sales talks and making suggestions.

I read both inspirational and how-to-do books, including *The Five Great Rules of Selling*. I took the Dale Carnegie Sales Course and went on to become an instructor.

I set aside fifteen minutes each morning to read something of an inspirational nature. I reserved Friday night, Saturday afternoon and night, and Sunday through noon for the family. Sunday afternoon was reserved for office detail, if necessary, otherwise for my family. Sunday night was for my wife.

Monday and Thursday nights were reserved for night calls, Wednesday night for a church supper, and Tuesday night for a civic club.

The year before I started really organizing my day's work I sold $600,000 of insurance. The first full year after I organized it, I sold $850,000—a gain of 41 per cent as a result of organizing my day's work. At the end of my second year of organizing my work, I sold $1,200,000!

The first step Roy Lockhart took in the direction of organizing his day's work was to start. That should be your first step.

The problem is: how to motivate yourself to *start!* Marcelene Cox made this wise observation about how some men start:

When a man does a household job, he goes thru three periods: Contemplating *how* it will be done; contemplating *when* it will be done; and contemplating.

So stop contemplating and start organizing.

"Shucks," you say, "I've organized my day's work already."

Good—now go back over your organization problem and see if you can't work out a better solution.

_____ CHAPTER 57

Selling is no job for a lazy man

Making a lot of calls will do almost anything for a salesman that super-salesmanship can do—and many things it can't.

This chapter tells you how to make more calls.

Knowing salesmen as I do, I'm not sure you *want* to know how to make more calls. Maybe you want to know merely how to make more sales.

For many of the readers of this book, the best, quickest, and easiest way to make more sales is to see more people. So let's consider how to do it.

Let's start by admitting that few salesmen make as many calls as they should. They suffer from what the psychologists call "voluntary inertia."

Don't say, "You can't mean *me*." I *do mean you*.

Are you making as many calls as you can?

No, and probably never did—not for any sustained period.

A lot of us are like the salesman I read about in the house magazine *Philnews*. A friend asked him, "How do you like your new job as a salesman?"

"Oh," replied the other, "it's swell. You meet some fine fellows at hotels and have lots of fun in the evenings. But what I don't like is calling on all those buyers."

In more than nineteen years as a sales manager, I have known but one salesman who worked as hard as he could for more than a couple of days at a time—or any sales manager either, including myself.

Many salesmen could make about twice as many calls as they do, if they were willing to punish themselves a little.

Maybe you, too, could make more calls!

I was chatting one day in Waco, Texas, with a man who represented a firm of public-relations counselors in Chicago. He said, "I'm tired."

"Why?" I asked.

"I usually make five calls a day," was his answer, "and I usually spend six days here in Waco. On account of a convention, I can get a room here for only three days. So I've been making ten calls a day."

This man seemed tired, but not exhausted. Yet if his boss had said, "Why not do it every day?" he would probably have fallen in a swoon!

This attitude is well illustrated by a prehistoric joke:

A certain salesman was in a Pullman smoker when the general pest approached him and attempted to start a conversation with the question, "How many salesmen work for your firm?"

"Oh," replied the salesman, putting out his cigarette and getting up, "I should say, roughly, about half."

Some salesmen have a remarkable talent for loafing—even when there's no work to do!

Take this example:

When my wife, Gene, and I are driving through the country, we often see a man driving along at 25 miles an hour, lolling back in the car, steering with two fingers, smoking a pipe, and obviously resting.

When we spot one of these "crawlers," we say, in unison, "Salesman."

In nine cases out of ten our diagnosis is right. The back of the crawling car will be filled with samples or other selling paraphernalia.

Salesmen who drive between calls at 25 miles an hour are trying to see how few—and not how many—calls they can make! They are more interested in sleep than they are in sales.

In fact, a top worry of many sales managers is the number of unemployed salesmen on the payroll!

Admittedly, only a small proportion of all salesmen are really lazy. Those who are energetic and ambitious try to see how many effective calls they can make in every business day.

Salesmen rarely die of exhaustion!

In all my years as a sales manager, I knew only one salesman who worked himself to death—though a lot claimed that they were close.

The exception was a Rockland schoolteacher. He came to work for our securities-selling force in Maine back in 1920. He was seventy-two years old—I hired him largely out of charity.

He proved to be a natural, a man who couldn't do a selling wrong. But he made the mistake of trying to make up in fifty-two weeks for the fifty-two years he had wasted teaching school—and he died trying.

Unless you too are seventy-two years old—or older—never fear that you cannot make more calls than you are making now without overtaxing your strength.

I've been asked, "What happens when a salesman under seventy works to the limit of his time, strength, and endurance?" I can truthfully give only one answer, "I don't know. I've never seen one do it."

Any salesman with brains enough to add two and two and make the answer come out four with reasonable regularity knows something about the law of averages. He knows what every salesman knows: that, if he makes more calls, he must inevitably make more sales.

An inquiry made as to the good qualities of 400 of the most successful salesmen of twenty large insurance companies showed that willingness to do a full day's work stood second in the list of qualities that made for success.

Of 624 salesmen who were discharged by members of the Chicago Sales Executives Club, nearly a third were parted from the payroll for lack of industry. In other words, they did not make the calls.

This must be wrong!

In our sales course we have a conference to consider the problem of why salesmen don't make more calls and what can be done about it. We ask salesmen in these conference groups why salesmen they know don't make enough calls. The first reason given is always the same: *laziness*.

Frank Bettger, in his book *How I Multiplied My Income*, said, "I firmly believe that comparatively few men fail in selling because they cannot sell. Our failure comes because we lack self-direction and self-discipline."

So maybe there's some reason why a gag like this has persisted from vaudeville days to the television era:

First sales manager: "Do you like lazy salesmen better than the other kind?"

Second sales manager: "What other kind?"

That gag does not apply to all salesmen—but it does to many. This is unfortunate, because selling isn't easy and—don't delude yourself—it never will be.

Most selling requires that you do more walking than sitting. In fact, most sales managers will not hire a salesman who buys suits with *two* pairs of trousers!

And from the booklet "We Love Salesmen" we gather this truism: "If a man works with his hands, his head, his heart, and *his feet*, he's probably a real salesman!"

Here's another example of the effectiveness of making a lot of calls, culled from a Westvaco publication:

"You gotta see a lotta people and you gotta see 'em often." That was Eddie Wilson's homespun way of saying that the surest way to get contracts is to make contacts.

Eddie grew up in the heart of the Berkshires. He walked right out of the tenth grade one day into an electric shop as an all-round helper.

It soon developed that he could sell, that he liked to sell, that he had to sell. Before he was twenty-two he was in Rutland working for a major utility company. Once there, he made Vermont sales history. Up at Montpelier you'll still hear the story about Eddie's appearance at a sales convention. He was to give a talk on "How I Tripled My Quota."

Eddie had never talked to a group. He was scared! In midafternoon he decided to resort to bottled courage. He reached the depths of the bottle, the heights of assurance!

Through the meal Eddie sat dazed, befuddled, bewildered. He was glowingly introduced. He stumbled to his feet and murmured: "See the people, see the people, see the people."

Then he sat down.

That was all he had to say to tell his story of sales success.

This shows what
a hard-working salesman can do!

If you think you work hard, take a look at the record of Harry S. Truman. In an interview with a reporter for *Printers' Ink*, Mr. Truman said:

I traveled 31,000 miles [in the campaign against Dewey], made 356 speeches, shook hands with half a million people and talked to 15 or 20 million in person and to 30,000,000 by radio.

[The *Printers' Ink* reporter adds, "Harry Truman not only defeated Dewey, he also beat down the predictions and reputations of the pollsters and the pessimism of his own advisers."]

[The Kansas City Advertising and Sales Executives Club gave Mr. Truman a free lifetime membership for a "remarkable performance by the world's greatest salesman."]

Surely, making a lot of calls, like political campaigning, is hard work—and so is everything else that's worth doing.

[Henry Ward Beecher once received a letter from a young man asking him to find "an easy place." This was his reply:]

"You cannot be an editor; do not try the law; do not think of the ministry; let alone all ships, shops and merchandise; be not a farmer nor a mechanic; neither be a soldier nor a sailor; don't work, don't study, don't think. None of these are easy. Oh, my son, you have come into a hard world! I know of only one easy place in it, and that is the grave."

CHAPTER 58

How to make more calls

> Hard work alone will accomplish remarkable results.
> But hard work with method and system will perform
> seeming miracles. No one can profit more by a realiza-
> tion of these truths than the man who sells goods for a
> living.   —W. C. HOLMAN

To make more calls:

1. You must *want* to.
2. You must *plan.*
3. You must *work.*

Let's take up these three *musts*—one at a time.

Requirement No. 1 for making more calls: Make yourself *want* to make more calls. Sell the idea to yourself—make repeated sales talks to yourself—affirm to yourself that you are eager to make more calls.

Don't think your job of selling yourself on making more calls is completed with one application. You may have to resell yourself five to ten times a day until you have built up in yourself an eagerness to make more calls. After that, your subconscious mind looks after it.

Don't think you can skip this step of selling yourself and yet find it easy to force yourself to make more calls.

Here is a good way to sell yourself: Sit down and figure the value of your time—how much you earned last year per hour worked. Then consider how much you will make if you work more hours.

When you have done this, set a goal—not of how many calls you are determined to make, but how much money you are determined to earn.

Then see yourself mentally as you enjoy the extra money.

See yourself as you pay off the mortgage on your house. See yourself driving the car you've always wanted and couldn't afford. See yourself bringing home to your wife the expensive frock she admired the other day in a store window. See yourself and your family sailing on the *Lurline* to Hawaii for a long vacation In other words, arouse your desire to make more calls by painting word pictures.

When you have the goal and the benefits clearly in mind, then figure out how many calls a day it will take you to reach that goal.

Then set a specific goal, in terms of sales calls per day. Don't set it too high—don't aim at the impossible. If you do, you are defeated before you start. If your first goal is not high enough don't worry—when you reach it, set a new and a higher goal!

Once your goal is set, your next job is to so organize your day's work that you can reach that goal. You will find some suggestions in the next chapter.

─────────────────────────────────── CHAPTER **59**

You have to work your brain, too

Don't expect to be paid 2 dollars an hr for your working hrs when you use your leisure hrs as tho they were worth 5¢ a doz. —HENRY L. DOHERTY

Requirement No. 2 for making more calls: You must *plan,* use your brain—think!

To make more calls, first analyze your time and set up a general plan.

You begin with twenty-four hours in a day! "Astounding," you remark. I know. Yet more human waste and human want and human suffering are due to a failure to recognize that fact than to almost any other failing.

A study by a scale manufacturer, made among a group of high-grade salesmen, all consistent business producers, shows that of the 8,760 hours in a year which each man has at his disposal—

5,110 are spent for sleep, meals, and recreation

1,040 Saturday and Sunday hours are nonproductive

210 holiday and vacation hours are not used for sales calls

100 hours are wasted during idle days

920 hours are lost because of the six-hour-day idea

460 hours are spent between calls, traveling, and waiting

920 hours—slightly over 10 per cent—are actually *spent with the buyer*. No wonder you have to use them frugally!

If the above figures are truthful, then the time a salesman spends face-to-face with his prospect is between two and three hours a day.

To organize you must analyze

Now is the time to make a more complete job analysis.

Below you will find a reasonably complete list of the duties and recreations of the average salesman.

Please take two steps to fill in the blanks against each item. First, go through the entire list and put down, without too much thinking about it, the amount of time you feel you should spend, in a normal day, on each item.

Total your figures.

Quite probably you will be startled to realize that you need more hours in every working day. What an ambitious salesman needs is a thirty-six-hour day!

Then go back and fill out the second (right-hand) column with revised figures—cut down those figures so that they will add up to the utterly inadequate twenty-four hours that we have at our disposal each day.

This exercise in arithmetic should bring home to you the

fact that you have to do a lot of organizing and scheduling to fit all your duties and recreations into each day and still have time enough left over for sleep.

NOTE: If you don't mind being startled and dismayed please fill in the table on this page.

The headings over the two columns will tell you how to make this time-study of your activities.

THE ACTIVITY	My offhand guess as to the amount of time I should spend on each activity in order to get everything done that I want to do.	My carefully considered opinion as to the amount of time I can afford to give to each activity, if I am to fit all of them into a 24-hour day.
Amusement		
Calling		
Civic activities		
Club activities		
Eating		
Making reports		
Office work		
Planning		
Prospecting		
Religious activities		
Sleeping		
Studying		
Television		
Thinking		
Traveling		
Waiting		

Ask yourself questions about your activities

Next, ask yourself a lot of questions which begin with *why*. Find out why you do things the way you do. For example: "Why do I get up at 7:00 A.M.—instead of perhaps 6:00 A.M.?" "Why do I get up so late that I don't have adequate time for breakfast?" "Why do I sit around the office for a half hour before I start calling?"

"What do I do—why do I do it?" That's what you need to ask yourself.

Before you do your job of planning, we urge you to sit down at the end of the day and ask yourself these questions:

1. Am I making enough calls? (How many are "enough?" In general, as many as you can crowd into the longest day you have the time and the strength to work—and don't underestimate your strength.)

As a preliminary to answering Question 1, ask yourself these three basic questions:

(*a*) How many actual complete sales presentations did I make today?

(*b*) Should I have made more?

(*c*) Why didn't I make more? (Be brutal with yourself in answering this question. Maybe it's all right to try to fool your sales manager, but it is plain idiocy to fool yourself.)

After you have asked yourself these basic questions, go to work to find out *why* you did not make more calls. Ask yourself the questions which follow:

2. Do I make good use of each hour of each working day? Do I cut down waiting time in prospects' offices? Do I study the problem? Do I analyze it? Do I think; do I use my brain? (I'm sure folks don't say about you, "Between his collar button and the sidewalk, he is the best salesman in his home town." You are equipped to think—so think!)

3. When do I plan my day's work—and is it the best time to do it?

4. How do I plan it? Do I call systematically or do I call helter-skelter? Do I prepare an itinerary before I start?

To be sure that your planning is systematic, ask yourself:

(*a*) On whom do I plan to call tomorrow?

(*b*) Why? (Maybe you ought to call on somebody else. Are you sure—and what makes you sure?)

(*c*) *When* will I call?

The man who is not willing to take time to prepare himself to do the job is like the woodchopper who, because he wasn't doing well, was urged to stop and sharpen his ax. He snorted: "It's tough enough now getting this job done without taking time out to grind an ax."

It's your time—but why waste it?

The next step in the direction of getting more calls made is to ask yourself:

5. Do I waste time—especially at our office? (Don't do it. Start. Get out of there. Get where the prospects are—fast. As Quintillian, who taught oratory in Rome in 68 A.D., said, "While we deliberate about beginning, it is already too late to begin.")

6. Do I get up early enough? (Ben Franklin said, "Early risers on the average live to a much older age and are more successful." Surely early-rising salesmen, on the average, sell more. Too many salesmen are like Mark Twain, who said, "Since forty I have been regular about going to bed and getting up ... I have made it a rule to go to bed when there wasn't anybody left to sit up with, and I have made it a rule to get up when I had to.")

Ask yourself:

(*a*) At what hour did I start making calls:

(1) Today?

(2) Yesterday?

(3) What time, through the past month, on an average, have I started to make calls?

(*b*) Why did I not start earlier?

C. H. Larrabee, chairman of the board of Printers' Ink Publishing Co., Inc., wrote an editorial last year under the heading "On Getting Up Early," part of which follows:

Some time ago I wrote an article, "Thirty-nine Tips to Better Salesmanship." Paul C. Bowman of Chicago offers a fortieth tip. He says, "I contend that in order to sell, successfully or otherwise, you must get up in the morning. That's my number one point."

I have always felt that one of the big fallacies which salesmen clasp to their breasts with loving tenderness is that you can't get anybody to listen to your sales talk before ten o'clock in the morning. Some salesmen, I suppose, really believe this. Others, I know, like to believe it because it allows them to get up late and still have plenty of time to chew things over with the boys in the office—and to get that morning cup of coffee.

If you are determined to make more calls, you will utilize the hours most often wasted by salesmen: those before 10 A.M. and those after 4 P.M. When you start trying to see how many effective calls you can make, you will probably learn that you can easily find people who will grant you an interview before 9 A.M. or after 5 P.M. and that you can sometimes find people—if you look hard—willing to listen to your sales talk even before 8 A.M. or after 6 P.M.

An English merchant from London arrived in Boston some years ago, where he had a branch of his business. One day, on looking over the salesmen's reports, he found that one salesman was making almost exactly three times as many calls as any other salesman connected with the company.

The merchant asked the salesman how he was able to do this. The salesman said that he did it by studying the grocers he was trying to sell. When pressed for specific details, the salesman said that he found which grocer in the neighborhood was the first to open up in the morning, so he went to him first. Then he found which was the last one to close at night. So he made his last call of the day on him.

The English merchant said to his American manager, "I want you to watch this man."

The English merchant was William Lever, the famous British soap manufacturer. And the hustling salesman—who was he? Well, he was Francis A. Countway, then an obscure salesman; later called "the greatest advertising man in the world."

When the United States tax statements were made up for 1938, the Hollywood movie stars were at the top. But Francis A. Countway led all businessmen with an income of $469,713.

Now let's go back to asking ourselves questions about saving time:

7. Do I eliminate unnecessary traveling?

(*a*) Today, for example, did I waste any time, in going from prospect to prospect, which I could have used more effectively in *talking* with prospects? (Some salesmen have no more sense of direction than a pretzel.)

(*b*) Do I try to cut down lost motion?

(1) Do I work in one neighborhood, city, or territory? That is, do I avoid jumping around?

(2) Do I avoid unnecessary trips to the office or to the hotel or to my home?

(3) Have I eliminated customers so remote that I can't afford to call on them?

Look for the time wastes

8. Do I waste time around the office or hotel? ("Sitting in an office chair ought to be a dull sort of amusement to a salesman who is losing money by doing it," says W. C. Holman.)

(*a*) Do I go to the office too often?

(*b*) Do I stay too long? (W. C. Holman used to tell the National Cash Register salesmen, "You ought to bounce into the office and out again as a rubber ball bounces out of a barrel.")

(*c*) What can I do to break myself of this bad habit of sitting around the office too long?

9. Do I work late enough in the afternoon? (A weakness of salesmen since the beginning of selling has been to quit too early in the day. Do *you* quit too early?)

(*a*) In the last six days, at what time (on the average) did I finish my last call?

The idea that sales can be made only at conventional times has cost many salesmen many sales. It is astonishing how a determined salesman can make sales at odd times.

For example: I once conducted an employee securities-selling campaign for the Northern Connecticut Light and Power Co., with headquarters at Thompsonville, Connecticut. We offered a prize for the employee who, during the drive, sold the most shares of the company's preferred stock.

The closing night of the contest I sat in the company's office with Walter B. Schwabbe, general manager, and Miss Anna Hannigan, his secretary. Mr. Schwabbe was checking the results of the campaign. It was after ten o'clock—which is late at night in Thompsonville. Finally Walter turned to Miss Hannigan and said, "Anna, if you can tip over one ten-share sale tonight, you will win the prize for the most sales."

Miss Hannigan turned to me and said, "If you'll go with me, I'll make one more try."

We went to the home of Dr. F. F. Simonton, rang the bell until we got him out of bed. He came to the door in his pajamas and dressing gown. Then and there—on the front porch, at nearly eleven at night—Anna Hannigan sold the doctor ten shares of stock, and got his check.

Anna displayed the qualities it takes to become a great sales-man—courage, determination, and a fine disregard for the time of day!

The next questions to ask yourself are:

(*b*) If I had really tried, could I have made just one more call today?

(*c*) As a rule, what time do I quit working?

(1) Why do I quit at that time?

(2) On whom could I have called later, if I were really trying to do a full day's work?

10. Do I quit when I don't feel quite fit?

When I was in Harvard, going on a hundred years ago, more or less, LeBaron R. Briggs was dean. One day a student explained his failure to do some assigned work by saying, "I wasn't feeling well."

Dean Briggs replied, "I think in time you may perhaps find that most of the work in the world is done by people who aren't feeling well."

11. Do I make night calls? (Obviously, night calls are impractical for salesmen in certain lines. If your line is something that can be sold at night, you will probably find that one night call is worth two or three daytime calls.)

Night is usually the perfect time to get husband and wife together in cases where you need their joint decision to close the sale. If you sell a product or service that can be sold at night, here are four questions for you:

(*a*) When did I make my last night call?

(*b*) On how many nights have I made calls in the past thirty days?

(*c*) Honestly now, am I making enough night calls—as many as I possibly can?

(*d*) How can I arrange to make more night calls?

12. Do I make enough calls on Saturday? Do I work all day, half a day, or not at all? Why? Are prospects available on Saturday? Do I have enough strength to work on Saturday? Is the salesman's theory that salesmen should rest on Saturday based on sound reasoning, fear, or old-fashioned laziness?

13. Do I make calls on holidays? (In some lines, holiday calling is impractical; in others—for example, insurance, automobiles, real estate—holidays are, I think, better than ordinary days. In such lines of selling, if you must have your day off, work on the holiday and take some other day off.)

14. Do I throw away any of my selling time:

(*a*) By going to moving pictures in business hours? (Why are some moving-picture houses open in the morning? For salesmen! How do I know? I see them there myself!)

(*b*) By friendly chats? (A garrulous salesman can easily waste many hours each week in idle blather.)

(*c*) By coffee breaks?

(*d*) By just sitting around?

15. Am I more interested in sailing, golfing, watching baseball games, fishing—than I am in making a success of my selling career?

Maybe you're like the two salesmen who had taken a day off without permission and were feeling a little guilty about it. One said to the other, "I suppose we should have stayed on the job and made a lot of calls today."

To this the other salesman replied, "Heck, I couldn't have worked today anyway; my wife is sick!"

Calls are only a means to the great end: *sales*

One last word of warning—don't let all I have said about making more calls confuse you as to the main issue. Your final objective is not to see how many *calls* you can make—but how many *sales* you can make.

16. When the day's work is over, do I forget it?

Emerson conveyed this message well when he said, "Finish every day and be done with it. You have done what you could. Some blunders and absurdities no doubt crept in; forget them as soon as you can."

_____ CHAPTER 60

Hurry! But hurry efficiently

If salesmen misused their cars as so many of them
misuse their time, they'd go broke on repair bills.

Now, let's consider how you can get all your jobs done faster
and better.

Speed-up Rule No. 1: Study ways to save time in doing all
your regular jobs.

Study routine jobs to learn the best, easiest, and quickest
way to do them. In general, split the big job into little ones
and then learn the best way to do the little ones. Once you
have learned the right way, force yourself to do the job the
right way until you have established the habit.

Speed-up Rule No. 2: Determine not to do anything that
will hurt your efficiency. Don't eat too much. Don't drink too
much.

Speed-up Rule No. 3: Don't skimp on your planning time
and on your study time.

You need a schedule

When you have accepted these rules you are ready to work
out a tentative daily schedule, with time allotted to all the
things you ought to do.

First consider how to figure out your daily schedule.

When should you make your plans for the day's work?

The possibilities are:

(*a*) Just before dinner at night.

(*b*) Just before going to bed.

(*c*) The first thing in the morning. This is the best time!
Also, to take advantage of this plan, you have to get up earlier

than you normally do! I know that most salesmen will find
the idea of getting up thirty minutes earlier quite revolting.
Try it anyhow.

All right, it's 7:00 A.M.—or maybe even 6:30—and you are
ready to plan a day's work.

How to plan a day's work

Here are the steps you must take:

A. Think. Have what Henry L. Doherty, who in his lifetime was immensely successful in both the utility and oil busi-
nesses, used to call "an old-fashioned brain sweat."

Not one salesman in ten million uses his brain as much as
he could—some don't seem to use it at all—for the purpose of
thinking.

A salesman suffered a stroke, but seemed to improve after the
crisis was over. A friend called to see how he was feeling.

"Fair to middlin' these days," confided the patient. "No pain;
eatin' and sleepin' right well, and I'm able to drive to town, fetch
the groceries, and go to church."

Then, as an afterthought, he added: "Of course, my mind is
gone, but I don't miss it much."

B. Determine your objective. Just what are you going to
try to do today?

C. Select the prospects you are going to call on.

D. Route your calls to cut down distance. The less distance
you travel, the more calls you can make. A Carnegie Institute
of Technology survey showed that 45 per cent of a salesman's
working time was taken up by walking and waiting. If practicable, make your hardest call first.

E. Eliminate unnecessary calls.

F. Next prepare a schedule for the day's calls. Have some
elasticity in your schedule. Determine what you will do if a
prospect is busy or away.

Speed-up Rule No. 4: Start early. It is amazing how many prospects arc astir at 7:00 A.M. if you take the trouble to locate them.

Speed-up Rule No. 5: Speed up your walking. Don't drag your feet. Walk briskly.

Speed-up Rule No. 6: Keep your sales talk as short as is practicable. Especially cut down all conversations except those about business. "Any businessman worth his salt," says *Printers' Ink,* "nowadays has but one real hobby. It's no sport-page hobby. It's a first-page hobby. It's business. Talk that."

Speed-up Rule No. 7: Make your lunch brief and light—but don't wolf it. Take time to chew your food.

Speed-up Rule No. 8: Keep calling briskly.

Speed-up Rule No. 9: Don't stop too early. The average salesman could get in from one to five more calls a day if he would just keep going.

Vincent F. Sullivan, in his book *How to Sell Your Way into the Big Money,* says, "Your fellow workers may, in the beginning, sneer at you for working longer hours than they, but their sneers will turn to dismay when they see you progressing ahead of them."

Speed-up Rule No. 10: Make night calls, if your business permits.

You know all those rules anyway. Of course you do! But can you honestly say that you live up to them?

Get more done with less effort

CHAPTER 61

Nobody can do this for you—
it's your own personal job

An inch of time cannot be bought with an inch of gold.
—CHINESE PROVERB

Requirement No. 3 for making more calls: Force yourself to do it.

"All right," you say, "admitting that I want to make more money and admitting that I'd like to observe the rules, how can I force myself to do it?"

I don't know.

The unsolved problem of all time is how to make people do what they ought to do. This point is well made in this little parable from *The Washington Review:*

With eagerness the young agent asked his manager how he could attain success.

"I'll tell you," the manager said, "how to obtain success by the use of two simple rules.

"The first is: Don't do the things you know you ought not to do."

The young man's face fell.

He had not expected a rule so hard to follow.

"The second is: Do all the things that you know you ought to do."

The young man turned away sadly.

He wanted to succeed without the personal discipline necessary for success.

You will find some suggestions in Chapter 53 for forcing yourself to do the things you ought to do. Here are two rules that will work.

1. Force yourself to make more calls.

You must be your own top sergeant—your own Simon Legree. Don't worry about starting to make more calls. Don't put it off. Just do it.

Stop "believing what you know ain't so!"

2. Stop believing in fairy tales, in salesmen's superstitions, in voodoos. Stop rationalizing, stop excusing yourself, stop salving your conscience with reasons as feeble as a moron's mind. For example:

(*a*) Stop believing that you can't sell in July and August.

When I started managing a securities-sales force in Maine in 1918, I knew nothing whatever about selling securities and my salesmen knew less! After three or four years of selling, I was astonished to find that our salesmen sold more securities per man in August than in any other month.

A little thought gave me the answer, and it was this: we were so ignorant that we didn't know that securities could not be sold in August! Smarter salesmen did know—so they stopped making calls. The result: we had the field to ourselves.

(*b*) Overcome your fear that you will break your health if you make too many calls.

H. W. Stafford, route supervisor, Dr. Pepper Bottling Co., Winston-Salem, North Carolina, told me this:

My men make from 100 to 150 calls a day. I myself have hit as high as 175 a day. My men start in the morning with a meeting at 6:30. They work until 5:30 P.M. or 6:30 P.M. or later. They have six jobs to do on each stop—and are asked to do them in 90 seconds: (1) greet merchant cheerfully, (2) check stock, (3) suggest quantity, (4) put bottles in box, (5) check inside advertising [Not inside the box—inside the store!], (6) thank dealer.

If some salesmen stand up under 100 calls a day, you can surely survive 10 a day—which is probably considerably more than you are making now if you sell insurance, securities, or automobiles.

(c) Stop deluding yourself that you will become so tired you can't make effective calls. It can happen—but it isn't likely to.

(d) Give up the idea that you need long week ends, long vacations; that you need to space out one-day holidays into three days and long week ends into five days.

(e) Quit telling yourself that rainy days are bad days to sell.

Acacia News reports that a purchasing agent told the editor recently that, in good weather, he is called upon by from ten to fifteen salesmen a day. "Believe it or not," he added, "during the rainy days about two weeks ago, I was called on by exactly three salesmen."

Some evidence of what a man can do in rainy weather was given me by Dale Carnegie, as follows:

T. D. McCall of Enid, Oklahoma, was out of a job. He wanted to sell farm machinery and wrote a letter of application to the district agent for one of the large companies. He promptly got back a form letter saying, "no dice."

He immediately wrote them another letter telling them that he was really a whacking good salesman, and even more promptly got back form letter number two saying, "*absolutely* no dice." This irritated Mr. McCall, so he went to the nearest stationery store, bought a set of order pads, and left for the nearest rural district to sell farm machinery "on spec"!

When he got to the small town that he picked for his headquarters, he found that two salesmen for rival companies were also staying there and preparing to work the district. Thought Mr. McCall, "Was ever a poor man so bedeviled!"

The next day was rainy. Mr. McCall found his two rivals playing pinochle while waiting for the weather to clear. [I don't know whether you have ever visited Oklahoma, but I can tell you from experience that waiting for an Oklahoma rainy spell to let up is a job that will sometimes take all of a salesman's energy and attention for as much as two or three weeks.] Anyway McCall figured that two salesmen working on the weather situation was enough and that he would take the opportunity to work on the farmers.

And opportunity it was!

McCall was frank with his prospects and told them that he was selling on speculation. They liked his spirit. The harder it rained the harder he sold.

At the end of two weeks the rain let up, and McCall hopped a train for the office from which he had received the form letters. Yes, he got the job.

(*f*) Stop believing you are in danger of saving too much time. If you do, you will be like the salesman that sent this testimonial to the makers of "Speedo—The Miracle Stuff": "Dear Sir: I have quit using Speedo. It saved so much time I got all worn out doing the things I never had time to do before."

(*g*) Stop believing that the early days of the week are the best for calling. The Babson Institute made a survey of the calling activities of 755 salesmen and found that these men made 75 per cent more calls on the first three business days of the week than they did on the last three.

Fairy tales! Myths! Rationalizations! Superstitions! They keep salesmen from selling.

Stop excusing yourself. Stop trying to sell the easy way. Don't weaken.

More calls will do it

Make more calls. Work harder.

Does an increased number of calls produce an increase in volume? In 1932, reports *Printers' Ink*, the American Enameled Brick Corporation found itself faced with a shutdown. General Manager Frank Geraghty said to his salesmen:

"Besides doing your regular work, each of you will make ten extra working calls, every working day, on architects and contractors." The men made more calls. And 10 per cent of these extra calls resulted in so many sales that the factory, instead of shutting down, went into day-and-night production.

Make more calls. This one act may solve all your pressing problems.

When I was a small boy living on a farm in Connecticut, I read in a mail-order paper a two-line advertisement that said: "How to get rich. Send 10 cents." It looked like a good buy, so I sent the dime.

I got back a piece of rough newsprint paper on which was crudely printed this stirring message: "Work like hell." I'm inclined to think that this is Rule 1 of successful selling.

FIFTEEN

Learn how to become enthusiastic
and how to stay enthusiastic

_____ CHAPTER 62

How to become enthusiastic

Men are failures, not because they are stupid but because they are not sufficiently impassioned....
—STRUTHERS BURT

You can do anything if you have enthusiasm. Enthusiasm is the yeast that makes your hope rise to the stars. Enthusiasm is the sparkle in your eye, it is the swing in your gait, the grip of your hand, the irresistible surge of your will and your energy to execute your ideas. Enthusiasts are fighters. They have fortitude. They have staying qualities. Enthusiasm is at the bottom of all progress! With it there is accomplishment. Without it there are only alibis—
—HENRY FORD'S FIREPLACE MOTTO,
AS GIVEN IN THE HOUSE MAGAZINE
Western Union

When I was general retail sales manager of the Securities Department of Henry L. Doherty and Company, we had, in Ohio, an amazingly successful and astonishingly ignorant securities salesman.

He really was ignorant! This man was successful in spite of his ignorance. His familiarity with correct English was slight, his supply of general information was meager, his knowledge

303

of Cities Service Company and its securities was sketchy—and mostly wrong!

One day I called with him on a prospect for Cities Service preferred stock. In the course of the sale, the prospect asked, "How much does Cities Service have in the way of assets?"

The salesman replied, "I can't rightly say how much assets Cities Service has, but I do know this: it has a hell of a lot."

Yet he made the sale—and hundreds of other sales of Cities Service preferred stock.

Why? Because he was wildly enthusiastic about his product. He got that way because he believed that the stock was good and that it would pay dividends and advance in price. He was convinced that every time he sold an investor any of that stock, he was doing that investor a real service. (P.S. It turned out that he was right!)

With a faith like that, this man could sell in spite of almost complete ignorance about the company and the security, and an almost total disregard for the rules of English and of selling.

The history of selling is crowded with examples of men who sold because of one quality they possessed: *enthusiasm.*

Enthusiasm sells insurance—and watermelons!

Dale Carnegie told in his newspaper column of the experience of Harry Wright, who was buried for three years behind the wires of a cashier's cage in an insurance broker's office.

Wright asked for a better job and was refused. He hated the work, he wanted to quit—but, even more, he wanted to eat.

So he stayed in the cage until his vacation time came. Then he did not go on a pleasure trip. Instead, he tried to sell life insurance. He was only twenty-two years old at the time. He knew virtually nothing about life insurance. Yet he sold three out of the first five men he called on. His unbounded enthusiasm did it.

He never went behind the wires again. He continued to sell —largely on enthusiasm. For sixteen years he sold over a million dollars' worth of insurance a year—still largely on enthusiasm.

Oh yes, enthusiasm *is* important to a salesman. If you asked a thousand salesmen or a thousand sales managers this question, "What is the most valuable personality trait a salesman can have?" I am convinced that at least 750 would reply, "Enthusiasm."

The following example of the miracle of enthusiasm in selling was given by Charles M. Achauer in a talk before a Dale Carnegie Sales Course class in Phoenix, Arizona.

Back in the early 1930's, my partner, E. E. Brown, and I were operating a country store in Scottsdale, Arizona, about twelve miles from Phoenix in the Salt River Valley.

One morning in the summertime a boy about twelve years old came in the store. He was carrying half a watermelon, cut lengthwise. He held it in front of me, looked up with pride and enthusiasm, and said, "Isn't it a beauty! I sent away and got some extra good seed. I planted them near the irrigation ditch so I could see that they got plenty of water. They got a little afternoon shade so they are not sunburned. And see, I put straw under each melon as it was growing, so there are no ground bruises, and they ripened evenly. They are delicious! Do you want two of them?"

"I sure do," I said, before I asked the price or realized that the refrigerator at home would take only one watermelon at a time!

Salesmanship? Yes, but repeat that boy's words without his tremendous enthusiasm and see what you have—very little!

Be enthusiastic! Your words and deeds will double—yes, triple—in effectiveness.

Since enthusiasm is so important to salesmen, let's find out how to develop it and how to retain it after it *is* developed.

Animation isn't *enthusiasm*, and vice versa!

Before we get into the question of how to develop enthusiasm, however, let's straighten out the confusion that exists in the minds of so many people between the words *animation* and *enthusiasm.*

In the first place, these words do not mean the same thing. You can be animated without being enthusiastic and you can be enthusiastic without being animated.

Animation is physical—a matter of muscles and vocal cords. You can turn it on and off instantly as you turn on or off an electric light.

Enthusiasm is not physical—it is a thing of the spirit. You can no more turn it on and off instantly, than, by an effort of the will, you can instantly increase your pulse rate or your blood pressure.

The big distinction between animation and enthusiasm is this: When you are enthusiastic, it is always *about something.* Look back through your own experience. Isn't it true that every time you were really enthusiastic it was always *about something?* It had to be, because you just can't be enthusiastic about *nothing.* You can be animated, however, for no better reason than that you have said to yourself, "Be animated."

"Before I learn how to be enthusiastic," you say, "please tell me how I can learn to be animated—since animation also is important in selling."

The answer takes just two words: "Act animated."

However, if you are enthusiastic about your product and what it does for people who use it, you do not have to bother to *act* animated, you *will be animated* without acting. Enthusiasm breeds animation.

So let's face the basic and all-important problem, "How do I become enthusiastic?"

How to go about becoming enthusiastic

To become enthusiastic and to stay enthusiastic you must observe two great rules and a few minor rules.

Here are the great rules:

Rule 1: To become enthusiastic, learn more about your product. (See Chapter 4 for suggestions for gaining product knowledge.)

This idea was well expressed by W. C. Holman in his book *Ginger Talks*. He said, in a talk to salesmen:

The reason you salesmen are not selling more goods to merchants is that you haven't sold yourselves yet.... It's no use to try to start a flame of enthusiasm in somebody else, if your own mind is full of icy doubts.

Why did that man over on the Avenue turn you down yesterday morning? Because he could tell by the look in your eye that you half expected him to do so. And the fellow you called on in the afternoon sized you up the same way. You didn't get anywhere near him. He listened to what you said—but it was with a cold and fishy eye.... When you came to put your finger on him at the end to get the order signed, he was like the Dutchman's famous flea—he wasn't there.

You had lost him. You hadn't impressed him—why? Because you hadn't been impressed yourself.... He didn't feel any electric sparks of enthusiasm jumping the space from your mind to his.

Consider the bearing of these two axioms on your problem of becoming enthusiastic:

(*a*) If you don't know about it, you don't like it.

(*b*) The more you know about a good product—and how it benefits your prospects, the more enthusiastic you become about it.

My friend Randy Howland, who used to run an employment agency, gave me this example:

My organization was asked by a big linoleum company to get a salesman for a difficult territory. I secured for this job a man who had been selling linoleum for another company—with only mediocre success.

The reason he had been selling so little, I told the company's sales manager, was that the salesman knew so little about linoleum that he had no enthusiasm for it.

The linoleum company did not send this man on the road at once, but instead kept him in the plant for three months. The salesman actually worked at various jobs in the factory. He helped to *make* linoleum. He saw cork being prepared for various uses.

He got the feel of cork, the smell of cork, the taste of cork—got interested in how linoleum was made and how it was used.

As a result of knowing so much about linoleum, he became thoroughly enthusiastic over it. When he started selling for the new company, he was successful almost at once. He was soon made sales manager of one of the company's important Western territories. At last report he was still there, still successful, and still enthusiastic.

This salesman became enthusiastic by learning more about his product—and so can you.

Incidentally, you should be excited, not only about your product but also about your job—the job of selling. If selling bores you, you will inevitably do a poor job. If you are enthusiastic about it—if you would rather sell than do any other work in the world—you will almost inevitably succeed at selling.

Wally Powell expressed it well in an article in *Specialty Salesman:*

Doing your job in a professional way means getting *excited* about it. Not the ranting, raving kind of excitement—but deep-down genuine enthusiasm for what you are doing.

I don't believe I know one successful professional man who's not genuinely excited about his job. That goes for lawyers, dentists, doctors and architects.

——————————————————————— CHAPTER 63

You must believe in miracles

*Thorough knowledge of the merchandise and apprecia-
tion for what it will do for the customer produce enthusiasm.*

—FROM *Successful Salesmanship*

Rule 2: To become enthusiastic, you must believe that your
product benefits the people who buy and use it—that it literally performs miracles for them!

The example which follows appeared in an article I wrote
for the magazine *Printers' Ink:*

It has taken me more than a third of a century—thirty-four and
a half years, to be exact—to discover the one sure way to get a
sales force enthusiastic and to keep it enthusiastic!

I made this discovery when I interviewed E. A. Nash, merchandising manager; J. A. Clarke, manager of sales training; and
John Linneman, merchandising department—all of the Airtemp
division of the Chrysler Corporation. In this interview, I was told
about one amazingly fine training technique that Airtemp uses.

When they are breaking in a new salesman and have given him
the necessary product knowledge, they hand him twenty or twenty-
five names of proprietors of retail stores and shops where Airtemp
air-conditioning equipment is used—for example, five hair-dressing
parlors, five butcher shops, five drugstores, five motion-picture
theaters. They instruct the neophyte salesman to call on these
users, to make one statement and to ask one question.

The statement: I am just starting in as a salesman for Airtemp.

The question: Do you like the results you are getting from your
Airtemp installation?

Mr. Nash reports that the salesman comes back fairly ablaze
with enthusiasm over what Airtemp does to increase the business
of users. Once the salesman is afire with enthusiasm, he is ready

to go out calling on prospects. He does not call as a mere peddler of air conditioners but as a missionary, eager to help retailers share in the blessings of air conditioning.

Men thus equipped are not self-conscious or timid. They can't be, because, when they call on a prospect, they are not thinking of themselves, but of the service they can render him.

If you do not believe that your product renders a real service to users, then you can hardly hope to sell it enthusiastically.

Why they weren't selling dog food

This was illustrated in a story which I heard Arthur H. ("Red") Motley tell:

It happened at a sales meeting—a real sawdust trail affair—conducted by a dog-food company.

Winding up the session in grand flag-waving style, the sales manager shouted, "Who's got the best company in the United States?" and the salesmen dutifully responded, "We have."

"And who's got the best sales force in the United States?" Again the same reply.

"And who's got the best advertising campaign to back them up?" The salesmen came through again.

"Then why can't we sell more dog food?" the sales manager demanded.

"Maybe," piped up a little guy in the front row, "the dogs don't like it."

If the dogs don't like the dog food, the dog-food salesman cannot be enthusiastic. In reverse—if the dogs relish the food and thrive on it, the dog-food salesman will be on fire with enthusiasm.

I once hauled a man out of an engine room of a Public Service of Colorado plant and gave him a full-time job selling the company's preferred stock.

That was about a third of a century ago. I have forgotten this man's name, and almost everything about him except his enthusiasm for the company's preferred stock.

To him, the fact that that stock paid $7 a year on an investment of $100 against $4 for the same amount then paid by a savings bank—almost double—was a miracle.

To him it was wrong, under those circumstances, for any man to keep money in the savings bank. And he set out to right that wrong!

I don't know how long he lasted or what became of him, but I know that, as long as I was with the company, he kept on selling stock. He sold a lot of stock—and I know why. It was because he felt that it worked miracles for those who bought it.

This man had discovered, by accident, one of the two great rules for developing enthusiasm. He had developed the missionary spirit. He was distressed and disturbed over all the people who could increase their income by owning this preferred stock—and didn't own it.

To repeat: to be enthusiastic, you must believe that the product you are selling works miracles for people who buy it and use it. You must feel sorry for people who do not buy it. You must have the missionary spirit—must try to sell, not because you will make money for yourself by selling, but *because you will benefit buyers.*

Is that too goody-goodyish, too altruistic, too Golden-Rule-ish for the average practical salesman?

Some of the most practical and successful salesmen in the United States don't think so. I know because they have told me.

Miracles come in several grades

Many salesmen will say, "I sell just staple groceries to dealers. My stuff doesn't perform miracles."

Naturally the miracles that such a product produces do not compare with the miracles sometimes performed by insurance, or efficiency systems, or a good, practical course in salesmanship. But your product may produce minor miracles just the same.

I was talking about enthusiasm to a man recently who sold "just toothbrushes" to dealers.

"My brushes don't perform miracles," he said.

I replied, "Didn't you tell me that you had a display stand that would increase toothbrush sales for druggists by 10 per cent?"

"Yes," was the answer.

"Isn't a 10 per cent increase in toothbrush sales a miracle to a druggist?" I asked.

The salesman had to admit that it was.

Perhaps you ask (anyway, I hope you do), "How do I go about finding miracles that my product or my company perform?"

Dig up your own examples

Here are my suggestions:

1. Be on the lookout for miracles among your own customers. When you find one, get the customer to write it out for you. It will not only increase your enthusiasm for what you are selling, but it will also prove a handy testimonial. (P.S.: If your customer will not write it, you should.)

2. Ask other salesmen in your organization to tell you miracles that they have observed. (Write them down or you will surely forget them.)

3. Ask your sales manager or any of the executives of your company—right up to the company president—for miracles they know about.

4. When you find a customer who is exceptionally enthusiastic about your product or service, ask him why. You will almost certainly find that he is enthusiastic because of some miracle your product has performed.

5. Keep a "Miracle Book." In it record every miracle you can find that your company or your product has performed. Then, when you feel that your enthusiasm is fading, dig out

the book and read it. Resell yourself—recharge your batteries.
W. C. Holman wrote in his book *Ginger Talks:*

Go off around a corner somewhere, where you can be alone, and
sell *yourself* a line of the article we make. Think over its value;
realize it; burn it into your mind.... Consider what our product
will do for a businessman, the money it will make for him, the
saving it will effect.... You are selling him something that he
needs. You are helping him to increase his profits.

Say these things over to yourself. Think them in your heart;
realize them—they're all true. Light the flame of your enthusiasm
and fan it into a good brisk blaze. Then, when you've sold yourself,
when you believe in your own proposition, heart and soul—go back
and tackle that man you failed to sell today.

I wish you could buy
Holman's book, but you can't

Quite possibly you will feel that I have taken an unusually
large number of excerpts from the book *Ginger Talks* by
Worthington C. Holman. I have—deliberately.

I have done it because the book, which was published fifty-
one years ago, is now out of print and because it contains so
much good material which you should not miss.

Dale Carnegie called the book to my attention, only a
couple of years before his death. Dale started as a salesman just
three years after the book was published. He bought it, liked
it, and tried to live up to Holman's teachings.

When Dale learned that I was planning to rewrite my book,
he had the country's secondhand book stores searched until
he was able to find a copy of Holman's book—which he presented to me.

My feeling is that, since the book contains so much good
material and since it is not available at bookstores, I am doing
a favor to the readers of my book to give them some helpful
extracts from Mr. Holman's stimulating book.

Now let's get back to our study of enthusiasm—and how to acquire it.

Here are some minor rules for building enthusiasm

In addition to the two great methods of arousing enthusiasm already given, there are several minor ways of building enthusiasm that will help. They are:

Minor Rule No. 1: Act animated. That is, act as you would normally act if you were enthusiastic.

Animation in selling is normally a symptom of enthusiasm. If you are enthusiastic you will usually be animated.

However, if you feel your enthusiasm begin to ebb, as you will now and then—especially after a turndown—it will help to act animated. By acting animated you will tend to become a person who is habitually animated.

Minor Rule No. 2: Give yourself both pep talks and faith talks. Tell yourself that you are going to succeed.

Minor Rule No. 3: If you feel yourself losing enthusiasm, *make more calls!*

"This just can't be right," you say. "Why, it upsets beliefs as old and respectable as the belief that nobody buys on Saturday morning, just before Christmas, or in August."

What does the average salesman do when he is turned down a couple of times and when he has about as much snap and crackle as wilted lettuce?

He quits and goes to a picture show—or fishing.

"What I need to get my pep back," he says, "is a little relaxation."

When he is through "relaxing," has he more enthusiasm to go back to work? No, he has less.

Years ago, William James taught that when you try to get things done you reach a fatigue point, where you don't seem to have enough energy to keep going. James insists that, if you will only keep on through the hard place, you find a new second wind of effort. Persist until you get your second wind.

If you are not too young, you will remember the time Ruth Nichols, the greatest woman aviator of her day, had a terrible crash and was in the hospital for weeks. She went up again in a plane before she could even walk; had herself carried to the field and lifted into a plane. Because she wanted to? No—but because she didn't dare to wait for fear to set in.

So, when your sales talk cracks up, don't run away. Stay and face it. Go right back up into the air. Don't just make the usual number of calls—try to make twice the usual number.

"As a cure for worrying," said Addison, "work is better than whisky." Also as a cure for fading enthusiasm.

Let's close this chapter on enthusiasm and how to get it by reprinting excerpts from an editorial by B. C. Forbes which appeared in *Forbes Magazine* on March 15, 1952.

THE MASTER KEY TO SUCCESS

What is the master key to success?

Enthusiasm is the all-essential human jet propeller. Without it the highest heights are rarely reached. It is the driving force that elevates men to miracle workers. White heat enthusiasm can melt the hardest problems, can vault Himalayan hurdles. It generates immeasurable powers. It begets boldness, courage; kindles confidence, overcomes doubts. It creates endless energy, the source of all accomplishment.

Perseverance withers and dies when not perpetually fed by enthusiasm. If you dig deeply enough into the history of America's most monumental enterprises of yesteryear and today, what do you discover? Almost invariably there was one master mind, one master mind who wedded herculean work to his dreams, visions, ambitions, spurred and succored and strengthened always by his enthusiasm.

"Faith without works is dead." It is enthusiasm that transmutes faith, ambition, aspiration into imperishable deeds.

Without enthusiasm, nothing.

SIXTEEN

You can sell yourself to your prospects if you will follow the rules

-- CHAPTER 64

Let's learn how to "sell ourselves"

None of us can have as many virtues as the fountain pen or half its cussedness but we can try.
        —PUDD'NHEAD WILSON (MARK TWAIN)

If somebody asks you, "Why did you buy that product rather than another?" you can probably think up several imaginary reasons. Often the real reason is that you liked one salesman better than another.

I ran into an example last summer that tends to prove that statement.

I stopped one day at the combination gas station, post office, and general store in the tiny town, The Glen, in the Adirondack region. A salesman walked out as I walked in.

Five minutes later, Mrs. Goodman, who manages the store, was complaining to me that she had forgotten to order something and that it was the salesman's fault. "He never suggests items to me or tries to find out what I need, the way the other salesmen do," complained Mrs. Goodman.

"Then why do you trade with him?" I asked.

"Because I like him," replied Mrs. Goodman. "He's such a nice young man."

Being a "nice young man" got business for that salesman that he didn't deserve.

He had "sold himself."

I wonder if he knows how he did it. Probably not. Few salesmen do.

Do you know how to "sell yourself"?

When I am speaking to sales groups, I often ask for a show of hands on this question: "How many of you feel that it is of vital importance to you to 'sell yourselves' to your customers and prospects?"

Always, every hand goes up.

Then I point to somebody in the group and ask, "John, how does a salesman 'sell himself'?" The answers I usually get to that question are so far from the correct answer they would make a plumber's assistant blush!

Thus, over the years, I have learned that virtually every salesman knows that it is important for him to "sell himself" —and that few salesmen know how to do it!

The man who invented a term so misleading as "selling yourself" deserves a place in "The Hall of Infamy."

It really isn't "selling" at all

This man deserves punishment because the phrase he invented has led beginners into so many ridiculous mistakes. A beginner is told he must sell himself—but isn't told how. So he tries to sell himself to prospects as he would sell a fish pole or a new brand of coffee. He talks about himself, he boasts, he tells how good he is—and tries to prove it.

Naturally, the result he gets by this kind of "selling" is just the opposite of the one he wants to get.

So remember this rule: in selling your *product*, talk about your product—in selling *yourself*, don't talk about yourself.

Here's the "self-selling" formula

Let's be sure we understand what we really mean by the expression "selling yourself."

As I understand it, you have "sold yourself" if people like to deal with you—if you have gained their good will and friendship.

People may like to deal with you for many reasons. The two most important reasons are:

1. You have a good personality.
2. You use good human relations.

What is personality? When I asked that question once in a Sales Course class, a man gave me this definition. "Personality is what it takes!"—which is true, but incomplete. Dale Carnegie defined personality as, "the effect you have on other people." Dr. Henry C. Link, the noted New York psychologist and writer, says, "Personality is the extent to which a person has developed habits which interest and serve others."

Now that you know for sure what personality is, you probably ask, "What do you mean by 'good human relations'?"

The best answer I know will be found by reading *How to Win Friends and Influence People.* Over four million people have bought this book—perhaps ten or twelve million have read it. It does not pretend to cover the entire subject of human relations. However, if you will observe the first nine rules in that book, you will find that people like you—and like to buy from you.

If you have a pleasing personality and if you observe the *How to Win Friends* rules, you will have no trouble in selling yourself—and little trouble in selling any worthy product.

I recommend this program for improving your personality

What are you going to do about it?

Here is a boiled-down program for developing the kind of personality that helps you to sell yourself.

1. Determine what undesirable qualities you want to get rid of—and what desirable qualities you need to develop.
2. Determine how you are going about it.

3. Decide when you are going to start on this program of self-improvement.

4. Start!

What are the desirable and undesirable qualities of salesmen?

Before you start to list your own personality imperfections, it might be well to consider some of the common weaknesses of salesmen.

However, we can consider only a few characteristics because, as Dr. W. W. Charters once wrote, "Your personality as a whole is determined by the degree to which *some six thousand* attributes are present or absent in your make up."

Since it isn't practical to work on all six thousand of your "attributes," your problem is to decide which negative qualities are hampering you in your efforts to "sell yourself."

Perhaps it will help you in your search for your own personality weaknesses to read the lists that various experts have prepared of the good and bad qualities of salesmen.

Here's a list prepared by salesmen

Which weaknesses do practiced and successful salesmen feel are the most harmful?

We have asked many thousands of the salesmen who have taken the Dale Carnegie Sales Course twenty questions about their personalities.

The ten qualities they feel they should work on—in the order of their importance—are:

1. They talk too much—listen too little.
2. They are self-conscious.
3. They are timid.
4. They have annoying mannerisms.
5. They have no goal in life.
6. They are not energetic.

7. They are not thrifty.

8. They lack enthusiasm.

9. They have poor memories.

10. They are not loyal to their bosses and to the companies which employ them.

We add to this list of unattractive qualities four which were suggested by Dick Carlson. They are:

1. Selfishness

2. Conceit

3. A tendency to complain

4. Shiftlessness

Surely, from this list of undesirable personality qualities, you can select those which you need to work on.

How to determine your weaknesses

Now you have to determine which personality qualities you will eliminate in order to become the kind of person you want to be. I recommend that you:

1. Sit down and list, say, thirteen of your worst qualities.

2. The next step to take in determining your weaknesses is to ask your relatives, your sales manager, your fellow salesmen, and ten or a dozen of your customers—those who know you well—to write down and hand you a list of the things about you that they don't like.

They'll do it, too, if you insist on it sincerely. I know, because for several years, we have been getting salesmen who are taking the Dale Carnegie Sales Course to do just that.

What salesmen have found out by asking others to point out weaknesses in their personalities has startled and helped thousands of salesmen.

If you suspect that prospects don't like everything about you, your first job is to find out who is to blame. Don't be startled if it turns out to be you!

Don't be like Eddie, the store clerk described in *Ad Club News*, who was the most inefficient and discourteous sales-

man ever. When he was absent one day, a regular customer
noted it with pleasure. "Eddie isn't just away," explained the
proprietor; "he doesn't work here any more."

"Do you have any one in mind for the vacancy?" asked the
customer.

"Nope," said the proprietor, "Eddie didn't leave any vacancy."

Now for the desirable qualities

Ten traits, according to M. K. Wischart, determine the effectiveness of your personality in action. These ten traits—
with comments of my own—are:

Group I. Traits of temperament

1. Self-confidence.
2. Friendliness—"The only way to have a friend," said
Emerson, "is to be one," and somebody else (I don't know
who) said, "Few salesmen are qualified to make scintillating
sales talks, but any salesman can be agreeable and friendly."
3. Cheerfulness.
4. Willingness to take criticism.
5. Tact.

Group II. Traits of self-management

1. Industriousness—that is, willingness to do a full day's
work.
2. Initiative.
3. Memory—especially for names, faces, and promises.
4. Adaptability.
5. Truthfulness—the truthful salesman neither prevaricates
nor exaggerates.

It is the old Ben Franklin method

Just exactly how do you go about the long, slow job of im-
proving your personality?

Just as you go about learning to use the rules in this book, as explained in Chapter 53.

1. Briefly stated, you:

(*a*) Pick thirteen of your personality qualities which you would like to improve.

(*b*) Work for a week on each quality. (That is, for example, a week on industriousness, a week on adaptability, and so on.)

(*c*) Keep a "box score." Score yourself each night on your failure or success in using that quality for that day.

(*d*) At the end of three months, start again with personality quality number one.

(*e*) Keep it up for several *years*. And that's not meant to be funny! You can't change your personality by wishing—you do it by working. As Aristotle said, "Our characters are the result of our conduct." You have spent twenty to fifty years building into your personality, by your conduct, the qualities you now want to change. You can't build them out again—and replace them with desirable qualities—in a few days or a few weeks.

If you follow this plan you will improve a little each week—and each week you will find it increasingly easy to "sell yourself."

2. The second step in learning how to "sell yourself" is to improve your skill in using the human-relations rules.

How?

Also by the Ben Franklin method: Work a solid week on each rule. Use it on every possible occasion. Then move on to the next one.

Hard work? Yes, indeed. As Dr. Henry C. Link wrote in his book, *The Return to Religion* (which every salesman should read), "You can't think, analyze or talk yourself out of the predicament [of having a poor personality]. A good personality is achieved by practice. . . . People don't need self-analysis —they need self-discipline."

"You must think," you say, "that I have nothing to do but to work on self-improvement!"

My answer is, "If you can find an easier way that will work, let me know. I'll write a book about it—and split the royalties, 10 per cent to me, 90 per cent to you."

Personality improvement pays

"Is it worth all this effort," you ask, "merely to improve my ability to sell myself?"

Paul W. Ivey and Walter Horvath, in their book *Successful Salesmanship*, say, "An improvement of only five per cent in personality may produce a fifty per cent increase in *sales*." If you would like to increase *your* sales 50 per cent, go to work on your personality.

Remember: no matter how good your personality is now, it can be better if you make it better.

_____ CHAPTER 65

Pay sincere compliments, because compliments pay salesmen

No verbal vitamin is more potent than praise.
—FREDERICK B. HARRIS

I called one day on an important official of an A.T. and T. company in upstate New York. His office was well hidden on the top floor and at the back of the telephone company building. When I reached this man's desk, I said, "On my trip up to see you, Mr. Blank, I had to ask the way of five of your employees—and every one of them gave me a big smile."

He responded with the biggest smile in the lot and replied, "If you knew how hard I have worked to get our employees to greet people with a smile, you would know how I appreciate that compliment"—and I was off to a good start because I had paid a compliment—and it paid me!

Lincoln once began a letter, Dale Carnegie tells us in *How to Win Friends and Influence People*, by saying, "Everybody likes a compliment."

In fact, Dale Carnegie tells us a great deal about compliments in his discussion of two of his rules:

Give honest, sincere appreciation.

Make the other person feel important, and do it sincerely.

I advise you to go back, right now, to *How to Win Friends* and read those two chapters. They are two of the most helpful chapters in the most helpful book for salesmen ever written—even if it wasn't written for salesmen!

Compliments can be paid in three different ways

Sincere compliments come in several forms—all useful—as follows:

The direct compliment. Given good material, anybody can pay that kind.

A. Kelly Fuson, freight agent of the Intercity Trucking Co., of Memphis, gave me this example of the effectiveness of a direct compliment:

Kelly had called again and again on a man named Bradford, who was traffic manager for Fownes Brothers in Little Rock—but made no progress. One day he said to Mr. Bradford, "Maybe you wonder why I call on you when I never get any business. I'd rather call on you and get nothing than to call on lots of men and get an order—because I always learn something when I talk to you."

He said that it was a sincere compliment—that Mr. Bradford was one of the best informed traffic men in the South—and he said further that the compliment led the way to business that he has been getting ever since.

The indirect (or "warmed-over") compliment. In this case you repeat something complimentary you heard somebody

else say. This kind is often more effective than the direct compliment—because the recipient is more likely to feel that it is
completely sincere. For example, you say, "I heard Bill Jones
pay you a mighty nice compliment the other day. He said. . . ."

Watch for opportunities to pass along compliments.

The "assist" compliment. It's an "assist compliment" when,
for instance, you say to a man's secretary, "Your boss is a
grand guy"—in the hope that she will pass the compliment
along to her boss. In that case she is scored with an *assist*—
and the boss gets the compliment.

Observe these rules
and you will make compliments pay!

Here are a few rules for paying compliments:

1. *If you can't pay a compliment sincerely, don't pay it!*

The great Elbert Hubbard pointed out one possible exception
when he wrote, "A woman will doubt anything you say,
except it be a compliment of herself. Here she believes you
are truthful and mentally admires you for your discernment."

Barring that possible exception, a compliment, to be effective, must be something you honestly believe. Unless it is true
and sincere, it is flattery—and flattery rarely makes a friend or
closes a sale.

The Greeks had a sentence for it, "Many know how to flatter—few know how to praise."

Admittedly it is easy to flatter—because in flattery you are
not handicapped by facts.

2. *Always be on the lookout for material for compliments.*

This material is not always easy to find—especially in dealing with curmudgeons, churls, cranks and crabs!

If you are alert, however, you can usually find material for
a sincere compliment—even in the most unpromising places.

In fact, some men are so mean they relish a compliment on
their cantankerousness. I recall that my late friend Walter R.
Jenkins was once harassed and insulted by the advertising man-

ager of a food account in upstate New York. Finally Walter broke down and told this man the truth about himself—as Walter saw it. I've forgotten Walter's exact words, but in substance they were, "I want you to know that all of us advertising solicitors consider you a mean, disagreeable, insulting old you-know-what! You are a disgrace to the advertising business. Everybody hates you. I hate you. The sooner you die off, the happier we shall all be."

The curmudgeon must have been flattered, because he broke through with one of his rare laughs—and gave Walter a nice order. They were on friendly terms from that day on!

I recommend specifically that you do *not* use that technique—but it worked for Walter Jenkins.

3. *Make your compliments specific.*

If you say to a man, "That was a good speech you made the other day," it is a compliment—but a rather feeble one.

Suppose you said instead, "I enjoyed the talk you made last Wednesday at the Rotary luncheon. So did the other members—to judge by the repeated applause. I like the way you opened—you had attention from the start by arousing their curiosity. I found your examples interesting—and illuminating. It was a good talk."

A compliment like that is specific enough to be convincing.

4. *Compliment people on things they are not sure about.*

If, for example, somebody complimented me on the whiteness of my hair, the compliment would be wasted. It sure is white! If, however, they complimented me on a speech I had made, I would appreciate it—because I am always more than a bit uncertain about my speeches—maybe with good reason!

Even the truly great appreciate and enjoy a compliment of this kind. Toscanini, according to Leonard Lyons, once said, with respect to a compliment paid him by Judith Anderson, "She didn't say I had conducted the concert well. I knew that. She said I looked handsome."

5. *Use a compliment when you are in a tight situation.*

If a man brings up a difficult objection, compliment him.

Say, for example, "Not many people think of that point, Mr. Jones. It never occurs to anybody unless he knows a lot about this business. Let me give you the facts." (Don't say it unless you can say it sincerely.)

Another situation in which a compliment often helps is in handling a complaint. Once when we were holding a sales school in Grand Rapids, Miss Inez Mead, who was employed by the Michigan Consumers Gas Co., gave this example:

Inez was floor salesman one day when a woman came in who had a torrid complaint about her gas stove and didn't mind telling the world about it.

Inez told me that this customer cursed and raved, snorted and steamed. She insulted everybody from the president down.

As the customer raved, Inez was thinking to herself, "When this woman stops for breath, what on earth shall I say to her?" Then she remembered what I had told the group the night before in the sales school about the miracle of compliments.

So when, finally, the customer had offered her last insults, Inez said sweetly and sincerely, "That's a lovely and becoming dress you have on!"

Inez said the woman turned red, then pale. Apparently nothing like that had ever happened to her before.

The conclusion of the story is: the customer bought a new gas stove.

To sum it up: pay compliments—to prospects, to customers, to fellow salesmen, to your sales manager. Pay compliments to friends and relatives. Yes, and above all, pay compliments *to your wife*. I'll bet men will read this book who pay ten compliments to their secretaries for every one they pay their wives.

"Appreciative words," says Dr. George W. Crane, "are the most powerful force for good will on earth."

Most of the high spots in our lives come about through encouragement. I don't care how great, how famous, how successful a man may be, he hungers for applause.

Encouragement is the oxygen of the soul.

—GEORGE MATTHEWS ADAMS

CHAPTER 66

How to get yourself promoted

The salesman who wakes up to find himself a sales manager hasn't been asleep.

Often, in sales meetings, I have asked, "How many here would like, some day, to be sales managers?"

Usually about one-third of those present do *not* put up their hands. I wonder why! Do they honestly prefer to be salesmen all their lives? It's quite possible. Surely it's no disgrace to live and die a salesman! Stuart Studwell, a successful insurance salesman, once told me, "I wouldn't wet-nurse a 'passel' of salesmen for the president's salary."

I suspect, however, that some of those men who say they never want to be executives feel that way because they are afraid. They are afraid of the thing that keeps men little—the fear of being big.

Perhaps somebody has told them this sad truth: you can have the title of sales manager or you can have peace—but you can't have both!

Maybe *you* aren't sure whether or not you would like to be a sales manager. If you are in doubt, check yourself. Ask yourself these questions:

1. Honestly now, do I want to be a sales manager—want it hard enough to pay the price?

The first requisite for getting ahead is ambition—the kind of ambition that fills a man's daytime thoughts and disturbs his dreams—that wakes him up on occasion in the dead of night and sets him to pacing up and down the floor—the divine discontent with present conditions that makes inaction an agony to him.

It takes force and fierceness, gimp, grit, and gumption to run down success. —w. c. holman in *Ginger Talks*

2. Am I reading the books and magazines which will help me to become a better salesman—and perhaps a good sales manager?

3. Do I take every practical salesmanship course that is available?

4. Have I taken a practical course in public speaking? Do I grab every opportunity to speak in public?

5. Am I loyal—do I work for my firm, think for my firm, root for my firm, always praise my firm and its executives? Do I help my boss to do a better job?

6. Do I observe the rules in Dale Carnegie's *How to Win Friends and Influence People?*

7. Do I keep my temper—always—or at least nearly always?

8. Have I decided between having a "good time" or leading a successful life? (You know you can't do both!)

9. Am I brave in the face of depressions, hard times, and selling slumps?

10. If a chance comes to make a sale on my day off—do I make it?

11. Am I willing to take responsibility? To make decisions? "Those who continue to shrink from responsibility," said the *Industrial Press Service,* "continue to shrink."

12. Can I dispatch things—get things finished?

13. Can I help a man to make a sale—and then give him full credit for it?

14. Am I willing to give credit to associates and subordinates for their share in any success I attain?

15. Do I dress, look, and act like a successful sales executive?

16. Do I have a reasonably happy home life? (Can the man who is at war at home be at peace at work?) Have I a wife who is willing to make sacrifices to help me succeed?

17. Do I shun detail?

The test is: Do I get my orders into the office in good shape? Do I keep the records I am asked to keep—no matter how I hate to do it? (Remember, a man who is not willing to take care of detail and routine jobs is never likely to be promoted to sales management—where he will have more detail and more routine jobs.)

18. Do I write a good letter?

19. Have I unshakable optimism? When I am hit, do I rebound or do I squash? Am I like the Arkansas hillbilly who was asked by a Yankee for directions to a certain town: "Well, let's see," said the native. "You go down the road a piece— no, you better go the other way till you reach a fork in the road—no. You know, mister, you just can't get there from here."

20. Have I learned as much as I can of my boss's job? (Remember, when you are an executive in a big company you will be responsible for three jobs: the one you are in, the one you left, and the one above.)

Benjamin F. Fairless, chairman of the board of U.S. Steel, said:

What is the recipe for successful achievement? To my mind there are just four essential ingredients: (1) Choose a career you love. (2) Give it the best there is in you. (3) Seize your opportunities. (4) Be a member of the team.

You must know *where, why,* and *when*

All right, if you have passed the foregoing test, you really want to be a sales manager. So, you now want to know how to become one.

To gain advancement, you must:

1. Know *where* you want to go. (Sales manager? Branch manager? Sales training manager?)

2. Know *why* you want to go there—what you want to get.

(*a*) More money. (How much?)

(*b*) Less legwork—more brainwork. (And if you think brainwork is easy, try it some time!)

(*c*) More prestige—things like titles, recognition—the things that add up to a "feeling of importance."

3. Know *when* you expect to get there: Now? One year? Three years? Five years? Ten years?

4. Prove to your superiors that you are worthy of promotion.

Some specific rules for getting ahead will be found in the next chapter.

—————————————————————— CHAPTER **67**

Here are some rules
for becoming a sales manager

No selling job has any future: the future is in the salesman.
—DR. FRANK CRANE (slightly modified—the quotation, not the Doctor!)

Here are some time-tried rules for winning promotion to a sales executive job:

Rule 1: Know more than any other salesman in your company about:

(*a*) Selling.

(*b*) Your company.

(*c*) The product you are selling.

(*d*) Your competitors and what they are selling.

Don't be held back by the idea that you already know it all. Remember Publilius Syrus' admonition, written in the first century B.C.! "He bids fair to grow wise who has discovered that he is not so."

Study, study, study! If you stop studying today, you will be ignorant tomorrow. Your education is not over until you are dead. As James Hilton said in the magazine *This Week:*

Mr. Chips wasn't often cantankerous, but he did once let fly over a letter from a parent containing the sentence, "After my son finishes his education he will enter my business."

It was the whole idea of "finishing an education" that did it. "Good Heavens," Mr. Chips exclaimed, "does the fellow think education is like measles—something you get over while you're young so that you don't have to be bothered with it ever afterwards?"

Read all the books on selling you can buy or borrow—including the bad ones. I used to get a laugh in one of my speeches to salesmen by saying, "Most books on selling were written by college professors and sold by misrepresentation to half-wits. I ought to know. I own over one hundred myself!"

I think Cervantes presented it better in *Don Quixote* when he said, "No book is so bad that something good may not be found in it."

Take every course in salesmanship that comes along—even lecture courses. The good ones are interesting—and the poor ones are better than none.

Store up lots of general information. Read books about economics, books about how surveys are made, books about current topics, about merchandising, about market research. "Where do I find time?" you ask. I don't know. But find it or fail.

Read books dealing with personality development and human relations. Read, and encourage your wife to read, Dorothy Carnegie's great book, *How to Help Your Husband Get Ahead.*

Read magazines dealing with business—especially advertising and selling. (I recommend *Printers' Ink*, 205 East 42 Street, New York 17, and *Sales Management*, 386 Fourth Avenue, New York 16. The best magazine devoted to all forms of selling is *The American Salesman*, 49 West 57th St., New York 19. Magazines published for door-to-door salesmen are *Specialty Salesman*, 307 North Michigan Avenue, Chicago, and *Salesman's Opportunity*, 850 North Dearborn Street, Chicago.)

Rule 2: Demonstrate that you can do the three big jobs of sales management: (1) hire 'em, (2) train 'em, and (3) work 'em. And of these three, working salesmen is the least important.

Don Herold wrote in the house magazine *The Crown:*

I was discussing the other evening with Jim Simpson, who has
the most successful bottling business in our town, the problem that
the owner of a carbonated beverage business has of multiplying
himself several hundred times.

"What's the biggest single factor in the successful selling of
carbonated beverages? Don't be too quick to answer. Think it
over," I asked Jim.

"I've already thought it over," answered Jim, without a moment's hesitation. "The answer is, the proper selection and training
of help."

If you asked your boss, "What is the biggest single factor
in selling?" you would get substantially the same answer that
Don Herold did.

How can you demonstrate to your sales manager and the
company higher-ups that you can successfully find and train
men? (Of course I mean, "and women, too.")

If the nature of your job and your company permits, get
your manager to let you take one man under your wing. Select
him, train him, then help him to be a successful salesman. By
the time you have done that for two or three men, you will
probably find the executives of your company ready to give
you the first opening as a sales executive.

Rule 3: Set a good example.

No sales executive will promote a salesman solely because
he is a steady churchgoer, a teetotaler, or a shining moral light.
Equally, however, no sales manager will knowingly promote a
salesman who: (*a*) drinks to excess, (*b*) gambles to excess,
(*c*) is notoriously loose as to morals, (*d*) is constantly and
hopelessly in debt, (*e*) gets a reputation for exaggeration,
fancy tales, or plain lying.

A sales manager must, whether he likes it or not, set an
example for his entire force. A salesman is not likely to be
made a manager if he constantly and conspicuously sets a bad
example.

Rule 4: Get out from under that bushel. You can't hope to be promoted, if you are never heard of—or from.

An old German proverb says: *"Modesty is an ornament, but you go farther without it."*

How can you bring yourself to the attention of executives? Well, here are some of the ways:

(*a*) Work hard. Executives notice it!

(*b*) Make a lot of sales. You don't have to be the top producer to win promotion, but you have to be a *salesman* and you must have proved it.

(*c*) Take an active part in sales meetings and conventions. To be a good sales executive you must be a good speaker and a good teacher. If you are, you can demonstrate it at meetings. Talk often—but briefly. Take part in everything. "The bashful always lose," says a French proverb—which is surely true of salesmen who want to get ahead.

(*d*) Be animated. No wise executive will ever promote, to a sales management job, a man who is listless and sleepy.

(*e*) Take a course in public speaking.

After you learn to speak, get yourself invited to speak at sales and advertising conventions, if possible—or wherever heads of companies gather. If you do not bring yourself to the attention of your employer, you may bring yourself to the attention of somebody else who needs a sales manager.

Rule 5: Make suggestions—even if they are bad. Let the boss know that you are around.

Rule 6: Keep everlastingly at it. If promotion is slow in coming, ask yourself if it is the company's fault—or yours. As Jerry Cole said:

Meeting the president of a large corporation, I asked his policy about promoting employees to better and more responsible positions.

"We never promote anybody," was his surprising reply.

"What do you mean?" I asked.

"Just what I say," he insisted. "We never promote anybody. No responsible firm in the country promotes an employee to a better job. *The employee promotes himself.*"

Rule 7: Ask for it. Go to your boss and tell him you are preparing yourself for the next executive job that opens up. He may be afraid that you are after his job—but probably he will not. Andrew Carnegie, when asked on one occasion whether he was not worried for fear some of the young men he was training would take his place, shook his head and replied, "All that worries me is that they won't."

Will you pay the price?

Let Herbert Francis DeBower sum it up:

The price of success is to force yourself to concentrate on the problem at hand and to plan.

To have a high and sustained determination to put over what you plan, not [merely] if circumstances are favorable to its accomplishment, but in spite of all adverse circumstances.

To refuse to believe that any circumstances are sufficiently strong to defeat you in the accomplishment of your purpose.

Every man should ask himself, "Am I willing to endure the pain of this struggle, for the comforts and rewards and glory that go with achievement?"

CHAPTER 68

Where do we go from here?

*Any fool can learn from experience. It takes a
smart salesman to learn from a book—but it pays.*

You didn't do quite your best yesterday, and the day before—
and neither did I. But what about tomorrow?

Unless you establish the habit of using, in your daily selling,
the rules you learn in this book, you have wasted your time
reading it.

Please, I beg of you, don't let this be true of this book. No
matter how good a salesman you are now, you can be a better
one by using the rules I have presented in this volume!

So again I urge you:

1. Pick out the one rule in the book which you need the
most.

2. Consciously and conscientiously use this rule in your day-
to-day selling.

3. Keep on using it until its use becomes habitual.

4. Then move on to the next rule.

Do it because the rules in this book *work!*

I have been gathering these rules through more than a third
of a century. All of them were picked up from my own experience or from successful salesmen. All have been tried out
—some of them by literally tens of thousands of salesmen under my supervision.

These rules are the rules that the winners use. They are the
rules that bring in the orders. They are the rules that will
increase your income and your chance for advancement.

If I can be sure that even a few of you who read this book
will use even a few of the rules, I shall feel that I have **not**
written in vain.

About the Author

Percy Whiting started his business career as an advertising manager and became a salesman almost by accident when he was asked to help raise capital for his company by selling stock. This led to stock-selling campaigns and eventually to his own investment securities business on Wall Street.

In 1935 Mr. Whiting took a Dale Carnegie Course in Effective Speaking and liked it so well that he joined the Dale Carnegie organization and is now Managing Director of the Dale Carnegie Sales Courses. He wrote *The Five Great Rules of Selling* because he and Dale Carnegie could not find a practical book suitable for these courses.

INDEX